KV-264-149

PERSONAL RELATIONSHIPS
DURING ADOLESCENCE

Edited by
RAYMOND MONTEMAYOR
GERALD R. ADAMS
THOMAS P. GULLOTTA

ADVANCES IN ADOLESCENT DEVELOPMENT
An Annual Book Series   Volume 6

SAGE PUBLICATIONS
International Educational and Professional Publisher
Thousand Oaks   London   New Delhi

HTUOMYJ9 2
830IVfl3≳

Copyright © 1994 by Sage Publications, Inc.

All rights reserved. No part of this book may be reproduced or utilized in any form or by any means, electronic or mechanical, including photocopying, recording, or by any information storage and retrieval system, without permission in writing from the publisher.

For information address:

SAGE Publications, Inc.
2455 Teller Road
Thousand Oaks, California 91320

SAGE Publications Ltd.
6 Bonhill Street
London EC2A 4PU
United Kingdom

SAGE Publications India Pvt. Ltd.
M-32 Market
Greater Kailash I
New Delhi 110 048 India

Printed in the United States of America

Library of Congress: 90-657291

ISSN 1050-8589

ISBN 0-8039-5680-0
ISBN 0-8039-5681-9

94 95 96 97 10 9 8 7 6 5 4 3 2 1

Sage Production Editor: Diane S. Foster

90 0220002 0

WITHDRAWN
FROM
UNIVERSITY OF PLYMOUTH

PERSONAL RELATIONSHIPS
DURING ADOLESCENCE

Charles Seale-Hayne Library
University of Plymouth
(01752) 588 588
LibraryandITenquiries@plymouth.ac.uk

ADVANCES IN ADOLESCENT DEVELOPMENT

AN ANNUAL BOOK SERIES

Series Editors:

Gerald R. Adams, *University of Guelph, Ontario, Canada*
Raymond Montemayor, *Ohio State University*
Thomas P. Gullotta, *Child and Family Agency, Connecticut*

Advances in Adolescent Development is an annual book series designed to analyze, integrate, and critique an abundance of new research and literature in the field of adolescent development. Contributors are selected from numerous disciplines based on their creative, analytic, and influential scholarship in order to provide information pertinent to professionals as well as upper-division and graduate students. The Series Editors' goals are to evaluate the current empirical and theoretical knowledge about adolescence, and to encourage the formulation (or expansion) of new directions in research and theory development.

Volumes in This Series

Contents

UNIVERSITY OF PLYMOUTH
LIBRARY SERVICES

Item No. 9ᴄᴏ .2 0 0 0 2Ó

Class No. i S S·5 PER

Contl. No. 08039756800

OF PLYMOUTH
SERVICES

Preface

Advances in Adolescent Development is a serial publication designed to bring together original summaries of important new developments in theory, research, and methodology on adolescents. Each chapter is written by experts who have substantially contributed to knowledge in their area or who are especially well qualified to review a topic because of their background or interests. The chapters in each volume are state of the art reviews of advances in adolescent studies. Some authors also present new data from their own research. The theme of each volume is selected by the senior editor of each volume and is based on reading of the latest published empirical work, discussions with the other editors, and ideas provided by colleagues. Chapter topics and authors are selected in a similar way. Readers with ideas for future themes should contact any of the editors.

Many people contributed to the completion of this volume. Our editors at Sage have been enormously important in this enterprise. C. Deborah Laughton continues to cheerfully and effectively nurture each volume along. Of course we gratefully express our gratitude to the authors who wrote and revised each chapter.

1. The Study of Personal Relationships During Adolescence

Raymond Montemayor
Ohio State University

The purpose of this volume is to examine recent theory and research on the development of personal relationships during adolescence. Personal relationships were defined broadly to include individuals with whom adolescents had regular contact and had formed an emotional bond or connection. In Chapter 2, Collins and Repinski define one important type of relationship examined in this volume, which they characterize as "close"—that is, a relationship with an enduring tie or connection between two individuals, comprising frequent, interdependent interactions that occur across diverse settings and tasks. Not every author focuses on a close relationship, but most do, and this type of relationship is the central relationship discussed in this volume.

A broad array of relationships are examined in this volume: They include not only parents and same-sex friends, but also romantic relationships between opposite-sex adolescents and same-sex adolescents, and relationships involving nonkin adults. That chapters were not written about siblings, grandparents, teachers, and many other important relationships in the lives of adolescents is a reflection of the small data base on these topics and on limitations of space in this volume. Authors were encouraged to examine relationship development, both continuity and change, as children made the transition into adolescence and moved into later adolescence. Some chapters have more of a developmental focus than others, which reflects authors' interests and the state of theory and research on a topic.

In addition to examining a variety of relationships, authors were encouraged to consider conceptual and methodological issues that cut across type of relationship. Among the recurrent conceptual themes discussed in this volume are the need to define terms to distinguish one relational concept from another and the problem of integrating the views of both individuals in a relationship. Several methodological issues are discussed and illustrated, including problems in assessing relationships and measuring relationship change. None of these conceptual or methodological issues are solved in this volume, but several authors present new ways of thinking about them that open up avenues for interesting empirical investigation. The authors are individuals who have made important conceptual and empirical contributions to the study of adolescent relationships. In addition, authors were selected to purposefully sample a diversity of relationships during adolescence. They were requested to examine theory and research on their topic and to present data from their own research program. They were given wide latitude in selecting and organizing material. Each chapter represents the particular view of its authors, and, as the reader will soon discover, these views reveal some overlap and a remarkable degree of difference.

Chapter 2, by Collins and Repinski, entitled "Relationships During Adolescence: Continuity and Change in Interpersonal Perspective," provides an overview of the theories and constructs that have guided research on parent and peer relations during adolescence. According to Collins and Repinski, two essential features of adolescent relationships are that they change and that they become more differentiated. These distinctive aspects of adolescent relationships have been examined from four perspectives: (a) *endogenous-change views,* which emphasize biological and motivational pressures toward alterations of relationships; (b) *social-psychological approaches,* which focus on external pressures toward change and the interplay of internal and external factors; (c) *attachment perspectives,* which address the pressures toward continuity and coherence in primary aspects of dyadic relationships; and, most recently, (d) *interdependency perspectives,* which emphasize the patterns of interaction and affect and the principles of exchange that characterize close relationships. These theoretical views have given rise to two clusters of relational constructs: those emphasizing relative distance during adolescence— conflict, individuation, psychological separation, and autonomy; and those emphasizing interpersonal connectedness—trust, intimacy, closeness, relative positive affect, and communication. The authors conclude that future research should be framed to include attention to interrelations among aspects of relationships, the social networks in which individual dyads are embedded, and changes in the functions of relationships as adolescents mature.

Patricia Noller's Chapter 3, entitled "Relationships With Parents in Adolescence: Process and Outcome," begins with a review of research by Noller and her colleagues on the differing perspectives that adolescents and their parents have on family relations. Across four studies, she reports that adolescents generally have more negative views of their families than do parents. Most of the chapter focuses on research on family processes and the outcomes of those processes for adolescents. Processes examined are parent-adolescent communication, conflict, punishment and violence, decision making, the development of autonomy and identity, and attachment. The main outcomes examined are adolescent psychopathology; problem behavior, such as smoking, abuse of alcohol and drugs, and sexual involvement; and adolescents' later relationships. From her review of the literature, Noller concludes that adolescents who have constructive, helpful relationships with their parents, in which internal rather than external controls are emphasized, are more likely to be well adjusted, to possess values similar to those of their parents, and to cooperate with parents. These adolescents are also less likely to focus on the peer group and to become involved in unhealthy behavior such as alcohol and drug abuse. They are also more likely to have secure attachments to parents and to form stable romantic relationships of their own.

In Chapter 4, entitled "Cultural Perspectives on Continuity and Change in Adolescents' Relationships," Catherine Cooper argues that adolescents develop ideas about the self and others out of experiences in relationships within family, peer, and school contexts. The theme of the chapter is that cultural perspectives are crucial to characterizing what develops in adolescence, and that goals and values, activities, personnel, and scripts are key dimensions of this process. Cooper argues that addressing each of these features of relationships in adolescence will enrich both our conceptual models and methodologies. For example, cultural variation exists in norms of respect by adolescents toward their parents. Recent portrayals of adolescents as renegotiating asymmetrical patterns of earlier parent-child relations toward peerlike mutuality may better characterize European-American families than families from Asia and Mexico. Examining development embedded within culture calls into question universalistic notions of social development. Cooper's goal in this chapter is to enrich the study of normative relational development during adolescence by explicitly examining cultural diversity, including gender, family structure, ethnicity, social class, and multicultural adaptation.

Chapter 5, by Youniss, McLellan, and Strouse, "'We're Popular, but We're Not Snobs': Adolescents Describe Their Crowds," examines theory and research on adolescent peer groups. They also present data from their own research on adolescents' views of peer culture. Descriptively, six core crowds emerged from adolescents' own descriptions of their peer world: *Populars* emphasized their social skills, involvement, and attractiveness; *Jocks* stressed their physical activities; *Brains* talked about their grades and intelligence; *Normals* discussed their averageness and lack of deviance; *Loners* felt alone or unaccepted; and *Druggies-Toughs* admitted to deviant conduct. Youniss and his colleagues go on to discuss several points about these crowds. First, rather than being a member of only one crowd, many adolescents claimed membership in several crowds. Thus crowd boundaries were not rigid. Second, crowd boundaries also were permeable in another way. Qualities considered important by adolescents for membership in one crowd, such as "getting along well with others," were also endorsed by adolescents in other crowds. Third, the adolescent culture is not essentially in opposition to adult society. Instead it encompasses a range of values from antiadult sensation seeking and drug taking to an adult-centered school orientation. Lastly, gender arrangements in the adolescent society were similar to those found in adult society, with females having more of an expressive orientation and males being more activity centered. The basic point to emerge from this chapter is that adolescent peer culture needs to be studied as a complex social organization and not as an immature and warped version of adult society.

Chapter 6, by Brown, Mory, and Kinney, entitled "Casting Adolescent Crowds in a Relational Perspective: Caricature, Channel, and Context," also examines adolescent crowds. Writers in this area have argued that teenage crowds facilitate identity development and socialize youth into salient roles in the teen or adult culture. Crowds also help structure social interaction among peers. In this chapter Brown and his colleagues explicitly attempt to examine crowds from a relational perspective. Drawing upon ethnographic and survey research, they examine three ways that crowds structure peer social interactions. First, teenagers *caricature* crowds so as to locate them in symbolic space; they can then use the resulting social map to predict the prospects for relationships with unknown peers. Second, crowd affiliations *channel* adolescents into associations with particular peers and away from relationships with others. Third, crowds provide a social *context* that rewards certain relational styles and disparages others. According to Brown and his colleagues, crowds differ in their typical features of peer relationships, and these differences help to establish crowds as disparate peer cultures operating in the same social context. Thus teenagers' crowd affiliation and their understanding of the crowd system both affect and reflect their choice of peer associates and the features of their peer relationships. Yet the crowd system is a dynamic phenomenon that is sensitive to contextual features of the social milieu. The nature of and interrelationships among crowds change across adolescence and differ from one community to the next. Brown and his colleagues argue that by employing this dynamic, relational perspective, investigators can expand their understanding of the role that peer crowds play in adolescent social development.

In Chapter 7, "Romantic Views: Toward a Theory of Adolescent Romantic Relationships," Furman and Wehner present a behavioral systems conceptualization of adolescent romantic relationships. This novel theory is based on an integration of attachment theories and Harry Stack Sullivan's theory of interpersonal development. The authors propose that the four behavioral systems of affiliation, attachment, caretaking, and reproduction play central roles in romantic relationships. A new key concept in their model is romantic "views," which are conscious and unconscious perceptions of particular romantic relationships. Views resemble the concept of "working models" from attachment theory and are based on previous experiences in romantic relationships that shape expectations about future relationships. Furman and Wehner go on to examine the links among romantic relationships, parent-child relationships, and peer relationships. Next they outline a series of hypothesized developmental changes in these relationships. Lastly, they describe results from two empirical studies that provide some support for their conceptualization.

Chapter 8, by Ritch Savin-Williams, "Dating Those You Can't Love and Loving Those You Can't Date," discusses the unique problems in defining and finding lesbian, gay male, and bisexual adolescents. According to Savin-Williams, these adolescents have not been highly visible in their social communities, nor have they been visible to the social science research community. Consequently, little is known about these romantic relationships, but what is known is reviewed in this chapter. Results from survey research on the sexual orientation of youth indicate that less than 1% define themselves as gay, lesbian, or bisexual. According to Savin-Williams, this percentage is lower than estimates for adults, which, he argues, indicates an unwillingness to admit to a gay identity. Gay romantic relationships need to be understood in the context of a social world that is intolerant of same-sex romantic relationships. Some of these barriers are examined, especially peer harassment, and the consequences for the development of gay youth are considered. Primarily, Savin-Williams argues, gay youth feel a deep sense of isolation from others, which impairs the development of a healthy self-concept.

Chapter 9, by Darling, Hamilton, and Niego, entitled "Adolescents' Relations With Adults Outside the Family," reviews the literature on adolescents' relations with nonkin adults. The authors argue that one reason why these relations have been neglected in research on adolescent development is that researchers have focused on the affective qualities of relationships, which are central in kinship relations, rather than on instrumental and activity-centered components, more commonly the basis for nonkin relations. Three questions are addressed in this chapter, which reviews and integrates research on relations between adolescents and unrelated adults. First, how often do adolescents establish close relations with unrelated adults? Second, how do adolescents describe their relations with unrelated adults, and how do these relations compare with their relations with significant others in other social roles? Third, what is the developmental impact of adolescents' relations with nonkin adults? Research is reviewed on the specific effects of mentoring programs, which match adolescents with nonkin adults whom they would be unlikely to know without the program. The authors argue that one key element that distinguishes adolescents' relations with nonkin adults from relations with other associates is the primacy of instrumental qualities and processes. They conclude that it is only by broadening the focus of research to include these dimensions that the role of unrelated adults in adolescents' lives can be understood.

2. Relationships During Adolescence: Continuity and Change in Interpersonal Perspective

W. Andrew Collins
University of Minnesota

Daniel J. Repinski
State University of New York, Geneseo

Relationships with family and friends have long been considered crucibles of adolescent development. Implicit in this view has been the idea that relationships during adolescence bear unique significance for the development of individuals. Ironically, much research on adolescence has focused on individual characteristics (e.g., autonomy, identity) without adequately attending to the salient relational contexts in which these same individuals participate. This chapter will provide an overview of conceptual perspectives on relationships, with particular attention to the distinctive features of adolescents' close relationships.

RELATIONSHIPS DURING ADOLESCENCE

Relationships are defined as more or less enduring ties or connections between two individuals, comprising frequent, highly interdependent action sequences that occur across diverse settings and tasks (Kelley et al., 1983). These interdependencies are natural products of shared histories and the complementary roles that emerge over time in both familial and close extrafamilial relationships (e.g., friendships).

Adolescent relationships bear some similarities to their childhood counterparts. In North America and Europe, parents and adolescents

AUTHOR'S NOTE: The authors wish to thank several anonymous reviewers and Raymond Montemayor for their constructive comments and suggestions on an earlier draft of this chapter. Support in completion of this chapter was provided by a grant from the National Institute of Mental Health to W. Andrew Collins and by an Eva O. Miller Fellowship from the University of Minnesota to Daniel J. Repinski.

7

commonly perceive their relationships with one another as warm and pleasant. Among the families that encounter difficulties in this period, a large proportion have had problems prior to adolescence (e.g., Kandel & Lesser, 1972; Offer, Ostrov, & Howard, 1981; Rutter, Graham, Chadwick, & Yule, 1976; for reviews, see Montemayor, 1983; Steinberg, 1990).

Relationships with peers during adolescence also show considerable continuity with peer relationships during childhood. Although specific friendships may not be stable across these two periods, several findings imply that relative success in forming and maintaining friendships in adolescence is highly correlated with childhood friendships. Stable friendships may be neither typical nor required during adolescence (Epstein, 1986; Savin-Williams & Berndt, 1990). Furthermore, stability with a "best" friend during adolescence appears to be more common than instability over the course of a school year (Berndt, Hawkins, & Hoyle, 1986), although some instability may be expected and indeed may be functional for individual development (Epstein, 1986; Savin-Williams & Berndt, 1990). Adolescents who experience peer difficulties frequently have a history of similar difficulties in relationships during childhood (Patterson, DeBaryshe, & Ramsey, 1989; Rubin, LeMare, & Lollis, 1990; see Hartup, in press, for a review).

Distinctive Features of Adolescents' Relationships

Two features of relationships during adolescence set the stage for assessing their significance and impact: (a) *changes* in the qualities of dyadic interactions in conjunction with the biological, cognitive, and social changes of adolescence; and (b) *differentiation* among the multiple dyadic relationships that comprise adolescents' social networks.

Changes in Relationships

The dyads and social networks in which adolescents participate undergo changes in response to the biological, cognitive, and social changes of adolescence. Although relationships show important common features from early to later adolescence, significant changes occur in the amount, content, and perceived meaning of the interactions occurring within them, in the expressions of positive and negative affect, and in the interpersonal perceptions of the interactors (for reviews, see Collins & Russell, 1991; Parker & Gottman, 1989). Feelings of positive regard increase toward parents, especially mothers, and perceptions of reciprocity with and acceptance by parents become more frequent (Youniss & Smollar, 1985), and adolescents' perceptions of self and others converge with those of parents (Alessandri & Wozniak, 1987) and friends (Furman & Bierman, 1984). At the same time, feelings of acceptance and satisfaction with family life and decision making have been found to be lower in middle adolescence than in childhood or young adulthood, and both parents and adolescents report more expressions of negative emotion, more instances of disagreement, and lower expressions of positive emotions and feelings of closeness in early and middle adolescence (for reviews, see Collins & Russell, 1991; Steinberg, 1990).

In friendships, intimacy is increasingly reported across the years from middle childhood to middle adolescence (Berndt, 1982; Bigelow & LaGaipa, 1975; Furman & Bierman, 1984; Furman & Buhrmester, 1992; Sharabany, Gershoni, & Hofman, 1981). Paradoxically, conflicts are more likely between friends than between acquaintances, but conflicts between friends are also resolved in distinctly different ways than conflicts between acquaintances. Furthermore, conflicts are less disruptive to friendships than to more casual acquaintanceships (for reviews, see Hartup, in press; Savin-Williams & Berndt, 1990).

Thus during adolescence some significant discontinuities in interactions coexist with important continuities in emotional ties to significant others. This pattern is often interpreted as evidence of transformations in close relationships in response to individual developmental changes during the transition to adolescence (e.g., Collins, 1990, in press). This transformation is thought to facilitate development of appropriate levels of individuation and autonomy as adolescents mature (Grotevant & Cooper, 1986; Wynne, 1984). Thus a key issue in studying relationships during adolescence concerns how dyads and systems adapt successfully to developmental changes in individuals.

Differentiation in Social Networks

Changes in the nature and course of relationships are accompanied by increasing differentiation among adolescents' close relationships. Relationships in adolescence are more extensive and diverse than those of childhood (Blyth, 1982; Csikszentmihalyi & Larson,

1984). Although family relationships remain salient during adolescence, an increasing proportion of time is devoted to interactions with nonfamily members (Csikszentmihalyi & Larson, 1984). Adolescents establish a wider range of casual friendships than children do, perhaps because of the more numerous possibilities available in school and at work. Romantic relationships also become common. These diverse relationships have different characteristics that serve both complementary and overlapping functions (see reviews by Collins & Russell, 1991; Hartup, in press).

Conceptual Perspectives on Relationships During Adolescence

Theories of adolescent development provide contrasting accounts of differentiation and change in relationships. In this section, we briefly outline four general theoretical perspectives: (a) endogenous-change perspectives, which emphasize biological and motivational pressures toward alterations of relationships; (b) social-psychological perspectives, which focus on external pressures toward change and the interplay of external and internal factors; (c) attachment perspectives, which address the pressures toward continuity and coherence in primary aspects of dyadic relationships; and (d) interdependency perspectives, which emphasize the patterns of interaction and affect and the principles of exchange that characterize close relationships.

Endogenous-Change Perspectives

Psychoanalytic and *evolutionary* views have in common two perspectives on relationships during adolescence. One is a focus on pubertal maturation in precipitating increased conflict and emotional distance in parent-child relationships and, correspondingly, an increased orientation to relationships beyond the family. The other is an emphasis on the functional significance of relationships and relationship changes.

Both Sigmund Freud (1923/1949) and Anna Freud (1969) assumed that hormonal changes and the subsequent surge of sexual excitation at puberty generated increased difficulties in impulse control. Distantiation from parents through rebelliousness and devaluation were seen as facilitating ego and superego controls in the face of strong pressures from the id. More recent psychoanalytic formulations (e.g., Blos, 1979) depict puberty as precipitating psychic pressure for individuation from parents in order to fulfill the social role demands of adulthood. Concomitant with these aspects of control and autonomy-striving are the issues of personal integration and mastery encompassed by Erikson's (1968) concept of ego identity. Evolutionary views (Steinberg, 1988) also emphasize the motivational force of autonomy-striving. From this perspective, perturbations in parent-child relationships at puberty serve to facilitate formation of sexual relationships outside of the family group and, particularly for males, to foster the socialization of autonomy. Steinberg (1988) has argued that the relation of puberty to family perturbations may be bidirectional, with pubertal changes actually being facilitated or intensified by family conflict and, conversely, impeded by family closeness.

These views give special importance to variables pertaining to the affective tone and subjective closeness of parent-child exchanges. In addition, the psychoanalytic emphasis on devaluation (in Blos's [1967] term, *deidealization*) of parents implies changes in attitude toward or confidence in parents as models and guides for action. With regard to parents, Erikson (1950) implies that evidence of a resurgence of identity issues might accompany the shift from rearing dependent children to facing an "empty nest" (Aldous, 1978; Silverberg & Steinberg, 1990).

The process of change implied by these formulations is a dynamic one, with degree of disruption fluctuating throughout the early and middle adolescent years. The hypothesis of hormonal disruption implies that the most pronounced parent-child conflict and anxiety should coincide with the most intense periods of pubertal change, although the evolutionary viewpoint suggests that pubertal change follows, rather than precedes, intensified relationship perturbations. Corresponding increases in orientation to relationships with peers are viewed as a shift toward interpersonal objects appropriate to adult roles (Blos, 1979).

Social-Psychological Perspectives

Social-psychological theories view family perturbations as a reflection of the stresses engendered by the multiple adaptations required during the transition to adolescence (Lewin, 1939; Simmons & Blyth,

1987). Also included in this category are perspectives from social-learning theory (Bandura, 1964), cultural anthropology (e.g., Benedict, 1938), and family-development theory (e.g., Aldous, 1978; Combrinck-Graham, 1985). The latter regard the life-cycle changes experienced by offspring as having ramifications for family systems, which in turn affect the individual development of both parents and children (Combrinck-Graham, 1985; Wynne, 1984).

The extensiveness of the transition is due partly to the physical changes of puberty and behavior commonly expected of physically adult, reproductively mature individuals. In addition, however, the transition to adulthood is partly determined by age-graded expectations, tasks, and settings. The confluence of maturational changes and age-graded shifts in tasks and settings can have greater effects on the psychosocial adaptation of individuals than either alone. A well-documented instance is the deleterious impact on seventh-grade girls' self-esteem from the combination of pubertal maturation, the onset of dating, and a shift from elementary to junior high school (Simmons & Blyth, 1987; Simmons, Burgeson, & Reef, 1988).

The impact of adolescent transitions on relationships has two major sources. One is the increase in ambient anxiety and tension associated with adapting to the multiple changes of early adolescence. Some difficulties in adjusting to the world beyond the family are imported into family relationships, perhaps because families provide relatively safe settings for manifesting bewilderment, anger, and frustration that cannot readily be expressed with nonfamily members (Hartup, 1979; Youniss, 1980). The second is the pressure to diminish dependency on the family in order to adapt successfully to the world beyond the family (Brooks-Gunn, Petersen, & Eichorn, 1985; Lerner, 1985). These latter pressures are likely to affect psychosocial variables (e.g., self-esteem, perceived independence, value placed on independence, perceived acceptance, methods of control, and implicit timetables for "acting older" [Collins, in press; Simmons & Blyth, 1987]) that may affect a variety of interpersonal relationships. Parental role confusion and satisfaction also have an impact upon the transitions of this period (Silverberg & Steinberg, 1990; Wynne, 1984). The convergence of life-course issues in the two generations has been frequently cited as a likely source of difficulties in parent-adolescent relationships (e.g., Hill, 1987; Rossi, 1987; Silverberg & Steinberg, 1990).

Although, like other perspectives, the social-psychological viewpoint implies an increase and then a decrease in relationship difficulties from early to late adolescence, the course may be more episodic than other theories would imply. From the perspective of social age grading, this episodic pattern would reflect the periodic occurrence of age-graded transitions; from a family systems perspective (e.g., Combrinck-Graham, 1985; Wynne, 1984), episodic change would recur in connection with changes in family status. An alternative, but conceptually consistent, prediction is that early adolescence might be the primary period of change, with gradual restabilization as appropriate accommodations are made to transitional status. Individuals may vary, moreover, as a function of timing of puberty. Hill (1988) has suggested that very early pubertal timing for girls may result in long-lasting perturbations in relationships, but the reasons for a different pattern of resolution for this group than for other timing-of-puberty groups are not based in theory.

Attachment Perspectives

Attachment approaches are directed toward understanding motivational tendencies that produce functional similarities in relationships across time. Bowlby (1982) predicted that *internal working models* of relationships formed in early caregiver-child interactions would be stable from one period of life to another. The stability occurs in the *qualities* of relationships. These qualities are based in emotions associated with feelings of security and insecurity and therefore undergo little change. Specific forms and modes of interaction between parent and child differ from one age period to another, reflecting the developing capabilities and needs of the child and the varying challenges associated with age-graded tasks and settings.

The view of change within this framework is that specific interactions vary as a function of changing developmental challenges from one age period to the next, but are still guided by internal working models that are essentially stable. For example, in longitudinal work (Sroufe & Fleeson, 1988), interactions and the management of emotions with teachers and peers in early and middle childhood can be predicted from assessments of caregiver-child attachment in infancy. These parallel patterns of behavior and affect across age periods have been attributed to stable *organizations* of behavior, mediated by internal working models formed in early caregiver-child relationships and repeatedly reconfirmed in subsequent interactions with others (Sroufe & Fleeson, 1988; Sroufe & Waters, 1977). Behavior change may be more marked from one age period to another in relationships marked by attachment security because adaptation to new situational constraints and demands may be mediated by feelings of security. In contrast, relationships marked by insecurity may be more repetitious despite changes in situational cues and expected behaviors.

Differentiation among relationships results from certain cues or signals regarding what is expected from a particular other person. Although there is considerable coherence in adolescents' reactions to certain types of actions by others, relationship partners nevertheless elicit different types of interactions. For example, aloof, ambivalent adolescents both elicit and actively respond to different types of overtures from peers than do more outgoing, relaxed, sociable children (Waters, Kondo-Ikemura, Posada, & Richters, 1991).

Interdependency Perspectives

Interdependency perspectives also emphasize the joint patterns in which the actions, cognitions, and emotions of each member of the dyad are significant to the other's reactions (Berscheid, Snyder, & Omoto, 1989; Hinde & Stevenson-Hinde, 1987; Kelley et al., 1983). In this perspective, however, close relationships are defined quantitatively, rather than qualitatively. Closeness is reflected in the interdependency between two persons, defined in terms of the frequency, diversity, strength, and duration of mutual impact (Berscheid et al., 1989; Kelley et al., 1983; Repinski, 1992). Thus a close relationship is one in which two persons interact with each other frequently, across a variety of settings and tasks, and exert considerable influence upon each other's thoughts and actions. Typically, such relationships are not transitory, but exist for periods measured in months or years. It should be noted that closeness is independent of the emotional content of the relationship; interdependency characterizes relationships in which affective expression is largely negative, as well as those in which warm, positive emotions predominate.

In this perspective, adolescence can be characterized as a period during which interdependencies in familial relationships continue, but often in different forms than in earlier life, whereas interdependencies with friends and romantic partners become more apparent. Some changes are required to create and maintain these interdependencies. In parent-child relationships, expectations must be adjusted on both sides in order to preserve the degree of interdependence that permits parents to continue to influence the child's development (Collins, in press). In peer relationships, skills must be developed for maintaining interdependence on the basis of shared interests, commitments, and intimacy, even when contact is relatively infrequent (Parker & Gottman, 1989). Mismatch between expectations about the relationship may stimulate conflicts, but these conflicts often stimulate adjustments of expectations that gradually restore harmony (Collins, 1990, in press). The process by which discrepant perceptions mediate changes in interactions has yet to be examined directly (see reviews by Collins & Laursen, 1992; Silverberg, Tennenbaum, & Jacob, 1992; Steinberg, 1990).

Differentiation is partly constrained by interrelations among the relationships in which most children and adolescents participate. For example, trust, communication, and conflict resolution within families have been found to be correlated with adolescents' intimacy and communication with peers (Cooper & Ayers-Lopez, 1985; Youniss & Smollar, 1985), and the intimacy experienced in friendship may provide a model that enhances capacities for intimacy within families as adolescents mature (Youniss, 1980). Nevertheless, differences in the frequency, diversity, strength, and duration of relationships with parents or siblings and those with friends and acquaintances clearly produce contrasts among these different relationship types.

ASPECTS OF ADOLESCENTS' RELATIONSHIPS

The foregoing implies two linked hypotheses about relationships during adolescence. One is that adolescent development is accompanied by increasing distance in parent-child relationships and decreasing distance in adolescents' friendships; the other is that adolescents increasingly form close relationships with persons outside of the family. Together these hypotheses have yielded two contrasting but overlapping groups of constructs. One group consists of aspects of behavior and emotion that imply interpersonal distance in relationships, and the other consists of constructs that emphasize interpersonal connections. For each construct, we address implications for the increasing differentiation among relationships during adolescence and the changing nature and processes of relationships with family members and friends.

Constructs Emphasizing Relative Distance

Constructs of distance are addressed in all conceptual perspectives on adolescents' relationships. Most closely identified with these ideas are psychoanalytically influenced views that psychological separation and individuation from parents during early and late adolescence are essential for healthy adjustment (Blos, 1979). The constructs emerging from these views include conflict, individuation, separation, and autonomy.

Conflict

Early interest in parent-adolescent conflict was rooted in the implication of inevitable storm and stress in psychodynamic theories of adolescence. Empirical findings have consistently indicated, however, that conflict varies considerably across relationships (Montemayor, 1986). Researchers have accordingly turned toward examining the nature, content, frequency, and function of conflict between parents and adolescents.

Conflicts are a normal and regular part of family-adolescent relationships. Adolescents report about two arguments with their parents and three arguments with siblings in an average week (Montemayor, 1982). Both females and males have more arguments with their mothers than with their fathers, and girls report more conflicts with their mothers than do boys (Montemayor, 1982; Montemayor & Hanson, 1985; Savin-Williams & Small, 1986; Smetana, 1988, 1989; Smith & Forehand, 1986; Youniss & Smollar, 1985). These sex differences, however, have not been found in parents' reports of disagreements with adolescents (Hill & Holmbeck, 1987).

Disagreements with parents during adolescence, like those of the prepubescent years, center around mundane aspects of family life (Csikszentmihalyi & Larson, 1984; Gehring, Wentzel, Feldman, & Munson, 1990; Montemayor, 1983; Smetana, 1988, 1989). Adolescents report frequent disagreements with both parents and siblings regarding interpersonal issues (e.g., personal eccentricities, competition for limited resources, etc.) and family rules (Montemayor & Hanson, 1985; Smetana, 1989; Youniss & Smollar, 1985). Parents of adolescents report dissatisfaction with the child's behavior at home (Achenbach & Edelbrock, 1981; Harris & Howard, 1984), as well as disagreements concerning peer relations, personal habits, and family obligations (Hill & Holmbeck, 1987). Until recently (see Gehring et al., 1990; Papini & Sebby, 1988), parents and adolescents rarely reported arguing about potentially explosive issues such as sex and substance abuse. Thus in most families parents and adolescents appear to argue about a small number of issues, with many aspects of their relationship remaining satisfying.

Studies examining parents' and adolescents' reasoning about conflicts (i.e., their understanding and construction of expectations and responsibilities) reveal that adolescents focus on issues of personal choice, whereas parents treat conflicts as issues that should be resolved with reference to social conventions (Smetana, 1989). In addition, observational studies have demonstrated that the adaptive function of parent-adolescent conflicts depends on the quality of the relationship itself. Parent-adolescent conflicts in a relationship characterized by trust, closeness, and positive emotional tone are associated with greater identity exploration and skills for interpersonal understanding (Grotevant & Cooper, 1985), whereas conflicts marked by hostility, inconsistency, and escalation to high intensity alienate the individuals from each other and limit the potential for positive interactions in the future (Patterson, 1986).

Differences between familial and extrafamilial relationships are apparent in research on the nature and content of conflicts in adolescent friendships. In contrast to parent-child relationships, conflicts between adolescent friends frequently involve violations of rules that govern the maintenance of friendships (Youniss & Smollar, 1985). These violations include untrustworthy acts, lack of sufficient attention, disrespectful acts, unacceptable behavior, and inadequate

communication. In adolescence, unlike earlier developmental periods, friendships are likely to continue through periods of conflict
rather than terminate (Youniss & Smollar, 1985).

Individuation

The concept of individuation was introduced by Mahler (1963/1979)
as a process that characterizes the young child's movement away from
the symbiotic mother-infant relationship. Blos (1967) proposed that a
second individuation process occurs during adolescence that serves to
further the development of a separate self. Current conceptualizations
of individuation imply a simultaneous process of *separation* from
parents, which facilitates the search for a distinctive definition of the
self, along with a continuing connectedness to parents through the
maintenance and elaboration of existing emotional bonds (Grotevant
& Cooper, 1985, 1986; White, Speisman, & Costos, 1983).

Psychological Separation

Using psychoanalytic theory (Blos, 1979; Mahler, 1963/1979) as a
foundation, Hoffman (1984) proposes that psychological separation
entails functional, attitudinal, emotional, and conflictual independence
from parents. *Functional independence* requires the management and
direction of one's personal affairs without the aid of parents. *Attitudinal
independence* concerns one's ability to have one's own set of unique
beliefs, values, and attitudes. *Emotional independence* is defined as freedom from excessive need for emotional support from parents. *Conflictual independence* is characterized as freedom from excessive guilt,
mistrust, or anger in relation to the mother and father.

Psychological separation has been studied most frequently in
older adolescents. Psychological separation has been found to increase during the college years (Lapsley, Rice, & Shadid, 1989; Rice,
1992). Male college students reported a greater degree of psychological
separation from parents than did females (Lapsley et al., 1989;
Lopez, Campbell, & Watkins, 1986; Rice, 1992). Several studies have
documented positive associations between conflictual independence
and healthy adjustment to college for both females and males (Lopez,
1991; Lopez et al., 1986; Rice, Cole, & Lapsley, 1990). Dependency
conflicts with parents, in combination with a diminished sense of

individuality, have been linked to eating disorders among young women (Friedlander & Siegel, 1990).

Autonomy

Autonomy includes both intrapsychic and interpersonal dimensions (Hill & Holmbeck, 1986) and implies independence and greater self-determination in thought, behavior, and affect. These dimensions have been defined and studied separately. With regard to *cognitive autonomy*, Piaget (1965) argued that autonomy develops within a cooperative relational context rather than being the result of cognitive individualism or independent thinking. Accordingly, the autonomous individual is able to accept ideas and principles that have been validated through the process of open and fair discussion (Youniss & Smollar, 1985). Youniss and Smollar (1985) criticize the conventional meaning of autonomous thinking as placing too much emphasis on the accomplishments of adolescent's own reasoning. In their view adolescents' reasoning and self-understanding develop within relationships with parents and friends. Cognitive autonomy has also been characterized as a subjective sense of self-reliance and a belief that one has control over one's life (Sessa & Steinberg, 1991; Steinberg & Silverberg, 1986).

A second dimension, *behavioral autonomy*, has frequently been operationalized in terms of independence of thought and self-governance of action in relationships with parents (Amato, 1987; Dornbusch, Ritter, Mont-Reynaud, & Chen, 1990; Feldman & Quatman, 1988; Feldman & Rosenthal, 1991; Poole & Gelder, 1984) and peers (Steinberg & Silverberg, 1986). For example, choosing how to spend money, which clothes to buy, and which friends to go out with are all decisions that purportedly reflect behavioral autonomy.

A third construct, *emotional autonomy*, is grounded in the psychoanalytic notion that the adolescent must relinquish childish dependencies on and conceptualizations of parents (Blos, 1979). This view has been operationalized (Steinberg & Silverberg, 1986) as consisting of four components: two cognitive components ("perceives parents as people" and "parental deidealization") and two affective components ("nondependency on parents" and "individuation"). Findings from a survey of early adolescents revealed that, with increasing age, adolescents are more likely to feel individuated, less likely to idealize their parents, and less likely to express childish dependency on them (Steinberg & Silverberg, 1986).

A controversy surrounds the meaning and function of emotional autonomy in adolescents' relationships. Ryan and Lynch (1989) have recently argued that Steinberg and Silverberg's (1986) measure of emotional autonomy actually reflects a sense of emotional detachment from the parents and a general reluctance to rely on the parents. In support of this criticism, Ryan and Lynch (1989) found that emotional autonomy was negatively associated with early adolescents' reports of the quality of attachment to parents and positively associated with high school students' experience of parental rejection. Steinberg and Lamborn (1992) maintain, however, that emotional autonomy is a relational quality and cite evidence that adolescent reports of emotional autonomy can have differing developmental consequences as a function of the underlying security of the parent-adolescent relationship.

Constructs Emphasizing Interpersonal Connectedness

Psychoanalytic theorists (e.g., Blos, 1979) hypothesized that as adolescents separate from their parents they turn to friends and peers as foci of emotional connections. In contrast, contemporary formulations of adolescent development (Collins, 1990; Grotevant & Cooper, 1985, 1986) emphasize the transformation of adolescents' relationships with both parents and friends. Of particular interest are the constructs of trust, intimacy, closeness, and communication.

Trust

Trust as a characteristic of adolescents' relationships with parents and friends has been characterized in one of two ways. First, trust as a subjective experience has been conceptualized as one's belief in the sincerity and truthfulness of the other's words and promises (Imber, 1973), the feeling of security that others will understand and respect one's needs and desires (Armsden & Greenberg, 1987), or one's own attributions of trust to others (Fine, Worley, & Schwebel, 1985; Rosenthal, Gurney, & Moore, 1981; Rotenberg, 1984). Adolescents' reports of mutual trust in their relationships with parents and peers are positively related to the quality of communication in these relationships and negatively associated with feelings of alienation and isolation (Armsden & Greenberg, 1987). Trust has also been conceptualized as an element of adolescents' relationships that emerges through interaction. In this view, mutual trust arises from a reciprocal pattern of cooperation (Rotenberg & Pilipenko, 1983). Trust is seen as developing in a relationship in which partners can depend on one another and rely on the other to participate according to agreed-upon norms (Youniss, 1980). In this view trust is the product rather than a determinant of the relationship. Although few studies exist, it seems likely that adolescents' experience of trust in relationships with parents and friends becomes more differentiated and sophisticated in acccord with developing cognitive abilities and an expanded repertoire of experience.

Intimacy

Intimacy as a quality of relationships appears to emerge between childhood and adolescence. With regard to friendships especially, intimacy becomes salient in descriptions of friendship that emphasize sharing of thoughts and feelings (e.g., Berndt, 1982; Buhrmester & Furman, 1987; Furman & Bierman, 1984). Adolescents display greater knowledge of such information about their best friends than do children (Diaz & Berndt, 1982). The development of intimacy in mother-adolescent relationships seems to parallel friendships (Youniss & Smollar, 1985). These findings support Sullivan's (1953) contention that the need for intimacy allows relationship partners to reveal themselves while seeking and expressing validation of each other's attributes and perspectives.

Reis and Shaver (1988) argue that intimate interpersonal interactions occur when two "partners experience and express feelings, communicate verbally and nonverbally, satisfy social motives, augment or reduce social fears, talk and learn about themselves and their unique characteristics, and become 'close'" (Reis & Shaver, 1988, p. 387). These two dimensions of intimacy (i.e., emotional communication and validation) are evident to varying degrees in research on friendships. In studies with early adolescents, intimacy has been defined in terms of disclosure of personal thoughts and feelings (Buhrmester & Furman, 1987; Bukowski, Newcomb, & Hoza, 1987). With older adolescents, intimacy has been characterized as the degree to which respondents feel accepted, understood, and satisfied with friendships (Crockett, Losoff, & Petersen, 1984; Fenzel & Blyth, 1986; Rosenthal et al., 1981), one's knowledge of the preferences and personality characteristics of a friend (Diaz & Berndt, 1982), as well as the degree to which friendships are reciprocal, stable, and characterized by honest communication and sensitivity to the needs and interests of the partners (Townsend, McCracken, & Wilton, 1988). Sharabany's Intimacy Scale (Sharabany et al., 1981) taps eight dimensions of intimacy with a best friend: frankness and spontaneity, sensitivity and knowing, attachment, exclusiveness, giving and sharing, imposing and taking, common activities, and trust and loyalty.

Studies examining the salience of intimacy in adolescents' relationships reveal both differentiation and change. Girls report more intimate knowledge (Diaz & Berndt, 1982) and more frequent intimate interactions with same-sex friends than do boys (Buhrmester & Furman, 1987; Fenzel & Blyth, 1986). Both male and female adolescents report greater intimacy in their relationships with their mothers than with their fathers (LeCroy, 1988). Intimacy in opposite-sex friendships and same-sex friendships increases with age (Diaz & Berndt, 1982; Sharabany et al., 1981). Finally, intimacy with close siblings remains constant during the adolescent years, but decreases across time in the parent-adolescent relationship (Buhrmester & Furman, 1987).

Closeness

Closeness in adolescence has been variously conceptualized in terms of emotional tone or cohesion, subjective opinions, and interdependence or mutual influence. When defined by strong positive affect, closeness has been likened to intimacy because of its characteristic emotional communication, self-disclosure, and personal validation (Blyth, Hill, & Thiel, 1982; Crockett et al., 1984; Paulson, Hill, & Holmbeck, 1991; Vanden Heuvel, 1988) and has also been characterized as positive feelings and attributions directed toward another (Daniels & Plomin, 1985). Subjective closeness is typically assessed by asking individuals to rate how close they feel to each other on a single 4- or 5-point scale (Bell, Avery, Jenkins, Feld, & Schoenrock, 1985; Cicirelli, 1980; Daniels, Dunn, Furstenberg, & Plomin, 1985). Findings have consistently revealed that adolescents experience greater closeness with mothers than with fathers; similarly, mothers, in comparison to fathers, feel closer to the adolescents (Cicirelli, 1980; Paulson et al., 1991; Paulson, Koman, & Hill, 1990; Repinski, 1992). In addition, emotional closeness and cohesion have been assessed with pictorial representations (Pipp, Shaver, Jennings, Lamborn, & Fischer, 1985) and figure placements (Gehring & Feldman, 1988). These procedures have revealed decreasing closeness with increasing age in adolescents' relationships with siblings (Gehring & Feldman, 1988) and parents (Gehring & Feldman, 1988; Pipp et al., 1985). In the interdependence view (Kelley et al., 1983) described earlier, closeness is defined in terms of mutual impact between two persons. Recent research indicates that interdependence in parent-adolescent relationships decreases from fifth to eleventh grade (Laursen, 1991; Repinski, 1992) and that interdependence with friends increases up to the early college years (Laursen, 1991). Interdependence, subjective closeness, and emotional tone are only moderately associated and thus are not simply redundant dimensions of parent-adolescent relationships (Repinski, 1992).

Relative Positive Affect

The experience of affect in relationships has frequently been conceptualized as a continuum with a positive and a negative pole (e.g., warm, supportive, and accepting versus hostile, stressful, and rejecting). The experience of warmth, support, and acceptance typically involves the communication of positive, benevolent feelings from one individual to another, whereas the experience of hostility and rejection connotes a dismissing and cruel attitude. This continuum is evident in much of the parent-child socialization literature (see Baumrind, 1991; Maccoby & Martin, 1983). In research on adolescents' relationships, this view has been applied both to relationships with parents (Amato, 1989; Daniels & Plomin, 1985; Papini, Datan, & McCluskey-Fawcett, 1988; Paulson et al., 1991; Repinski, Conger, & Whitbeck, 1992) and with friends (Brown, Eicher, & Petrie, 1986; Bukowski et al., 1987; O'Brien & Bierman, 1988).

In general, findings indicate that positive and negative emotions are not polar opposites, but emotions that coexist in relationships (Kelley et al., 1983). Adolescents' relationships with family members are characterized by overall increases in emotionally expressive exchanges, with relative declines in the expression of positive emotions and relative increases in negative emotions around the time of puberty (Hill, 1988; Papini et al., 1988; Steinberg, 1988; see review by Collins & Russell, 1991). This general pattern affects a variety of forms of emotional experience in relationships with parents and with friends: perceptions of emotional support, problem-focused support, behavioral support (Cicirelli, 1980; Frankel, 1990; Hoffman, Ushpiz, & Levy-Shiff, 1988), physical affection (Barber & Thomas, 1986), and relationship quality (Richardson, Galambos, Schulenberg, & Petersen, 1984). The experience of negative affect in relationships has also been manifested in rising incidence of general stress, hurt feelings, and embarrassment (Frankel, 1990).

Communication

Communication has been conceived of as the process and content of information exchange. Process questions have focused on the quality of interactions, whereas interest in content has focused on topics of discussion. Many common measures of family functioning include a scale or dimension of communication, characterized as direct discussion, open conflict resolution, and a mechanism for sharing preferences, needs, and feelings.

Most of these measures assess communication at the level of the family (e.g., Family Adaptability and Cohesion Evaluation Scales [Olson, 1986]; McMaster Family Assessment Device [Epstein, Baldwin, & Bishop, 1983]; Family Assessment Measure [Skinner, Steinhauser, & Santa-Barbara, 1983]; Self-Report Family Inventory [Beavers, Hampson, & Hulgus, 1985]). Some, however, are specific to parent-adolescent relationships (e.g., the Parent-Adolescent Communication Scale [Barnes & Olson, 1982]). Noller and Bagi (1985) have examined six process dimensions (i.e., frequency, initiation, recognition, domination, self-disclosure, and satisfaction) and 14 content areas of communication varying in intrafamilial or extrafamilial focus and degree of specificity. Adolescents' perceptions of parental criticism directed toward the adolescent have also been studied (Harris & Howard, 1984), as have perceptions of the quality of communication with parents and friends (Armsden & Greenberg, 1987).

Differentiation within family relationships is evident in that adolescents typically discuss a wider range of topics with their mothers and friends than they do with their fathers (Richardson et al., 1984; Youniss & Smollar, 1985). If one compares family and extrafamily relationships, adolescents appear to seek communication opportunities with parents regarding topics that entail a long-term perspective and parents' greater authority and experience. By contrast, communication with friends is sought regarding evaluations within shared social goals and value systems (Hunter, 1985; Rawlins & Holl, 1988; Youniss & Smollar, 1985). Change is apparent in a generally greater orientation to mutual understanding with both parents and friends (Hunter, 1985).

TOWARD FURTHER RESEARCH ON RELATIONSHIPS DURING ADOLESCENCE

This review of constructs encompassing both changes and differentiation in relative distance and in interpersonal connectedness provides some useful guidelines for how future research might be framed. In this section, we attempt to answer the question, What should be contained in a useful conceptual framework for research on relationships during adolescence?

First, the framework should include an emphasis on interrelations among aspects of relationships. Researchers have frequently focused on discrete constructs of interactions, emotions, or cognitions. For example, measures of relative distance have often been the focus of studies, but these have rarely been assessed in conjunction with measures of connectedness. Consequently, the links between specific constructs and the multiple changes that occur in relationships during adolescence have rarely been explored. In studies in which multiple constructs have been assessed (e.g., Flannery & Montemayor, 1991; Hill, 1988; Steinberg, 1987, 1988), constructs such as positive affect and subjective closeness, as measured by reports of parents and adolescents, were negatively related to pubertal status, whereas negative affect was directly related to pubertal maturation. At the same time, these studies leave open the question of the role of conflict in distancing, because conflict was not assessed independent of affective measures (Collins & Laursen, 1992). A recognition that the meaning of single constructs is often conditional on measures of other constructs should encourage research on the multifaceted nature of relationships and relationship changes during adolescence.

Second, the framework should attend to the social networks in which individual dyads are embedded. The rapid expansion and increasing diversity of social networks during adolescence entail greater possibilities for interactive effects: relationships are likely to affect and be affected by other relationships in which the members participate. Interactions in one parent-child dyad are often influenced by interactions between the parents or between parents and other children (e.g., Gjerde, 1986; Vuchinich, 1987). Moreover, behavior in parent-child dyads is often correlated with behavior toward friends and acquaintances (e.g., Cooper & Ayers-Lopez, 1985).

Attention to links among relationships, in addition to studies of particular types of dyads, is needed to further our understanding of the characteristics and processes of relationships during adolescence. As an example, consider findings about intimacy in adolescents' relationships with parents and with friends. Intimacy more clearly becomes a defining characteristic of friendships in adolescence. Although this might be attributed to distancing from parents and relatively greater connectedness to peers, studies have also consistently shown that adolescents perceive considerable intimacy with mothers, although less so with fathers (e.g., Youniss & Smollar, 1985). When multiple dyads are considered, intimacy in adolescent relationships seems less a matter of shifts in orientation from parents to peers than evidence of greater differentiation in relationships. Along with increased differentiation, there may also be (a) a general increase in capacity or desire for intimacy (or both), and (b) greater selectivity in the relationships in which intimacy is attempted and experienced.

Some key questions about the nature and impact of relationships during adolescence await attention to interrelations among significant relationships. As an example, consider questions of relative influence by parents and by peers in adolescence, which reflect concerns about increasing parent-child distance and increasing connectedness in peer relationships. Some findings indicate complementarity between these two types of relationships, with peers and parents influencing adolescents in different spheres, whereas others imply that increasing cross-pressures accompany differentiation of relationships during this period (see Hartup, 1983, for a review). Considering parent-child and peer relationships simultaneously may provide insights into the conditions under which functional complementarity, rather than competitive influence, occurs.

Third, future research should pay consistent attention to the functions of relationships and to changes in those functions as adolescents mature. Much work on adolescent development has included measures of the behaviors and attitudes of others as cor-relates of social competence. These studies have largely implied static, one-way models in which adolescents are passive recipients of the actions of others (Collins, in press). Yet the influences of others are most likely to occur within the joint patterns of action, emotion, and thought between adolescents and their parents or friends.

Some evidence supports this view. Characteristics of problem-solving interactions between parents and adolescents have been found to be correlated with measures of adolescents' ego develop-ment and identity exploration (Grotevant & Cooper, 1985, 1986; Hauser et al., 1984; Leaper et al., 1989). Furthermore, differentiation of dyads was clearly apparent within these families. Fathers of adolescents who were rated as high in identity exploration and in role-taking skill characteristically expressed high levels of sensitiv-ity and respect for others' views, but also expressed separateness by being willing to disagree with others.

Social development in and beyond adolescence requires the con-tinuation of bonds between adolescents and their close relationship partners, with simultaneous adjustments in response to physical, social, and cognitive changes in the adolescents. Collins (in press) has recently proposed that adaptation in relationships is stimulated by repeated experiences of violations of expectations in close rela-tionships. Particularly in the case of parent-child relationships, de-viations from expected behavior patterns give rise to conflict be-tween parents and children during the transition to adolescence. These conflicts in turn provide an impetus for both parent and children to form new age-appropriate expectations, behaviors, and responses with respect to their interactions. Variations in responses to violated expectations may be an important basis for distinguish-ing among relationships during adolescence and for predicting differences in the developmental sequelae of those relationships.

CONCLUSION

A relationships approach represents an innovation in the study of individual development during adolescence. Many of the pronounced individual changes that historically have been the main focus of re-search on adolescence can be understood more fully in the context of relationships with significant others. It is now clear, for example, that conflict does not merely reflect intrapersonal turmoil, but also contributes to interpersonal adaptations to the changing capabilities and needs of adolescents. Relational perspectives also challenge the simplistic view that adolescents turn away from parents toward peers; rather, both are elements of an expanding network of relationships in which their influences are interrelated and complementary.

The key task for the future is to understand the interplay between individual growth and change during adolescence and the nature and developmental significance of relationships with others. Of particular concern is a better understanding of those aspects of relationships that are maintained over time because they are important to healthy development in and beyond adolescence. Equally significant are aspects that are modified in the service of the same developmental purposes. Such research may reveal the distinctive significance of relationships during adolescence and ultimately may illuminate their place in individual development across the lifespan.

REFERENCES

Achenbach, T. M., & Edelbrock, C. S. (1981). Behavioral problems and competencies reported by parents of normal and disturbed children aged four through sixteen. *Monographs of the Society for Research in Child Development, 46* (No. 188).

Aldous, J. (1978). *Family careers: Developmental change in families.* New York: John Wiley.

Alessandri, S. M., & Wozniak, R. H. (1987). The child's awareness of parental beliefs concerning the child: A developmental study. *Child Development, 58,* 316-323.

Amato, P. R. (1987). Family processes in one-parent, stepparent, and intact families: The child's point of view. *Journal of Marriage and the Family, 49,* 327-337.

Amato, P. R. (1989). Family processes and the competence of adolescents and primary school children. *Journal of Youth and Adolescence, 18,* 39-53.

Armsden, G. C., & Greenberg, M. T. (1987). The inventory of parent and peer attachment: Individual differences and their relationship to psychological well-being in adolescence. *Journal of Youth and Adolescence, 16,* 427-454.

Bandura, A. (1964). The stormy decade: Fact or fiction? *Psychology in the School, 1,* 224-231.

Barber, B. K., & Thomas, D. L. (1986). Dimensions of fathers' and mothers' supportive behavior: The case for physical affection. *Journal of Marriage and the Family, 48,* 783-794.

Barnes, H. L., & Olson, D. H. (1982). Parent-adolescent communication scale. In D. H. Olson, H. I. McCubbin, H. Barnes, A. Larsen, M. Muxen, & M. Wilson, *Family inventories: Inventories used in a national survey of families across the family life cycle* (pp. 33-48). St Paul: University of Minnesota, Dept. of Family Social Science.

Baumrind, D. (1991). Effective parenting during the early adolescent transition. In
   P. A. Cowan & M. Hetherington (Eds.), *Family transitions.* Hillsdale, NJ:
   Lawrence Erlbaum.
Beavers, W. R., Hampson, R. B., & Hulgus, Y. F. (1985). Commentary: The Beavers
   Systems approach to family assessment. *Family Process, 24,* 398-405.
Bell, N. J., Avery, A. W., Jenkins, D., Feld, J., & Schoenrock, C. J. (1985). Family
   relationships and social competence during late adolescence. *Journal of Youth
   and Adolescence, 14,* 109-119.
Benedict, R. (1938). Continuities and discontinuities in cultural conditioning. *Psy-
   chiatry, 1,* 161-167.
Berndt, T. J. (1982). The features and effects of friendship in early adolescence. *Child
   Development, 53,* 1447-1460.
Berndt, T. J., Hawkins, J. A., & Hoyle, S. G. (1986). Changes in friendship during a
   school year: Effects on children's and adolescents' impression of friendship and
   sharing with friends. *Child Development, 57,* 1284-1297.
Berscheid, E., Snyder, M., & Omoto, A. M. (1989). The Relationship Closeness
   Inventory: Assessing the closeness of personal relationships. *Journal of Person-
   ality and Social Psychology, 57,* 792-807.
Bigelow, B. J., & LaGaipa, J. J. (1975). Children's written descriptions of friendship:
   A multidimensional analysis. *Developmental Psychology, 11,* 857-858.
Blos, P. (1967). The second individuation process of adolescence. *Psychoanalytic
   Study of the Child, 22,* 162-168.
Blos, P. (1979). *The adolescent passage.* New York: International Universities Press.
Blyth, D. A. (1982). Mapping the social world of adolescents: Issues, techniques,
   and problems. In F. Serafica (Ed.), *Social cognitive development in context* (pp. 240-
   252). New York: Guilford.
Blyth, D. A., Hill, J. P., & Thiel, K. S. (1982). Early adolescents' significant others:
   Grade and gender differences in perceived relationships with familial and
   non-familial adults and young people. *Journal of Early Adolescence, 11,* 425-450.
Bowlby, J. (1982). *Attachment and loss: Vol. 1. Attachment* (2nd ed.). New York: Basic
   Books.
Brooks-Gunn, J., Petersen, A. C., & Eichorn, D. (1985). The study of maturational
   timing effects in adolescence. *Journal of Youth and Adolescence, 14,* 149-161.
Brown, B. B., Eicher, S. A., & Petrie, S. (1986). The importance of peer group
   affiliation in adolescence. *Journal of Adolescence, 9,* 73-96.
Buhrmester, D., & Furman, W. (1987). The development of companionship and
   intimacy. *Child Development, 58,* 1101-1113.
Bukowski, W. M., Newcomb, A. F., & Hoza, B. (1987). Friendship conceptions
   among early adolescents: A longitudinal study of stability and change. *Journal
   of Early Adolescence, 7,* 143-152.
Cicirelli, V. G. (1980). A comparison of college women's feelings toward their
   siblings and parents. *Journal of Marriage and the Family, 42,* 111-118.
Collins, W. A. (1990). Parent-child relationships in the transition to adolescence:
   Continuity and change in interaction, affect, and cognition. In R. Montemayor,
   G. Adams, & T. Gullotta (Eds.), *Advances in adolescent development: Vol. 2. From
   childhood to adolescence: A transitional period?* (pp. 85-106). Newbury Park, CA:
   Sage.

Collins, W. A. (in press). Relationships and development: Dyadic adaptation to individual change. In S. Shulman & S. Strauss (Eds.), *Relationships and socioemotional development*. New York: Ablex.

Collins, W. A., & Laursen, B. (1992). Conflict and relationships during adolescence. In C. U. Shantz & W. W. Hartup (Eds.), *Conflict in child and adolescent development* (pp. 216-241). New York: Cambridge University Press.

Collins, W. A., & Russell, G. (1991). Mother-child and father-child relationships in middle childhood and adolescence: A developmental analysis. *Developmental Review, 11,* 99-136.

Combrinck-Graham, L. (1985). A developmental model for family systems. *Family Process, 24,* 139-174.

Cooper, C. R., & Ayers-Lopez, S. (1985). Family and peer systems in early adolescence: New models of the role of relationships in development. *Journal of Early Adolescence, 5,* 9-22.

Crockett, L., Losoff, M., & Petersen, A. C. (1984). Perceptions of the peer group and friendship in early adolescence. *Journal of Early Adolescence, 4,* 155-181.

Csikszentmihalyi, M., & Larson, R. (1984). *Being adolescent: Conflict and growth in the teenage years.* New York: Basic Books.

Daniels, D., Dunn, J., Furstenberg, F. F., Jr., & Plomin, R. (1985). Environmental differences within the family and adjustment differences within pairs of adolescent siblings. *Child Development, 56,* 764-774.

Daniels, D., & Plomin, R. (1985). Differential experience of siblings in the same family. *Developmental Psychology, 21,* 747-760.

Diaz, R. M., & Berndt, T. J. (1982). Children's knowledge of a best friend: Fact or fancy? *Developmental Psychology, 18,* 787-794.

Dornbusch, S. M., Ritter, P. L., Mont-Reynaud, R., & Chen, Z. (1990). Family decision making and academic performance in a diverse high school population. *Journal of Adolescent Research, 5,* 143-160.

Epstein, J. L. (1986). Friendship selection: Developmental and environmental influences. In R. C. Mueller & C. R. Cooper (Eds.), *Process and outcome in peer relationships* (pp. 129-160). New York: Academic Press.

Epstein, N. B., Baldwin, L. M., & Bishop, D. (1983). The McMaster Family Assessment Device. *Journal of Marital and Family Therapy, 9,* 171-180.

Erikson, E. H. (1950). *Childhood and society.* New York: Norton.

Erikson, E. H. (1968). *Identity: Youth and crisis.* New York: Norton.

Feldman, S. S., & Quatman, T. (1988). Factors influencing age expectations for adolescent autonomy: A study of early adolescents and parents. *Journal of Early Adolescence, 8,* 325-343.

Feldman, S. S., & Rosenthal, D. A. (1991). Age expectations of behavioral autonomy in Hong Kong, Australian and American youth: The influence of family variables and adolescents' values. *International Journal of Psychology, 26,* 1-23.

Fenzel, L. M., & Blyth, D. A. (1986). Individual adjustment to school transitions: An exploration of the role of supportive peer relations. *Journal of Early Adolescence, 6,* 315-329.

Fine, M. A., Worley, S. M., & Schwebel, A. I. (1985). The parent-child relationship survey: An examination of its psychometric properties. *Psychological Reports, 57,* 155-161.

Flannery, D. J., & Montemayor, R. (1991, April). *Impact of puberty versus age on affective expression, negative communication, and problem behavior in parent-adoles-*

cent dyads. Paper presented at the meeting of the Society for Research in Child Development, Seattle.

Frankel, K. A. (1990). Girls' perceptions of peer relationship support and stress. *Journal of Early Adolescence, 10,* 69-88.

Freud, A. (1969). Adolescence as a developmental disturbance. In G. Caplan & S. Lebovici (Ed.), *Adolescence: Psychological perspectives* (pp. 5-10). New York: Basic Books.

Freud, S. (1949). *Collected papers: Vol. 2. The infantile genital organization of the libido.* London: Hogarth, 1949. (Original work published 1923)

Friedlander, M. L., & Siegel, S. M. (1990). Separation-individuation difficulties and cognitive-behavioral indicators of eating disorders among college women. *Journal of Counseling Psychology, 37,* 74-78.

Furman, W., & Bierman, K. (1984). Children's conceptions of friendship: A multidimensional study. *Developmental Psychology, 20,* 925-931.

Furman, W., & Buhrmester, D. (1992). Age and sex differences in perceptions of networks of personal relationships. *Child Development, 63,* 103-115.

Gehring, T. M., & Feldman, S. S. (1988). Adolescents' perceptions of family cohesion and power: A methodological study of the Family System Test. *Journal of Adolescent Research, 3,* 33-52.

Gehring, T. M., Wentzel, K. R., Feldman, S. S., & Munson, J. (1990). Conflict in families of adolescents: The impact on cohesion and power structures. *Journal of Family Psychology, 3,* 290-309.

Gjerde, P. F. (1986). The interpersonal structure of family interaction settings: Parent-adolescent relations in dyads and triads. *Developmental Psychology, 22,* 297-304.

Grotevant, H. D., & Cooper, C. R. (1985). Patterns of interaction in family relationships and the development of identity formation in adolescence. *Child Development, 51,* 415-428.

Grotevant, H. D., & Cooper, C. R. (1986). Individuation in family relationships: A perspective on individual differences in the development of identity and role-taking in adolescence. *Human Development, 29,* 82-100.

Harris, I. D., & Howard, K. I. (1984). Parental criticism and the adolescent experience. *Journal of Youth and Adolescence, 13,* 113-131.

Hartup, W. W. (1979). Two social worlds of childhood. *American Psychologist, 34,* 944-950.

Hartup, W. W. (1983). Peer relations. In E. M. Hetherington (Ed.), *Handbook of child psychology: Vol. 4. Socialization, personality and social development* (pp. 103-196). New York: John Wiley.

Hartup, W. W. (in press). Adolescents and their friends. In B. Laursen (Ed.), *New directions for child development: Close friendships in adolescence.* San Francisco: Jossey-Bass.

Hauser, S. T., Powers, S. I., Noam, G. G., Jacobson, A. M., Weiss, B., & Follansbee, D. J. (1984). Familial contexts of adolescent ego development. *Child Development, 55,* 195-213.

Hill, J. P. (1987). Research on adolescents and their families: Past and prospect. In C. E. Irwin, Jr. (Ed.), *Adolescent social behavior and health. New Directions for Child Development* (No. 37). San Francisco: Jossey-Bass.

Hill, J. P. (1988). Adapting to menarche: Familial control and conflict. In M. R. Gunnar & W. A. Collins (Eds.), *Development during the transition to adolescence:*

Minnesota symposia on child psychology (Vol. 21, pp. 43-77). Hillsdale, NJ: Lawrence Erlbaum.

Hill, J. P., & Holmbeck, G. N. (1986). Attachment and autonomy during adolescence. *Annals of Child Development, 3,* 145-189.

Hill, J. P., & Holmbeck, G. N. (1987). Disagreements about rules in families with seventh-grade girls and boys. *Journal of Youth and Adolescence, 16,* 221-246.

Hinde, R. A., & Stevenson-Hinde, J. (1987). Interpersonal relationships and child development. *Developmental Review, 7,* 1-21.

Hoffman, J. A. (1984). Psychological separation of late adolescents from their parents. *Journal of Counseling Psychology, 31,* 170-178.

Hoffman, M. A., Ushpiz, V., & Levy-Shiff, R. (1988). Social support and self-esteem in adolescence. *Journal of Youth and Adolescence, 17,* 307-316.

Hunter, F. T. (1985). Individual adolescents' perceptions of interactions with friends and parents. *Journal of Early Adolescence, 5,* 295-305.

Imber, S. (1973). Relationship of trust to academic performance. *Journal of Personality and Social Psychology, 28,* 145-150.

Kandel, D., & Lesser, G. (1972). *Youth in two worlds.* San Francisco: Jossey-Bass.

Kelley, H. H., Berscheid, E., Christensen, A., Harvey, J. H., Huston, T. L., Levinger, G., McClintock, E., Peplau, L. A., & Peterson, D. R. (1983). *Close relationships.* New York: Freeman.

Lapsley, D. K., Rice, K. G., & Shadid, G. E. (1989). Psychological separation and adjustment to college. *Journal of Counseling Psychology, 36,* 286-294.

Laursen, B. (1991, July). Close relationships across adolescence. Paper presented at the meeting of the International Society for the Study of Behavioral Development, Minneapolis, MN.

Leaper, C., Hauser, S. T., Kremen, A., Powers, S. I., Jacobson, A. M., Noam, G. G., Weiss-Perry, B., & Follansbee, D. (1989). Adolescent-parent interactions in relation to adolescents' gender and ego development pathway: A longitudinal study. *Journal of Early Adolescence, 9,* 335-361.

LeCroy, C. W. (1988). Parent-adolescent intimacy: Impact on adolescent functioning. *Adolescence, 23,* 137-147.

Lerner, R. M. (1985). Adolescent maturational changes and psychosocial development: A dynamic interactional perspective. *Journal of Youth and Adolescence, 14,* 355-372.

Lewin, K. (1939). Field theory and experiment in social psychology. *American Journal of Sociology, 44,* 873-884, 895-896.

Lopez, F. G. (1991). Patterns of family conflict and their relation to college student adjustment. *Journal of Counseling and Development, 69,* 257-260.

Lopez, F. G., Campbell, V. L., & Watkins, C. E. (1986). Depression, psychological separation, and college adjustment: An investigation of sex differences. *Journal of Counseling Psychology, 33,* 53-56.

Maccoby, E. E., & Martin, J. A. (1983). Socialization in the context of the family: Parent-child interaction. In P. H. Mussen (Ed.), *Handbook of child psychology* (Vol. 4, pp. 1-101). New York: John Wiley.

Mahler, M. S. (1979). Thoughts about development and individuation. In M. S. Mahler, *Selected papers: Vol. 2. Separation and individuation* (pp. 34-55). New York: Jason Aronson. (Original work published 1963)

Montemayor, R. (1982). The relationship between parent-adolescent conflict and the amount of time adolescents spend alone and with parents and peers. *Child Development, 53,* 1512-1519.

Montemayor, R. (1983). Parents and adolescents in conflict: All families some of the time and some families most of the time. *Journal of Early Adolescence, 3,* 83-103.

Montemayor, R. (1986). Family variation in parent-adolescent storm and stress. *Journal of Adolescent Research, 1,* 15-31.

Montemayor, R., & Hanson, E. (1985). A naturalistic view of conflict between adolescents and their parents and siblings. *Journal of Early Adolescence, 5,* 23-30.

Noller, P., & Bagi, S. (1985). Parent-adolescent communication. *Journal of Adolescence, 8,* 125-144.

O'Brien, S. F., & Bierman, K. L. (1988). Conceptions and perceived influence of peer groups: Interviews with preadolescents and adolescents. *Child Development, 59,* 1360-1365.

Offer, D., Ostrov, E., & Howard, K. (1981). *The adolescent: A psychological self portrait.* New York: Basic Books.

Olson, D. H. (1986). Circumplex model VII: Validation studies and FACES III. *Family Process, 25,* 337-351.

Papini, D. R., Datan, N., & McCluskey-Fawcett, K. A. (1988). An observational study of affective and assertive family interactions during adolescence. *Journal of Youth and Adolescence, 17,* 477-492.

Papini, D. R., & Sebby, R. A. (1988). Variations in conflictual family issues by adolescent pubertal status, gender, and family member. *Journal of Early Adolescence, 8,* 1-15.

Parker, J. G., & Gottman, J. M. (1989). Social and emotional development in a relational context: Friendship interaction from early childhood to adolescence. In T. J. Berndt & G. W. Ladd (Eds.), *Peer relationships in child development* (pp. 95-132). New York: John Wiley.

Patterson, G. P. (1986). Performance models for antisocial boys. *American Psychologist, 41,* 432-444.

Patterson, G. R., DeBaryshe, B. D., & Ramsey, E. (1989). A developmental perspective on antisocial behavior. *American Psychologist, 44,* 329-335.

Paulson, S. E., Hill, J. P., & Holmbeck, G. N. (1991). Distinguishing between perceived closeness and parental warmth in families with seventh-grade boys and girls. *Journal of Early Adolescence, 11,* 276-293.

Paulson, S. E., Koman, J. J., & Hill, J. P. (1990). Maternal employment and parent-child relations in families of seventh graders. *Journal of Early Adolescence, 10,* 279-295.

Piaget, J. (1965). *The moral judgment of the child.* New York: Free Press.

Pipp, S., Shaver, P., Jennings, S., Lamborn, S., & Fischer, K. W. (1985). Adolescents' theories about the development of their relationships with parents. *Journal of Personality and Social Psychology, 48,* 991-1001.

Poole, M. E., & Gelder, A. J. (1984). Family cohesiveness and adolescent autonomy in decision-making. *Australian Journal of Sex, Marriage and the Family, 5,* 65-75.

Rawlins, W. K., & Holl, M. R. (1988). Adolescents' interaction with parents and friends: Dialectics of temporal perspective and evaluation. *Journal of Social and Personal Relationships, 5,* 27-46.

Reis, H. T., & Shaver, P. (1988). Intimacy as an interpersonal process. In S. Duck, (Ed.), *Handbook of personal relationships* (pp. 367-389). New York: John Wiley.

Repinski, D. J. (1992). *Closeness in parent-adolescent relationships: Contrasting interdependence, emotional tone, and a subjective rating*. Manuscript submitted for publication.

Repinski, D. J., Conger, R. D., & Whitbeck, L. B. (1992). *Parent behavior and adolescent self-esteem: The role of method variance*. Manuscript submitted for publication.

Rice, G. (1992). Separation-individuation and adjustment to college: A longitudinal study. *Journal of Counseling Psychology, 39*, 203-213.

Rice, K. G., Cole, D. A., & Lapsley, D. K. (1990). Separation-individuation, family cohesion, and adjustment to college: Measurement validation and test of a theoretical model. *Journal of Counseling Psychology, 37*, 195-202.

Richardson, R. A., Galambos, N. L., Schulenberg, J. E., & Petersen, A. C. (1984). Young adolescents' perceptions of the family environment. *Journal of Early Adolescence, 4*, 131-153.

Rosenthal, D. A., Gurney, R. M., & Moore, S. M. (1981). From trust to intimacy: A new inventory for examining Erikson's stages of psychosocial development. *Journal of Youth and Adolescence, 10*, 525-537.

Rossi, A. (1987). Parenthood in transition: From lineage to child to self-orientation. In J. Lancaster, J. Altmann, A. Rossi, & L. Sherrod (Eds.), *Parenting across the life span: Biosocial dimensions* (pp. 31-81). New York: Aldine.

Rotenberg, K. J. (1984). Sex differences in children's trust in peers. *Sex Roles, 9/10*, 953-957.

Rotenberg, K. J., & Pilipenko, T. A. (1983). Mutuality, temporal consistency, and helpfulness in children's trust in peers. *Social Cognition, 2*, 235-255.

Rubin, K. H., LeMare, L. J., & Lollis, S. (1990). Social withdrawal in childhood: Developmental pathways to peer rejection. In S. R. Asher & J. D. Coie (Eds.), *Peer rejection in childhood* (pp. 217-249). Cambridge, UK: Cambridge University Press.

Rutter, M., Graham, P., Chadwick, O., & Yule, W. (1976). Adolescent turmoil: Fact or fiction? *Journal of Child Psychology and Psychiatry, 17*, 35-56.

Ryan, R. M., & Lynch, J. H. (1989). Emotional autonomy versus detachment: Revisiting the vicissitudes of adolescence and young adulthood. *Child Development, 60*, 340-356.

Savin-Williams, R. C., & Berndt, T. J. (1990). Friendship and peer relations. In S. Feldman & G. Elliot (Eds.), *At the threshold: The developing adolescent* (pp. 277-307). Cambridge, MA: Harvard University Press.

Savin-Williams, R. C., & Small, S. A. (1986). The timing of puberty and its relationship to adolescent and parent perceptions of family interactions. *Developmental Psychology, 22*, 342-347.

Sessa, F. M., & Steinberg, L. (1991). Family structure and the development of autonomy during adolescence. *Journal of Early Adolescence, 11*, 38-55.

Sharabany, R., Gershoni, R., & Hofman, J. E. (1981). Girlfriend, boyfriend: Age and sex differences in intimate friendship. *Developmental Psychology, 17*, 800-808.

Silverberg, S. B., & Steinberg, L. (1990). Psychological well-being of parents with early adolescent children. *Developmental Psychology, 26*, 658-666.

Silverberg, S. B., Tennenbaum, D. L., & Jacob, T. (1992). Adolescence and family interaction. In V. B. Van Hasselt & M. Hersen (Eds.), *Handbook of social development: A lifespan perspective* (pp. 347-370). New York: Plenum.

Simmons, R. G., & Blyth, D. A. (1987). *Moving into adolescence: The impact of pubertal change and school context*. New York: Aldine.

Simmons, R., Burgeson, R., & Reef, M. (1988). Cumulative change at entry to adolescence. In M. Gunnar & W. A. Collins (Eds.), *Development during the transition to adolescence: Minnesota symposia on child psychology* (Vol. 21, pp. 123-150). Hillsdale, NJ: Lawrence Erlbaum.

Skinner, H. A., Steinhauser, P. D., & Santa-Barbara, J. (1983). The Family Assessment Measure. *Canadian Journal of Community Mental Health, 2*, 91-105.

Smetana, J. G. (1988). Concepts of self and social convention: Adolescents' and parents' reasoning about hypothetical and actual family conflicts. In M. R. Gunnar & W. A. Collins (Eds.), *Development during the transition to adolescence: Minnesota symposia on child psychology* (pp. 79-122). Hillsdale, NJ: Lawrence Erlbaum.

Smetana, J. G. (1989). Adolescents' and parents' reasoning about actual family conflict. *Child Development, 60*, 1052-1067.

Smith, K. A., & Forehand, R. (1986). Parent-adolescent conflict: Comparison and prediction of the perceptions of mothers, fathers, and daughters. *Journal of Early Adolescence, 6*, 353-367.

Sroufe, L. A., & Fleeson, J. (1988). The coherence of family relationships. In R. A. Hinde & J. Stevenson-Hinde (Eds.), *Relationships within families: Mutual influences* (pp. 27-47). Oxford, UK: Clarendon.

Sroufe, L. A., & Waters, E. (1977). Attachment as an organizational construct. *Child Development, 48*, 1184-1199.

Steinberg, L. D. (1987). Impact of puberty on family relations: Effects of pubertal status and pubertal timing. *Developmental Psychology, 23*, 451-460.

Steinberg, L. D. (1988). Reciprocal relation between parent-child distance and pubertal maturation. *Developmental Psychology, 24*, 122-128.

Steinberg, L. (1990). Interdependency in the family: Autonomy, conflict, and harmony. In S. Feldman & G. Elliot (Eds.), *At the threshold: The developing adolescent* (pp. 255-276). Cambridge, MA: Harvard University Press.

Steinberg, L., & Lamborn, S. D. (1992, March). Autonomy redux: Adolescent adjustment as a joint function of emotional autonomy and relationship security. In S. J. Frank (Chair), *Adolescent autonomy: Is it all it's cracked up to be?* Symposium conducted as the biennial meeting of the Society for Research on Adolescence, Washington, DC.

Steinberg, L., & Silverberg, S. B. (1986). The vicissitudes of autonomy in early adolescence. *Child Development, 57*, 841-851.

Sullivan, H. S. (1953). *The interpersonal theory of psychiatry*. New York: Norton.

Townsend, M. A. R., McCracken, H. E., & Wilton, K. M. (1988). Popularity and intimacy as determinants of psychological well-being in adolescent friendships. *Journal of Early Adolescence, 8*, 421-436.

Vanden Heuvel, A. (1988). The timing of parenthood and intergenerational relations. *Journal of Marriage and the Family, 50*, 483-491.

Vuchinich, S. (1987). Starting and stopping spontaneous family conflicts. *Journal of Marriage and the Family, 49*, 591-601.

Waters, E., Kondo-Ikemura, K., Posada, G., & Richters, J. E. (1991). Learning to love: Mechanisms and milestones. In M. R. Gunnar & L. A. Sroufe (Eds.), *Self processes* and development: The Minnesota symposia on child development (Vol. 23, pp. 217-256). Hillsdale, NJ: Lawrence Erlbaum.

White, K. M., Speisman, J. C., & Costos, D. (1983). Young adults and their parents. In H. D. Grotevant & C. R. Cooper (Eds.), Adolescent development in the family: New directions in child development (pp. 61-76). San Francisco: Jossey-Bass.

Wynne, L. (1984). The epigenesis of relational systems: A model for understanding family development. Family Process, 23, 297-318.

Youniss, J. (1980). Parents and peers in social development. Chicago: University of Chicago Press.

Youniss, J., & Smollar, J. (1985). Adolescent relations with mothers, fathers, and friends. Chicago: University of Chicago Press.

3. Relationships With Parents in Adolescence: Process and Outcome

Patricia Noller
University of Queensland, Australia

Researchers and theorists disagree about the role of the family in adolescence. The crucial disagreement is between those who see the peer group as more important than the family, and those who see the family as continuing to be important throughout adolescence and into adulthood. Whereas psychoanalytic theorists tend to emphasize the need for adolescents to separate themselves from their parents, with parent-adolescent conflict an essential part of that process, other writers emphasize the fact that many adolescents do not report high levels of conflict between themselves and their families (Offer & Sabshin, 1984). Grotevant and Cooper (1985) note the importance of focusing on the changes that need to take place in the parent-offspring relationship during adolescence, rather than just on levels of conflict.

Some theorists have argued that adolescents move away from the family toward their peers, but others (e.g., Jurkovic & Ulrici, 1985; Mussen, Conger, & Kagan, 1974) have shown that for most adolescents, family relationships endure and remain important throughout the entire period of adolescence. In addition, both peers and parents occupy important places in the adolescents' lives, and adolescents move comfortably between the two groups. Sheppard, Wright, and Goodstadt (1985), in fact, reject the notion that adolescents are necessarily more influenced by peers than parents. They maintain that "the peer group, contrary to what is commonly believed, has little or no influence as long as the family remains strong. Peers take over only when parents abdicate" (p. 951).

In this chapter I discuss the research that has been carried out on families with adolescents, including work from my own laboratory. The focus will be on family processes and the outcomes of those processes for adolescents. Although in the first part of the chapter the emphasis will be mainly on family processes, and in the second part of the chapter the emphasis will be more clearly on outcomes, there are some sections where it has proved difficult to separate processes and outcomes, and both must be considered as important. I will discuss family processes such as patterns of communication, conflict, punishment and violence, decision making, and identity development. The outcomes of interest include adjustment, psychopathology, moral development, problem behaviors, and later relationships.

Before focusing on these issues, however, I want to consider the question of differing perspectives on the family. Because adolescents are able to speak for themselves, it is possible to compare their views of the family with those of their parents, and to raise the question of whose perspective is likely to be the most reliable and valid. These differences between family members (see also Jessop, 1981; Niemi, 1974) tend to be discussed in terms of the generational stake hypothesis. Niemi (1974) has argued that neither parents nor adolescents provide objective accounts of family life, but that adolescents provide a more objective account of family life than parents. Bengtson and his colleagues (Bengtson & Kuypers, 1971; Bengtson & Troll, 1978), on the other hand, argue that each generation views family life in terms of its own bias or stake. Parents, because of their level of investment in the family, are likely to see the family in a positive light and to minimize differences between family members. Adolescents, who are motivated to contrast themselves and their parents and to emphasize their own individuality and independence, may be more likely to maximize differences between themselves and their parents and to see the family in a more negative light. This is an issue that we have examined in our laboratory over several studies.

PARENTS' AND ADOLESCENTS' DIFFERING VIEWS OF THE FAMILY

Across four different studies, we have found quite systematic patterns of difference, with adolescents generally having more negative views of the family than their parents. In our initial study (Noller & Callan, 1986), we used FACES II (Family Adaptability and Cohesion Evaluation Scales; Olson et al., 1983) to explore parents' and adolescents' perceptions of family functioning as well as the levels of cohesion and adaptability they would consider ideal for their own family. Overall, adolescents saw their families as less cohesive and less adaptable than their parents did, although there were some differences related to age. Adolescents were also less satisfied than their parents with the level of adaptability in the family, and both adolescents and parents were equally dissatisfied with the levels of cohesion in the family.

Although both the adolescents and their parents wanted their families to be more cohesive, adolescents wanted lower levels of cohesion than their parents. In addition, whereas cohesion scores were in the moderate to high range for both actual and ideal cohesion, mean scores for ideal adaptability were very high, falling in Olson's chaotic category. In other words, adolescents seem to want high levels of support from their parents, but also want the family to be highly adaptable and continually changing in response to their needs. This desire of adolescents for both high cohesion and high support could well be at the heart of many problems in parentadolescent relationships.

In a second series of studies (Callan & Noller, 1986; Noller & Callan, 1988), we used a very different methodology to explore differences between parents and adolescents in their perceptions of family interaction. Parents and adolescents engaged in an interaction that was videotaped and then worked through the videotape, making ratings of each family member on scales of anxious-calm, involved-uninvolved, strong-weak, and friendly-unfriendly at 15-second intervals. (See Callan & Noller, 1986, for detailed descriptions of the methods used.) Again adolescents were generally more negative than parents in their perceptions of family members, seeing them as more anxious, less involved and weaker than did parents. There were no differences between mothers and fathers in their ratings of family members.

When family members were asked to rate another family involved in the study in the same way as they had rated their own family (Noller & Callan, 1988), another bias was evident, with family members systematically rating their own family more positively than they rated the outsider family across all four variables, although ratings of anxiety were also affected by which family member was being rated. Interestingly, however, the adolescents tended to adopt a more negative view than their parents whether they were rating their own or another family. For example, the ratings by the adolescent from the insider family matched the negative ratings of the outsider family, providing some support for the view that adolescents' negative views of their families are a result of their objectifying their families and adopting an outsider's view.

Comparisons between ratings by family members (insider ratings), those of the members of another family (outsider ratings), and those of a trained observer indicated complex relationships between the different ratings. On the basis of the correlational data, it seemed that ratings of the outsider family were closer to those of the trained observer and different from those of the insider family. However, taking into account the mean ratings as well as the patterns of correlations, the trained observer seemed to follow a similar pattern in making ratings as the outsider family but to use the same metric as the insider family. There was also evidence that family members were more objective in rating themselves than other family members.

In another study (Noller, Seth-Smith, Bouma, & Schweitzer, 1992), we compared ratings of family functioning by parents and adolescents from both clinic and nonclinic families. Whereas the results for the nonclinic families were similar to those already reported, with parents' perceptions of family functioning being more positive than those of their adolescents, this difference was not present in the clinic families. Both parents and their adolescents had negative views of their families, seeing those families as less intimate and more conflicted than was true for the parents in the nonclinic families. There were no differences between the two groups of adolescents, however, despite the fact that these two groups of adolescents were very different in terms of their self-concepts, with the clinic group obtaining lower scores for self-esteem, emotional stability, and quality of parental and opposite-sex relationships. In addition, ratings of family functioning were strongly related to the self-concepts of the adolescents. Higher levels of conflict were associated with a more negative self-concept, and higher levels of intimacy and a more democratic parenting style were associated with a more positive self-concept.

In this study, the generational stake hypothesis was supported for nonclinic families but not for clinic families. In other words, adolescents in the nonclinic families were more negative in their ratings of the family than were their mothers; in the clinic families, adolescents and mothers were equally negative. One way to interpret this finding is to suggest that in clinic families, mothers are unable to maintain their rosy picture of the family and are forced to see the family in the same negative way that their adolescents do. It is possible that these parents give up their stake in the family and thus are no longer concerned about maintaining their positive view. On the other hand, they are bringing their children for help, suggesting that they do still have strong involvement in the family, and they may see giving up their positive view and facing the problems in the family as an important step toward improving the situation.

In terms of answering the question of whose view of the family is likely to be more reality based, however, these data suggest the possibility that the parents may be better reporters than the adolescents. The parents' perceptions of family functioning differs depending on whether the family is attending a clinic for problems with the adolescent's behavior, whereas that of the adolescents does not, and it seems unlikely that there would be no difference in family functioning between those families where the adolescent's behavior is in the normal range and those where it is causing so much concern to the parents that they are seeking professional help.

PATTERNS OF COMMUNICATION
IN FAMILIES WITH ADOLESCENTS

We will begin our discussion of communication processes in families with adolescents by looking first at the patterns of communication in the family: who talks to whom about what, and how do adolescents and their parents view the communication in their families? A number of researchers have used questionnaire measures to explore these issues.

Youniss and Smollar (1985) studied parent-adolescent communication in a sample of adolescents aged 15 to 18 years across six different areas (school-career, societal views, intrafamily issues, friendship, sex and marriage, doubts and fears) and four different process variables, including the openness between family members, the extent to which family members were able to negotiate about their disagreements and come to mutually satisfactory solutions, the extent to which they were guarded in their communication with one another, and the extent to which they tried to impose solutions on one another.

Adolescents had quite different views of their communication with each parent. Daughters, in particular, reported generally stronger relationships with mothers than fathers. Mothers were seen as more open, understanding, and accepting and more willing to listen to their adolescents' attitudes and opinions. They were also seen as more interested in the day to day problems of their teenagers than fathers, and more able to negotiate agreements when conflicts arose. Fathers, on the other hand, were seen as more judgmental; less willing to be involved in discussions of feelings, self-doubts, and problems of adjustment; and more likely to try imposing their authority on the adolescents. Adolescents claimed that they were more likely to limit their communication with fathers and to be more defensive and guarded with them. Even males who were strongly identified with their fathers generally believed that their mothers understood them better emotionally (Offer, 1969).

Following up many of these issues, Noller and Bagi (1985) also examined differences in communication between adolescent university students and their parents. Communication was assessed across 14 topic areas and six process dimensions. The 14 topic areas were chosen to represent two basic dimensions: reference (whether the issue was an intrafamily one or involved views and attitudes of the community as a whole) and specificity (whether the topic involved general principles or more specific issues). Sex roles, for example, could be discussed at the societal level or at the intrafamilial level (the relevance of sex roles in your family). Similarly, sexuality could be discussed in terms of general principles (attitudes towards sexuality) or in terms of specific information (information concerning sexuality). The full set of topics is described in Table 3.1.

The six process dimensions were the frequency of communication, the extent to which the adolescents disclosed their real feelings, the extent to which their views were recognized by their parents, who initiated discussion of various issues, who dominated discussions, and how satisfied the adolescents were with their communication with their parents.

Results from this study showed that discussions with parents were not very frequent, with most topics being rated between 2 and 3 on a 6-point scale from 1 = *rarely discuss this* to 6 = *frequent long discussions*. The topics discussed most with mothers were general problems, plans, and interests (all above 4), and those discussed least were sex information and sex problems (both below 2). Plans, politics, and general problems were discussed most frequently with fathers (above 3), and sex attitudes, sex information, and sex prob-

Table 3.1 Potential Topics of Discussion Between University Students and Their Parents (Noller & Bagi, 1985)

General philosophy of man: includes discussion of such issues as the nature of human existence and various religious perspectives.

Rules and conventions of society: includes discussion of rules, conventions, laws, etiquette, and the importance or otherwise of such rules.

Politics: includes discussion of the implications and functions of various political ideologies as well as the voting preferences and political behavior of family members.

Sex roles in society: includes discussion of the function of sex roles in society and whether they are beneficial or detrimental, as well as the role of women in both the workplace and the home.

Current social issues: includes discussion of issues such as drug and alcohol addiction, crime, and abortion.

Relationships: includes discussion of attitudes to the family and to related issues such as marriage and divorce.

Attitudes towards sexuality: includes discussion of the importance and function of sex in relationships, and issues of dating and premarital sex both in the society and in the family.

Information concerning sexuality: includes discussion where parent is giving specific information about sexual behavior or development.

Implications of family's philosophy of man for the family itself: includes discussion of the family's attitudes toward religion or other belief systems and the effects of such beliefs on the family.

Sex roles in the family: includes discussion of the roles of husband and wife and father and mother in the family; also issues of different expectations for male versus female children.

The adolescent's interests: includes discussion of your tastes in music, fashion, sport, or social interests.

The adolescent's plans: includes any discussion of your plans for the future in terms of education, work, or relationships.

The adolescent's general problems: includes discussion of any problems (apart from sexual) to do with work, home, university, or friends.

The adolescent's sex-related problems and queries: includes discussion of your questions about sexual behavior and your sexual experiences.

lems were discussed least. More self-disclosure tended to occur in the most frequently discussed areas, and adolescents were generally more satisfied with those areas that were discussed frequently and on which they were more likely to disclose. Disclosure ratings ranged from 3 to 4.7 for discussions with mothers and from below 3 to 4.5 for discussions with fathers. Adolescents were generally only slightly to somewhat satisfied with their communication with their parents.

Frequency and self-disclosure were the only dimensions where there were clear differences related to sex of parent and sex of adolescent. Daughters reported more frequent discussions with their mothers about sexual attitudes and relationships and reported disclosing more to them about interests, family sex roles, relationships, sexual information, sexual problems, and general problems. Daughters not only disclosed more to their mothers than did sons, but also disclosed more to their fathers, particularly about societal rules, general problems, and plans. Adolescents talked more to mothers than fathers over 9 of the 14 areas. Results confirmed that mothers are quite active in communication with their adolescents, whereas fathers are only minimally involved. Not surprisingly, mothers were better able than fathers to predict their adolescents' responses to the questionnaire (Parent-Adolescent Communication Inventory, Noller & Bagi, 1985).

In a follow-up study, Noller and Callan (1990) obtained data using the same instrument from adolescents ranging in age from 12 to 17 years. These younger adolescents, unlike the older adolescents in the earlier study, saw their mothers as both initiating more discussions with them and recognizing and accepting their opinions more than their fathers. Females reported more disclosure to mothers than fathers and tended to be more satisfied with interactions with mothers than interactions with fathers. Males reported more talk with fathers than did females about interests, sexual issues, and general problems. Males tended to report disclosing at similar levels to mothers and fathers and expressed equal, although only moderate, levels of satisfaction with their interactions with both parents. These findings again support the view that adolescents, especially daughters, generally have more positive interactions with their mothers than their fathers throughout adolescence.

Other research (Barnes & Olson, 1985; Olson et al., 1983) also supports this picture of greater openness in communication between mothers and their adolescents than between fathers and their adolescents. Mothers agree, describing their communication with their adolescents as more open than fathers do. Such findings fit with the adolescents' perceptions of their mothers as understanding them better and being more willing to recognize and accept their differing points of view.

There is also evidence that adolescent sons and daughters disclose about different issues to their parents (Jourard, 1971; Komarovsky, 1974). Davidson, Balswick, and Halverson (1980) found that females revealed more general and personal information, whereas males revealed more information regarding their sexuality to parents. Males also seem to disclose more about work and study, attitudes, and opinions, whereas females disclose more about aspects of their personalities (Mulcahey, 1973).

When asked about problems in communicating with their parents, adolescents reported low but equivalent levels of problems in communicating with each of their parents. Although the level of problems reported by parents was much higher than that reported by the adolescents, mothers and fathers reported equal levels of problems in their attempts to communicate with their adolescents (Barnes & Olson, 1985). On the other hand, adolescents report having more conflicts with their mothers than their fathers, an issue we will discuss in the next section.

CONFLICT IN FAMILIES
WITH ADOLESCENTS

The majority of arguments between parents and adolescents seem to be about day to day living and relationships within the family: personal hygiene, disobedience, school work, social activities and friendships, chores around the house, and conflicts with siblings (Caplow, Bahr, Chadwick, Hill, & Williamson, 1982; Csikszentmihalyi & Larson, 1984; Montemayor, 1982, 1983). Montemayor (1983) shows that the arguments between parents and adolescents in the 1970s and 1980s are basically about the same topics that parents and adolescents argued about in the 1920s.

Most conflicts between parents and their adolescents tend to be about minor matters such as style of dress and social life (see review by Montemayor, 1983). For instance, Ellis-Schwabe and Thornburg (1986) found more mother-daughter conflict than mother-son conflict and more conflict between mothers and adolescents than between fathers and adolescents. The parent with whom the adolescents are most likely to be in conflict depends on the type of conflict. Adolescents tend to be in conflict with mothers about personal manners, choice of friends, and clothes. With fathers, they argue about money, use of leisure time, and attitudes to school. Home responsibilities tend to be a source of conflict with both parents.

On the other hand, parents and adolescents tend not to argue about some topics of greatest difference between them, such as sex, drugs, religion, and politics (Bengtson & Starr, 1975). For example, research has shown a general lack of sex-related communication in families, with mothers being primarily responsible for what communication about sex occurs (Gebhard, 1977), even with sons (Fox & Inazu, 1980). A real paradox exists over communication about sex, in that so little seems to occur (Fox, 1980; Walters & Walters, 1980) even though parents want to be seen as active in providing sexual information for their own children (Abelson, Cohen, Heaton, & Slider, 1970; Roberts, Kline, & Gagnan, 1978) and even though adolescents report that they would like to have better sex-related communication with their parents (Sorenson, 1973). In our research (e.g., Noller & Bagi, 1985), we have also found very little communication about sex between parents and adolescents, although the communication about sex that did occur was between mothers and daughters.

Montemayor and Hanson (1985) compared adolescents' reports of conflicts with parents and their reports of conflicts with siblings. To minimize the problems of self-report, adolescents were interviewed over the telephone about the conflicts that had occurred the previous day.

Forty-four percent of all conflicts reported in this study occurred with siblings. Most arguments were with mothers or same-sex siblings. Whereas a greater proportion of conflicts about rules occurred with parents, a greater proportion of interpersonal conflicts took place with siblings. According to the adolescents, arguments with parents and siblings were least likely to be resolved through negotiation and were most often resolved by withdrawal. According to Montemayor and Hanson, "The close living conditions, competition for limited resources, and personal eccentricities of family members who daily interact with each other appear to be the primary causes of most of the discord between adolescents and their parents and siblings" (p. 28).

PUNISHMENT AND VIOLENCE
IN FAMILIES WITH ADOLESCENTS

Physical punishment seems to have particularly negative effects on adolescent functioning. Douvan and Adelson (1966) found that boys were most vulnerable and were likely to experience such negative consequences as poor internalization of control, low self-confidence, social isolation and covert resentment or rebellion. Whereas healthy families are characterized by a quasidemocratic approach (Jurkovic & Ulrici, 1985), families with problematic youngsters tend to be characterized by lax, neglectful, and inconsistent discipline. On the other hand, autocratic parenting tends to make adolescents more dependent and less self-assured (Elder, 1963). Thus once again it seems clear that the balance between support and control is the crucial issue in parenting adolescents. High support and low to moderate control seem to provide the ideal environment for healthy adolescents. Rebellion is most likely to occur when the authority structure is patriarchal and unequal, discipline is severe or inconsistent, and the parents' marriage is perceived as unhappy (Balswick & Macrides, 1975). Perception of discipline as extreme (strict or permissive) tends to be associated with lack of closeness between parent and child, and diminished regard for the parents (Balswick & Macrides, 1975; Middleton & Putney, 1963).

The negative relationship between punishment and feelings about parents is strongly supported in the literature on discipline. For example, Baumrind (1971) contends that high levels of discipline, with the accompanying unjust, arbitrary, and restrictive parental demands, seem to generate rebelliousness and hostility toward parents and even fear. Ironically, Smith (1970) has shown that parents' power and influence over children are based on the children's positive feelings toward the parents. Thus parents who overuse discipline and punishment are likely to minimize, rather than increase, their influence over their children.

In a study by Amoroso and Ware (1986), the degree of punishment and perceived parental control seemed to lower self-esteem and generate hostility in the adolescents. It seems clear that close supervision and other manifestations of parental control do provoke negative attitudes and behavior in adolescents. Martin, Schumm, Bugaighis, Jurich, and Bollman (1987) examined the relations between family violence and adolescents' perceptions of the outcomes of family conflict and their satisfaction with family relationships after a conflict episode. Nonviolent families seemed to resolve conflicts more effectively than violent families, whether the violence was verbal or physical. In addition, as the level of family violence increased, so did the adolescents' anger toward their parents, and their satisfaction with family relationships decreased.

Being physically abused has a number of consequences for adolescents, apart from the actual physical damage that may ensue. There is evidence for physical abuse of adolescents being linked to low self-esteem, poor social relationships, lack of empathy, drug or alcohol abuse, suicide, delinquency, and homicide (Garbarino & Gilliam, 1980); acting-out behavior, depression, generalized anxiety, extreme adjustment problems, emotional and thought disturbances, helplessness, and dependency (Farber & Joseph, 1985); low selfesteem, high anxiety, poor school performance, aggression, and lack of empathy for others (Galambos & Dixon, 1984); and less pleasure in life (Herrenkohl, 1977). We will discuss these issues in more detail when we focus more directly on outcomes in later sections.

In a study of homeless youth (Pears, 1992), we found that many children and adolescents reported leaving home because of conflict and abuse in the family. Family violence was given as the main reason for leaving home by 42% of the homeless young people in the study. Studies in other countries (e.g., McLeod's [1987] Canadian study) have also shown family violence to be one of the most important precipitators of adolescents' leaving home, although arguments with parents, even without violence, are also important reasons for leaving home. Adams and his colleagues (Adams, Gullotta, & Clancy, 1985) found that only 5% of the homeless young people in their sample reported that abuse was the main reason for leaving home, with the majority emphasizing arguments with parents as the main problem.

Although fewer than 50% of the young people in Pears' study gave violence as their main reason for leaving home, 73% reported being victims of family violence, with 48% of the abused group reporting that the abuse occurred on a daily basis and 52% reporting that they had needed medical treatment for injuries received as a result of family violence. In this sample, most of the abuse was physical abuse, although 17% of the abused group reported being victims of both physical and sexual abuse.

DECISION MAKING AND THE ADOLESCENT

Decision making is likely to be a problem in adolescence for two related reasons. First, adolescents are generally wanting to have more control over their lives and to make most of the decisions that directly affect them. At the same time, these decisions can have far-reaching consequences for both the adolescents and their families. Major decisions include whether to continue education, which peer group to spend most time with, whom to date and/or marry, whether to be involved in sexual activity and with whom, and whether to continue to live at home or to move out. Parents are likely to get anxious about the young person's ability to make such decisions and try to have more influence than the adolescent sees as reasonable. Ironically, such parents can lose what influence they have if they alienate their offspring by trying to control their decision making. The problem may be further exacerbated by the adolescents' lack of communication about their activities. This refusal to communicate often further raises their parents' anxieties. Again, undue anxiety on the part of parents may only serve to increase the chances that the adolescent will make the decisions the parent fears most.

Poole and Gelder (1985) explored the perceptions of family decision making of 15-year-olds. These adolescents generally saw themselves as making most of the decisions affecting their lives, although the influences of the family were still evident, depending on sex, social class, and ethnic background. Female adolescents considered their mothers' opinions as more important than did adolescent boys. On the other hand, the boys tended to be more influenced by their fathers' opinions than were girls. In addition, girls tended to make more decisions for themselves than boys.

Forming one's own opinions and taking note of the opinions of other family members, including both parents, were considered more important by high socioeconomic groups than by low socioeconomic groups. Families from ethnic backgrounds tended to be more cohesive than Australian families, to encourage autonomy in their adolescents less, and to put less store by the opinions of outsiders.

Whether parents or peers are considered the most important influence on decision making for adolescents depends on the relationship a young person has with parents and with peers, and the particular type of decision being made (Biddle, Bank, & Marlin,

1980). Wilks (1986) found that university students considered their parents as the most important influences in their lives, but that parents tended to be more important in future-oriented decisions such as educational and vocational choices (see also Sebald & White, 1980). Peers were more important in current decisions such as social activities, hobbies, and reading material.

Both parents and peers tend to agree that parents' opinions are more important when considering educational and vocational choices, as well as decisions about money. Of course, parents' involvement may be important in these areas because they are also likely to be important sources of financial support. Parents were also considered important in decisions about choosing a spouse, although many subjects were not sure whose opinion should count the most here. Although most young people would want their parents to approve of their choice of partner, whether they would actually give up a partner that the parents didn't like is another question altogether.

Friends were the clearly preferred reference group for decisions about social events, books to read, clubs to join, hobbies to pursue, and clothes to wear, and parents supported the use of the peer group as a reference for most of these decisions. Fathers, however, thought that they should be consulted about dress, and both parents thought that they should be used as guides about alcohol use, dating, and sex. At the same time, adolescents considered friends were more important sources of advice in these areas. In addition, when problems arose, these tended to be discussed more with their closest friend than with parents.

AUTONOMY, IDENTITY, AND ADOLESCENTS

Central to theoretical formulations of adolescence are the desires by teenagers for more autonomy, less control by parents, and less involvement in family life. Whether adolescents actually want to break away from their families or merely want an opportunity for the gradual renegotiation of roles and relationships within the family (Grotevant & Cooper, 1985) is, as we noted earlier, a hotly debated issue. There is also considerable disagreement about whether their main goal is to break away from the family or to engage in identity exploration and develop and stabilize their sense of who they are. The desire to break away from the family may just involve a temporary phase during which the adolescent requires distance from the family to engage in identity exploration.

The idea that the establishment of a stable identity is a crucial aspect of adolescence comes primarily from the work of Erikson (1968) but has since been developed by such theorists as Marcia (1966) and Waterman (1982). The basic hypothesis of identity development is that the transition to adolescence involves a progressive strengthening in the sense of identity. "Personal identity is like a blueprint for future commitments and life choices. It is a set of beliefs and goals about one's relationship with family members, lovers and friends, one's roles as worker, citizen and religious believer and one's aspirations for achievement. . . . Individuation suggests a clear sense of personal boundaries, a capacity to recognize one's values, and an ability to reflect on one's own thoughts and behaviors" (Newman & Murray, 1983, p. 294).

Marcia (1966) conceptualizes identity in terms of a self-structure involving "the dynamic organization of drives, abilities, beliefs and individual structure" (p. 159). Marcia comments, "The better developed this structure is, the more aware individuals appear to be of their uniqueness and similarity to others and of their own strengths and weaknesses in making their way in the world. The less developed this structure is, the more confused individuals seem about their own distinctiveness from others and the more they have to rely on external sources to evaluate themselves" (p. 159).

Marcia (1966) developed a model involving four identity statuses based on the two dimensions of crisis (whether the person has been through some kind of identity crisis or not) and commitment (whether the person is committed to their present identity). Identity Achievers have been through an identity crisis and are presently committed. Foreclosures are committed to their present identity, which tends to reflect the wishes and goals of adults close to them, although they have not been through a crisis or spent much time in the consideration of alternatives. Moratoriums are currently involved in an identity crisis and are actively involved in identity exploration, and Identity Diffusions have neither been through a crisis nor committed themselves to a particular identity. (See Figure 3.1.)

Identity formation and identity status are seen as important because of the increased level of self-esteem, increased stability of self-concept, and lower levels of anxiety that seem to come as a consequence of identity formation (Bernard, 1981). Waterman (1982)

Experienced Crisis

	Yes	No
Yes Committed to Identity	Identity Achieved	Foreclosure
No	Moratorium	Identity Diffusion

Figure 3.1 Four Stages of Identity Development
SOURCE: Adapted from Marcia (1966).

claims that during the adolescent years more consideration will be given to identity alternatives than at any other time, with personally meaningful commitments likely to be formed during this period. Such commitments may involve career decisions, religious and political affiliations, and personal relationships.

Theorists and researchers tend to agree that family factors affect the process of identity exploration (Noller & Callan, 1991). Families differ in the extent to which they provide an environment that is conducive to identity exploration, and some family environments actually inhibit such exploration. Family factors that are most relevant seem to be family closeness or connectedness, the emphasis in the family on autonomy or individuation, and the use of power in the family. As we shall see later, these same factors are also important in the development of self-esteem and affect the extent to which adolescents are likely to be involved in the problem behaviors of adolescence, such as alcohol and drug abuse and early sexual intercourse, as well as the probability of developing psychopathology.

Family Closeness Versus
Autonomy and Adolescent Development

Adolescents in different identity status groups report quite different levels of closeness in their families (Adams & Jones, 1983;

Bernard, 1981; Campbell, Adams, & Dobson, 1984). Foreclosures report having the closest relationships with parents. Identity Diffusions of both sexes report the most distance from their families. Parents of Identity Diffusions are seen as indifferent, inactive, detached, not understanding, and rejecting. Such an environment does not encourage identity exploration on the part of the adolescent. These findings suggest that where families are either very close or very distant, adolescents have problems with identity exploration. Where families are very close, adolescents seem to adopt the views of their parents as their own, often without adequately exploring alternatives. On the other hand, adolescents seem to also have problems with identity achievement where families are distant and rejecting. It seems likely that identity exploration and achievement require at least a minimal level of acceptance and understanding from parents

Grotevant and Cooper (1985) emphasize the balance between family closeness and the family's focus on issues of individuation and autonomy as having the major effect on identity exploration. Grotevant and Cooper measured the individuality variables of self-assertion and separateness and the connectedness variables of mutuality (sensitivity to and respect for the views of others) and permeability (openness and responsiveness to the views of others). Females in particular were more prepared to engage in identity exploration in families where separateness or individuality were emphasized.

The extent to which permeability and mutuality affected identity exploration depended on the sex of the adolescent and the sex of the parent. Higher levels of identity exploration in daughters were negatively related to the mother's responsiveness to the adolescent and the adolescent's respect for the mother's views. High identity exploration in sons was positively related to the adolescent's responsiveness to the father and the father's respect for the son's views. In other words, girls who have responsive mothers whose views they respect are likely to accept those views and not explore for themselves. (Thus they are more likely to be in the Foreclosure status.) On the other hand, boys explore better with a responsive father who respects their views.

The encouragement of autonomy versus control in the family is related to identity achievement, particularly for females (Adams & Jones, 1983). Adolescent females high in identity status report that mothers encourage independence and autonomy, whereas diffused females rate mothers high on control and regulation, as well as very high on encouragement of independence. These latter mothers seem to want their adolescent to be independent but also to want to control the process by which they achieve such independence. It is no wonder these adolescents struggle with identity achievement.

Family Power and Adolescent Identity Development

Writers like Newman and Murray (1983) see the parents' use of power in the family as a crucial determinant of adolescent identity exploration and achievement. Coercive power is less likely to nurture the development of personal identity and more likely to lead to external, rather than internalized moral standards, lower self-confidence, and problems in using one's own judgment as a guide to behavior. Adolescents whose parents adopt an inductive, democratic communication style, on the other hand, are more likely to be able to make their own decisions and formulate appropriate plans. Indeed, there is the paradox that democratic homes tend to produce adolescents who are strongly identified with their parents and have internalized their parents' rules and values.

On the other hand, it seems that some parent-adolescent conflict is necessary to identity exploration and achievement. Both males and females in the Moratorium and Identity Achievement statuses tend to be critical of their parents and to report conflict between themselves and their parents. Tensions seem related to ambivalence on the part of both parents over the teenager's attempts at individuation. Those adolescents who are encouraged to be assertive and to adopt their own points of view seem to achieve higher levels of identity development (Hauser et al., 1984). Whether adolescents actually need to separate from their parents, however, is a debatable point. Grotevant and Cooper (1986) emphasize the importance of the family environment changing its communication gradually through negotiation. If the parents come to show greater respect for the opinions of their growing adolescents and allow them more control, then separation will not be necessary. On the other hand, where parents try to force their opinions on the adolescent, rebellion and a break with the parents is a real possibility.

It also seems clear that adolescents still want the love and support of their parents, even while striving for these goals of individuation and autonomy (Erikson, 1968; Grotevant & Cooper, 1985; Noller & Callan, 1986; Olson et al., 1983). Certainly, older adolescents seem to change their relationships with their parents, developing new forms of interaction that involve reduced levels of conflict (Jacob, 1974; Steinberg & Hill, 1978). They renegotiate their status in the parent-child relationship (Hunter, 1985; Hunter & Youniss, 1985) so that they are treated more as equals whose opinions are respected and who are free to make their own decisions.

Unfortunately, in some situations adolescents may develop a negative rather than a positive identity. Erikson's (1959) concept of "negative identity" involves a lack of concern about being adversely evaluated by others and a tendency to engage in behaviors that are the opposite of what the parent would like. Harris and Howard (1984) found that high levels of parental criticism of adolescents accompanied by a sense of rejection by the parent were highly likely to be related to "negative identity." Adolescents whose parents are critical and rejecting tend to seek their parents' attention or try to punish their parents through negative behaviors. Chronic young offenders are also often caught in "negative identities."

Clearly, both individuality and connectedness are emphasized in those families that best promote adolescent identity exploration and status. Adolescent maturity is achieved through progressive and mutual redefinition of the parent-adolescent relationship and does not require that the adolescent leave or break away from the relationship. The balance between connectedness or closeness in the family and the encouragement of individuality and autonomy is crucial (Campbell et al., 1984; Cooper, Grotevant, & Condon, 1984). Overuse of power and criticism by parents seems to have negative consequences for both the adolescent and the family as a whole.

THE FAMILY AND
ADOLESCENT ADJUSTMENT

A crucial aspect of communication between parents and adolescents involves the extent to which communication promotes or inhibits the development of positive attitudes toward the self. A number of studies have shown positive relationships between parental support or nurturance and self-esteem (Buri, Kirchner, & Walsh, 1987; Gecas & Schwalbe, 1986; Hoelter & Harper, 1987; see also Rollins

& Thomas, 1979, for a review of early research). Self-esteem is positively related to the use of support and induction techniques by parents and negatively related to their use of coercion. Coercive parenting seems to give only negative messages to young people about themselves and their own worth, whereas parents' use of induction techniques seems to indicate that the young person is competent and worthwhile.

Openshaw, Thomas, and Rollins (1984) investigated whether predictions from symbolic interactionist theory or social learning theory offered the most useful explanations of adolescent self-esteem. To symbolic interactionists, adolescent self-esteem is related to the reflected appraisals adolescents receive from their parents: that is, the extent to which their parents' behavior toward them confirms them as worthwhile and lovable individuals. Social learning theorists, on the other hand, would claim that adolescents model the self-esteem of their parents. That is, adolescents who have parents who behave confidently will also behave confidently, whereas those who have parents who lack confidence and doubt their own abilities will show the same self-doubt in their own competence and coping skills. Openshaw and his colleagues found that the self-esteem of adolescents was more strongly related to their perceptions of the support they received from their parents than it was to the selfesteem of their parents. Thus there was more support for the symbolic interactionist model than for the social learning model.

In another study, Gecas and Schwalbe (1986) explored whether adolescent self-esteem was more closely related to the actual support adolescents received from their parents or to the adolescents' perceptions of support. Adolescents' perceptions of parental support and nurturance were more highly correlated with adolescent self-esteem than were parents' reports of their parenting behaviors. In addition, perceptions of fathers' support and nurturance were more strongly related to self-esteem in adolescents than perceptions of mothers' nurturance, particularly for boys.

As already mentioned, Noller et al. (1992) looked at the relations between family functioning (as perceived by the adolescents) and their self-concepts. The self-concept measure used, the Self-Description Questionnaire (Marsh, Parker, & Barnes, 1985), assessed general self (or self-esteem), emotional stability, physical appearance, parent relations, peer relations, and mathematics, verbal, and general ability. All of these self-concept variables (except mathematics) and the three measures of family functioning (Intimacy, Conflict, and Parenting Style) contributed to the discrimination between those with positive and negative self-concepts. Higher levels of intimacy and a more democratic parenting style were associated with more positive scores on the dimensions of self-concept, whereas higher levels of conflict were associated with more negative scores on the self-concept scales.

Gecas and Schwalbe (1986) found evidence for differences in the aspects of family life affecting self-esteem, depending on the sex of the adolescent. The self-esteem of sons was most strongly affected by the degree of autonomy allowed to the adolescent and the amount of control exerted by the parent. When sons were encouraged to be autonomous and control was low to moderate, they were likely to be high in self-esteem. Where control was very high and there was little encouragement of autonomy, self-esteem was likely to be low. The self-esteem of girls, on the other hand, was most affected by the parents' support and nurturance and hardly affected at all by control or autonomy. Girls with highly supportive parents were more likely than those with distant or rejecting parents to have high self-esteem.

As might be expected, there is evidence (e.g., Eskilson, Wiley, Muehlbauer, & Dodder, 1986) that high levels of pressure to succeed from parents negatively affect adolescents' self-esteem, although parental pressure seems unrelated to academic performance. On the other hand, feeling able to meet the goals set by parents contributes positively to self-esteem. Eskilson and her colleagues also found that adolescents under high pressure from their parents to achieve were more likely to get involved in deviant behaviors such as alcohol abuse, drug taking, and vandalism.

ATTACHMENT AND ADOLESCENT ADJUSTMENT

According to Bowlby (1969, 1973, 1980), early experience with caregivers is crucial to development because, on the basis of the responsiveness of their caregivers, children construct inner working models of themselves and others. Important aspects of these inner working models include whether the self is worthwhile and whether others can be trusted. More recently the principles of Bowlby's attachment theory have been applied to the study of adult romantic relationships (Hazan & Shaver, 1987). These researchers argue that working models established in early childhood produce relatively enduring differences in relationship styles that affect attitudes to romantic relationships during adolescence and adulthood. Hazan and Shaver differentiated three styles of attachment (Secure, Avoidant, and Anxious-Ambivalent), which are similar to those found in child populations by Ainsworth and her colleagues (Ainsworth, Blehar, Waters, & Wall, 1978). Secures tended to be comfortable with intimacy and able to trust other people and depend on them when appropriate. Avoidants tended to be uncomfortable with intimacy and closeness and to have problems trusting others or depending on them. Anxious-Ambivalents sought extreme closeness with others and tended to worry a lot about the possibility of being abandoned or of not being loved enough.

Researchers have generally shown that attachment style in adolescents and young adults is related in theoretically expected ways to family history. Feeney (1991) used the same adjective checklist to measure family history and found, as did Hazan and Shaver (1987), that secure and insecure subjects could be discriminated in terms of their perceptions of the parenting they received, with insecure subjects having more negative views of the ways they were treated by both their mothers and fathers. In addition, Feeney and Noller (1990) found that Avoidant subjects were more likely to report being separated from either parent during childhood than were either of the other groups.

Noller (1990) compared the three attachment groups in a sample of college students from a large West Coast U.S. state university in terms of their general level of psychological adjustment, using measures of self-esteem, trait anxiety, and loneliness. Self-esteem was measured using the Self-Esteem Inventory (Coopersmith, 1975), which measures personal self-esteem, social self-esteem, and family selfesteem (Noller & Shum, 1988). Trait anxiety was measured using the State Trait Anxiety Scale (Spielberger, Gorsuch, & Lushene, 1968), and loneliness was measured using the UCLA Loneliness Scale (Russell, Peplau, & Cutrona, 1980). The attachment groups differed on four of the five scales. Anxious-Ambivalents scored lower than both other groups on both personal and social self-esteem and higher than both other groups on anxiety and loneliness. Avoidants scored higher than Secures on anxiety and loneliness, but were not different from them in self-esteem. It seems clear from these findings

Table 3.2 Mean Scores for Attachment Groups on Measures of
Adjustment (American College Sample)

Adjustment Measure	Secure	Avoidant	Anxious/ Ambivalent	Probability
Total Self-Esteem	19.7	18.2	12.6	.001
Personal Self-Esteem	8.8	8.4	4.8	.001
Social Self-Esteem	5.8	5.3	3.8	.001
Family Self-Esteem	5.2	4.6	4.1	n.s.
Trait Anxiety	36.8	40.3	49.3	.001
Loneliness	31.7	40.1	44.5	.001

that the general psychological adjustment of Anxious-Ambivalents
is quite problematic, with Avoidants also having problems with
anxiety and loneliness but not self-esteem. (Sée Table 3.2 for mean
scores for the three groups on each of the measures of adjustment.)

Continuous measures of the extent to which adolescents believed
that each of the attachment styles was characteristic of them were
also taken and were correlated with the adjustment measures. (See
Table 3.3.) As would be expected, the measures of self-esteem were
positively correlated with Security and negatively correlated with
Avoidance and Anxious-Ambivalence, whereas the measures of
anxiety and loneliness were negatively correlated with Security and
positively correlated with Avoidance and Anxious-Ambivalence.
All but one of the 18 correlations was significant, with the weakest
relationships being found between Anxious-Ambivalence and social and family self-esteem. This finding almost certainly reflects the
fact that Anxious-Ambivalents have positive attitudes toward others (Bartholomew & Horowitz, 1991), but negative attitudes toward
themselves.

Attachment has also been related to personality characteristics.
Feeney, Noller, and Hanrahan (in press) had high school children
complete the Attachment Style Questionnaire, which measures five
attachment dimensions (Confidence in Self and Others, Need for
Approval, Discomfort with Closeness, Preoccupation with Relationships, Relationships as Secondary to Achievement) and the Eysenck
Personality Questionnaire (Eysenck & Eysenck, 1975), which measures Toughmindedness, Extraversion, Neuroticism, and Social Desirability (by means of the Lie Scale). They found strong relations

Table 3.3   Correlations Between Attachment Dimensions and
Adjustment Measures (American College Sample)

Adjustment Measures	Security	Avoidance	Anxious-Ambivalence
Total Self-Esteem	.39***	−.33**	−.31**
Personal Self-Esteem	.33**	−.25**	−.36***
Social Self-Esteem	.38***	−.27**	−.22*
Family Self-Esteem	.27**	−.30**	−.12
Trait Anxiety	−.43***	.35***	.40***
Loneliness	−.59***	.52***	.42***

*p < .05; **p < .01; ***p < .001

between the attachment dimensions of Preoccupation with Relationships and Need for Approval with the personality dimension of
Neuroticism. Those scoring higher on Preoccupation with Relationships and Need for Approval were also likely to be higher in Neuroticism. There were also clear relations between the attachment dimensions of Confidence in Self and Others, Discomfort with Closeness, and
Relationships as Secondary and the personality dimension of Extraversion. Those scoring higher on Extraversion were more likely to be
high in confidence, high in comfort with closeness, and less likely
to see relationships as secondary to achievement.

The importance of the recent work on adult attachment is that it
provides connections between family relationships and later romantic relationships, and thus between generations of families. The
empirical work carried out so far does seem to support the view
that early experiences in the family lead to fairly stable attitudes
to the self and to others that affect both the stability and quality
of later relationships, and hence the stability and quality of family life in the next generation. In a later section we will look at the
relations between attachment style and adolescent and adult romantic relationships.

ADOLESCENTS' PERCEPTIONS
OF DIFFERENTIAL TREATMENT BY PARENTS

Another issue related to adolescent adjustment is the extent to
which adolescents see their parents as having treated them better or

worse than their siblings. Differential parental treatment is related to children's feelings of competence and self-worth, especially for those who believe that they receive less affection than their sibling (Dunn, Stocker, & Beardsall, 1989; Dunn & Plomin, 1990). These effects hold even when the effects of the child's personality are controlled. We explored the effects of differential parenting in a study using adolescent twins as subjects (Sheehan & Noller, 1992). We particularly used same-sex twins for this study because this procedure enabled us to control for age and birth order, which are generally problematic when ordinary siblings are used. Adolescents rated the extent to which they believed they had been treated better or worse than their twin, using a modified version of the Sibling Inventory of Differential Experience (Daniels & Plomin, 1985), which measures perceptions of affection and control. We also assessed perceptions of family functioning, attachment, and the outcome measures of self-esteem and anxiety. Adolescents who believed they had received more affection and less control than their twin had more negative views of the family, were more likely to be insecure in attachment style, and tended to have lower self-esteem and to be more anxious than those who saw themselves as receiving similar or better treatment from their parents than their sibling.

FAMILY COMMUNICATION AND PSYCHOPATHOLOGY

Studies of family interaction and psychopathology tend to implicate similar family variables to those already discussed: power structures and control, closeness and cohesion in the family, and family communication and conflict. Power variables of relevance include excessive dominance of one partner over other members (Rodick & Henggeler, 1982) or mothers' having difficulty taking the role of parent and being too permissive (Barton, Alexander, & Turner, 1988). Thus a balance between authoritarianism on the one hand and excessive permissiveness on the other seems to be an important factor in maintaining the mental health of family members.

Inappropriate hierarchies (e.g., Hetherington, Stouwie, & Ridberg, 1971) and inappropriate coalitions in the family have also been implicated in the development of psychopathology in adolescents. Minuchin (1974) particularly emphasizes the need for clear separation between the parent subsystem and the child subsystem and the importance of parents' taking a clear leadership role.

Adaptability is also an important aspect of family functioning (Beavers & Voeller, 1983; Epstein, Bishop, & Levin, 1978; Olson et al., 1983). Family roles and rules should not be rigidly upheld, but should be able to change with the changing needs and abilities of family members. Roles and rules must also be able to accommodate to individual circumstances and special needs. Communication becomes crucial here in that adolescents have to be prepared to make their needs and issues known, and family members need to be able to negotiate new rules or amendments to old ones.

A related issue centers on the level of closeness in the family. A concern among family theorists is the level of closeness in the family, whether families can be too close (Beavers & Voeller, 1983; Olson et al., 1983), and the consequences of too much closeness (see Steinhauer, 1987, for a discussion of this issue). Epstein et al. (1978) describe an extreme level of symbiotic (or enmeshed) involvement as "so intense that the boundaries between two or more individuals are blurred" and as "extreme involvement that blurs individual differentiation" (p. 26). The main issue is whether individuals are clearly differentiated (able to separate self from nonself) and able to function as separate autonomous beings. The assumption of many theorists seems to be that high closeness always involves low or nonexistent autonomy (e.g., Bowen, 1978; Minuchin, 1974). Of course, the relationship between autonomy and closeness is an empirical question and should be treated as such. We suspect, however, as Beavers and Voeller (1983) comment, that capable families are able to respect individual choice, as well as maintain high levels of closeness. Although there has been little empirical work connecting the adolescent issues of individuation/differentiation, identity achievement, and attachment, such work is clearly needed.

Clarity of communication is also implicated in the development and maintenance of psychopathology in adolescents (Goldstein & Strachan, 1987; Jacob, 1975; Liem, 1980). Data consistently show that families of schizophrenics communicate with less clarity and accuracy than normal families, both with one another and with the schizophrenic patient. (See also Alexander & Parsons, 1982; Klein, Alexander, & Parsons, 1977.) There is also evidence for lower levels of facilitative information exchange and extremes of conflict (Barton et al., 1988) in these families. Goldstein and Strachan (1987) note that across a number of studies, parents of schizophrenics have difficulty maintaining a shared focus of attention, communicating meaning clearly and accurately, and taking the perspective of another person. In a 15-year follow-up, Goldstein (1985) showed that schizophrenia spectrum disorders were most likely in families where parents had difficulty communicating clearly, used a negative affective style, and were high in emotional expressiveness (harsh criticism and intrusiveness). He and his colleagues were also able to show that the communication difficulties were present before the onset of the disorder.

Some theorists also argue (e.g., Beavers & Voeller, 1983) that different types of problematic family interaction (or different family styles) produce different types of psychopathology in adolescents. According to Beavers and his colleagues, families that are extremely family focused and have little interaction with the outside world (centripetal) are likely to produce adolescents with internalizing disorders such as depression or schizophrenia. On the other hand, families that are focused strongly on the outside world, with only loose bonds between family members (centifugal), are likely to produce adolescents with externalizing disorders, that is, delinquent and conduct-disordered young people.

FAMILY RELATIONSHIPS AND MORAL DEVELOPMENT

Effective family communication also seems to facilitate the development of higher moral reasoning in adolescents (Stanley, 1978) and to increase the adolescent's ability to take the perspective of another (Cooper et al., 1984). The use of inductive disciplinary techniques by parents combined with the expression of affection is highly correlated with an internalized moral code (Hoffman, 1980). Power assertion techniques, on the other hand, lead to a moral code based on fear of detection and punishment.

Observational research of family discussions of moral dilemmas (Jurkovic & Prentice, 1974) has also shown that moral maturity in adolescents is related positively to parental encouragement and negatively to hostility and dominance on the part of parents. Where parents are willing to explain to their adolescent offspring the moral implications of particular actions and the consequences that are likely to ensue in a positive atmosphere of love and caring, the adolescents learn about the way the world works, the likely effects of their behavior on others, and appropriate ways of solving disagreements with others. Where parents merely "lay down the law," there is little opportunity for adolescents to develop the appropriate skills.

FAMILY RELATIONSHIPS AND PROBLEM BEHAVIORS OF ADOLESCENCE

Similar family variables to those that affect identity exploration and self-esteem also seem to affect the extent to which adolescents are involved in various problem behaviors. Family support and closeness and parental attitudes to autonomy and control seem to be the crucial issues. Family closeness, particularly the extent to which adolescents feel free to talk over problems with their parents, affects the extent to which adolescents become involved in smoking, drinking, and the use of other drugs. Where the famliy is not close and supportive, adolescents seem to turn more to their peers for support and to engage in more problem behaviors.

Smoking, Alcohol, and Drugs

Barnes, Farrell, and Cairns (1986) related adolescent patterns of alcohol consumption to the socialization practices in the family, particularly the levels of support and control. Alcohol problems among the adolescents were particularly prominent where mothers were low in both support and control and at their lowest when mothers were high in support and low or medium in control. Alcohol problems occurred at high levels when fathers were low in support and high in control and at low levels when fathers were high in support and exerted a medium level of control.

McCubbin, Needle, and Wilson (1985) examined the effects of family stressors and strains and family and adolescent coping on the likelihood of the adolescent becoming involved in problem behaviors. Adolescents who experienced a buildup of family stressors and strains were more likely to get involved in smoking, drinking, or drugs than other adolescents. On the other hand, those who coped with these strains by talking with their parents, trying to work out difficult issues with family members, and generally being more involved with the family were much less likely to engage in these health-risk behaviors.

Adolescents who were most at risk for heavy involvement in drugs of one sort or another were those who tended to "ventilate" or externalize in response to stress—blaming others, getting angry, yelling, and complaining. Those adolescents who saw their friendship group as providing close emotional support also had higher levels of smoking, drinking, and marijuana use. Such findings support the view that adolescents who rely on the peer group rather than the family for their main support are particularly vulnerable to peer pressure to engage in problem behaviors (Sheppard et al., 1985).

A review of the literature by Jurich, Polson, Jurich, and Bates (1985) underlines a range of family factors that are related to drug use and abuse. Conflict between the parents, absence of one or both parents when the child was growing up, little closeness between parent and child, parental rejection and hostility, lack of communication in the family, problematic discipline procedures in the family, and the parents' own use of drugs all have been implicated as causes of adolescent drug abuse.

In their own work, Jurich and his colleagues compared a drug-using group (infrequent or occasional use of legal or nonaddictive drugs) with a drug abusing group (almost daily ingestion of dangerous drugs). Families of drug abusers had more problems with communication in the family and talked of a communication gap between themselves and their parents. Parents of drug abusers were less likely to use democratic parenting and more likely to use either authoritarian discipline techniques or laissez-faire techniques. Authoritarian techniques are likely to increase parent-adolescent conflict and adolescent frustration and to lead to acting out on the part of adolescents. Laissez-faire discipline, on the other hand, is likely to allow adolescents more freedom than they can handle responsibly and may encourage a hedonistic use of drugs (Barnes, 1977; Jurich et al., 1985). Lax discipline techniques can also signal parental lack of interest or even rejection to adolescents, with the consequent effects on self-esteem and behavior.

Relationships with parents can even predict changing patterns of drug use over a 2 year period (Norem-Hebeisen, Johnson, Anderson, & Johnson, 1984). Increasing drug use between Grades 9 and 11 was associated with strong parental disapproval of the adolescent, little expression of caring and affection by parents, anger and rejection from the father, and increasing attempts to control the teenager's comings and goings. The adolescents who did not use drugs reported more positive relationships with their parents between the 9th and 11th grades, with more affirmation from both mothers and fathers and less hostility between themselves and their fathers.

Involvement in Sexual Intercourse

Family variables related to involvement in sexual intercourse include poor parent-child relationships and poor parent-child communication, especially difficulty in confiding in parents. As we have already noted, little communication about sex occurs in the average family, but it also seems clear that where communication is generally problematic, adolescents are more at risk for becoming involved in sexual relationships at an early age. These adolescents are also more likely to have a strong emphasis on independence, be unconcerned about academic achievement, be more tolerant of deviant behaviors, and be more critical of society in general (Callan & Noller, 1987; Chilman, 1980; Jessor, Costa, Jessor, & Donovan, 1983; Jessor & Jessor, 1977). They are also more likely to come from single-parent families and to be looking for affection.

Having permissive parents also increases the chances of adolescents' being involved in sexual intercourse at an early age. These adolescents may have less parental supervision and thus more opportunities for getting into situations where sexual intercourse is a likely outcome. It is also possible that permissive parents don't discuss the issues with the adolescent, pointing out possible problems and consequences.

Another serious concern is the lack of accurate information among teenagers. Morrison (1985) cites studies indicating quite clearly that adolescents are "a mine of misinformation" about sexuality and conception. Although those who have had some form of sex education tend to have more accurate knowledge than those who do not, the appalling ignorance among adolescents does not seem to be totally alleviated by such classes (Morrison, 1985). Parents are usually the least important sources of sex information, especially for sons; this is not surprising, given what we have said earlier about the lack of communication about sex in the family. However, those adolescents who have talked to their parents are more knowledgeable than those who have not (Rothenberg, 1980). Some researchers have, however, commented on the lack of knowledge of many parents (Fox & Inazu, 1980; Rothenberg, 1980), who may even be a source of some of the misinformation that adolescents have. Another problem is that adolescents often think they know it all when they don't, and may not be prepared to consult their parents or believe what they tell them. Providing good reading material for adolescents may be an important way that parents can help.

THE FAMILY AND ADOLESCENTS' LATER RELATIONSHIPS

The effects of the family on later relationships of adolescents can be examined from at least two theoretical perspectives: identity development (Erikson, 1968; Marcia, 1966) and attachment theory (Ainsworth et al., 1978; Bowlby, 1969, 1973, 1980; Hazan & Shaver, 1987). In the following sections we will examine the implications of these two perspectives.

Identity Development and Later Relationships

Erikson (1968) emphasized the importance of identity achievement in adolescence because those who do not achieve a clear sense of their own identity are likely to have problems in their relationships with others. Those who have a firm sense of their own identity are likely to relate best to others, particularly in intimate relationships. Erikson believed that a person could only be a caring partner to another person when he or she had first established a clear sense of his or her own identity.

Erikson's theorizing would have acccurately predicted the findings of Orlofsky, Marcia, and Lesser (1973), who related identity status to measures of depth and mutuality in interpersonal relationships. Identity Achievers and Moratoriums were more likely to be involved in intimate relationships, whereas no Diffusions and few Foreclosures were. Foreclosures and Diffusions tended to be involved in stereotyped relationships, and the Diffusions were most likely to be involved in isolated relationships that included little group involvement.

In a report of a longitudinal study of a group of art students over an 18-year period, Kahn, Zimmerman, Csikzentmihalyi, and Getzels (1985) provide data about the students' identity development during their time in college and then information about their personal, family, and professional life since leaving college. Marital status 18 years later was related to identity status in college, but in different ways for men and women. For men, there was a strong relationship between identity status and remaining single, with most of those scoring low on the identity scale in college reporting that they had never married. For women, there was no relationship between identity status and whether they married, but there was a clear relationship between identity status and marital stability. Women who scored low on the identity scale were more likely to experience marital disruption. Thus having a clear sense of identity does have important implications for long-term relationships for both men and women.

Attachment and Later Relationships

The definitions of the different attachment styles imply quite different styles of relating to others, whether we use the three-category system (Hazan & Shaver, 1987) or the four-category system (Bartholomew & Horowitz, 1991). Secures, for example, are characterized as generally comfortable with closeness and as able to trust other people and to depend on them. Anxious-Ambivalents tend to be clingy in their relationships and tend to be anxious and preoccupied with their relationships, fearing that they will be abandoned or not loved enough. Avoidants, on the other hand, are uncomfortable with closeness and tend to prefer to depend on themselves rather than other people. In their four-category system, Bartholomew and Horowitz distinguish between those with a dismissing style, who have a positive view of themselves, are very self-sufficient, and devalue relationships, and fearful Avoidants, who have negative views of both themselves and others and whose avoidance of relationships is anxiety driven.

Research comparing the different styles (Collins & Read, 1990; Feeney & Noller, 1990, 1991; Levy & Davis, 1988; Pistole, 1989) has enabled us to pinpoint more clearly the differences between the groups. Secure attachment tends to be associated with intimacy and relationship satisfaction; Avoidant attachment is associated with lower levels of intimacy and emotional intensity, and lower levels of commitment and satisfaction; Anxious-Ambivalent attachment is associated with high levels of passion, but also with dependence, idealization, and anxiety.

HELPING PARENTS COPE
WITH THE PROBLEMS OF ADOLESCENCE

It is clear from much that we have said that most adolescents want and need a close, warm relationship with their parents. Constructive, helpful parenting aims to provide such a relationship. Adolescents who feel comfortable about their relationship with their parents are more likely to reflect their parents' values, to disclose to them, and to cooperate with them. After all, where adolescents cooperate with their parents, obedience becomes a nonissue, and parents and adolescents generally have far fewer problems relating to one another.

Authoritarian parenting styles may increase conformity and obedience in the short term, but children are at risk for developing more external styles where they lack internal controls on their own behavior. Authoritarian parenting is also more likely to lead to rebellion and a complete breakdown of the parent-adolescent relationship. Many kids are on the street because of this type of breakdown in their relationships with their parents.

Adolescents also do much better when they feel accepted by their parents and are able to talk to them about their problems and issues and to negotiate changes in roles and rules. Many problems stem from the difficulties parents and adolescents have in communicating their feelings and needs and working out mutually acceptable solutions. Adolescents also need to be able to come to their parents to get information they need and to discuss issues with them. An accepting environment also helps adolescents to engage in the more basic tasks of identity exploration and development.

Parents need to be flexible in their dealings with adolescents and to be prepared to change role expectations and rules when they are no longer appropriate. Although it is important that adolescents know what the important family rules are, they should also expect that parents will take into account their individual needs and circumstances and to negotiate changes. For example, if a family rule that says that all family members should be present at breakfast precludes a family member from training for the school swimming team as she would like to, then such a rule may need to be revised. A further important consideration is that adolescents who are able to talk with their parents about their issues and rely on them for emotional support are likely to rely less on the peer group for both their emotional support and guides to appropriate behavior. Those whose main focus is on the peer group are more likely to be pressured into using less constructive means of coping such as drinking or drugs. In addition, the buildup of unresolved stressors and strains on the adolescent makes them increasingly at risk for using health-risk behaviors. Parenting styles encouraging the development of problem-solving approaches that involve talking to family members and trying to find ways of resolving the issues are much more constructive.

It is important for both adolescents and their parents to recognize that adolescents have to be responsible for their own behavior, and not to blame others or circumstances when they get involved in undesirable behaviors. The only real protection an adolescent has when confronted with the opportunity to engage in illegal, immoral, or undesirable behaviors is the ability to say no and to withstand pressure. Parents therefore should emphasize internal rather than external controls and discourage inappropriate attributions of blame to external sources. They should also take care that the implicit messages sent to the adolescent are ones that encourage good judgment and competence.

REFERENCES

Abelson, A. S., Cohen, R., Heaton, E., & Slider, C. (1970). *Public attitudes towards an experience with erotic materials* (Technical Report No. 6). Washington, DC: Commission of Obscenity and Pornography.

Adams, G. R., & Jones, R. M. (1983). Female adolescents' identity development: Age comparisons and perceived child-rearing experience. *Developmental Psychology, 19,* 249-256.

Adams, G. R., Gullotta, T., & Clancy, M. A. (1985). Homeless adolescents: A descriptive study of similarities and differences between runaways and throwaways. *Adolescence, 20,* 715-724.

Ainsworth, M. D. S., Blehar, M. C., Waters, E., & Wall, S. (1978). *Patterns of attachment: A psychological study of the strange situation.* Hillsdale, NJ: Lawrence Erlbaum.

Alexander, J., & Parsons, B. V. (1982). *Functional family therapy.* Monterey, CA: Brooks/Cole.

Amoroso, D. M., & Ware, E. E. (1986). Adolescents' perceptions of aspects of the home environment and their attitudes towards parents, self and external authority. *Adolescence, 21,* 191-204.

Balswick, J. O., & Macrides, C. (1975). Parental stimulus for adolescent rebellion. *Adolescence, 10,* 253-266.

Barnes, G. M. (1977). The development of adolescent drinking behavior: An evaluation review of the impact of the socialization process within the family. *Adolescence, 12,* 571-591.

Barnes, H. L., & Olson, D. H. (1985). Parent-adolescent communication and the circumplex model. *Child Development, 56,* 437-447.

Barnes, G. M., Farrell, M. P., & Cairns, A. (1986). Parent socialization factors and adolescent drinking behaviors. *Journal of Marriage and the Family, 48,* 27-36.

Bartholomew, K., & Horowitz, L. M. (1991). Attachment styles among young adults: A test of a four-category model. *Journal of Personality and Social Psychology, 61,* 226-244.

Barton, C., Alexander, J. F., & Turner, C. W. (1988). Defensive communication in normal and delinquent families: The impact of context and social role. *Journal of Family Psychology, 1,* 390-405.

Baumrind, D. (1971). Current patterns of parental authority. *Developmental Psychology Monographs, 4*(1).

Beavers, W. R., & Voeller, M. N. (1983). Family models: Comparing and contrasting the Olson Circumplex Model with the Beavers Systems Model. *Family Process, 22,* 85-98.

Bengtson, V. L., & Kuypers, J. A. (1971). Generational differences and the developmental stake. *Aging and Human Development, 2,* 240-260.

Bengtson, V. L., & Starr, J. M. (1975). Contrast and consensus: A generational analysis of youth in the 1970's. In R. J. Havighurst & P. H. Dreyer (Eds.), *Youth: The Seventy-Fourth Yearbook of the National Society for the Study of Education* (pp. 224-266). Chicago: University of Chicago Press.

Bengtson, V. L., & Troll, L. (1978). Youth and their parents: Feedback and intergenerational influence in socialization. In R. M. Lerner & G. B. Spanier (Eds.), *Children's influences on marital and family interaction: A life-span perspective* (pp. 106-130). New York: Academic Press.

Bernard, H. S. (1981). Identity formation during late adolescence: A review of some empirical findings. *Adolescence, 16,* 349-358.

Biddle, B. J., Bank, B. J., & Marlin, M. M. (1980). Parental and peer influence on adolescents. *Social Forces, 58,* 1057-1079.

Bowen, M. (1978). *Family therapy in clinical practice.* New York: Jason Aronson.

Bowlby, J. (1969). *Attachment and loss: Vol. 1. Attachment.* New York: Basic Books.

Bowlby, J. (1973). *Attachment and loss: Vol. 2. Separation: Anxiety and anger.* New York: Basic Books.

Bowlby, J. (1980). *Attachment and loss: Vol. 3. Loss.* New York: Basic Books.

Buri, J. R., Kirchner, P. A., & Walsh, J. M. (1987). Familial correlates of self-esteem in young American adults. *Journal of Social Psychology, 127,* 583-588.

Callan, V. J., & Noller, P. (1986). Perceptions of communication in families with adolescents. *Journal of Marriage and the Family, 48,* 813-820.

Callan, V. J., & Noller, P. (1987). *Marriage and the family.* Sydney: Methuen.

Campbell, E., Adams, G. R., & Dobson, W. R. (1984). Family correlates of identity formation in late adolescents: A study of the predictive utility of connectedness and individuality in family relations. *Journal of Youth and Adolescence, 13,* 509-525.

Caplow, T., Bahr, H. M., Chadwick, B. A., Hill, R., & Williamson, M. H. (1982). *Middletown families.* Minneapolis: University of Minnesota Press.

Chilman, C. S. (1980). Social and psychological research concerning adolescent childbearing: 1970-1980. *Journal of Marriage and the Family, 42,* 793-805.

Collins, N. L., & Read, S. J. (1990). Adult attachment, working models and relationship quality in dating couples. *Journal of Personality and Social Psychology, 58,* 644-663.

Cooper, C. R., Grotevant, H. D., & Condon, S. M. (1984). Family support and conflict: Both foster adolescent identity and role-taking skills. In H. D. Grotevant & C. R. Cooper (Eds.), *Adolescent development in the family: New directions for child development.* San Francisco: Jossey-Bass.

Coopersmith, S. (1975). Building self-esteem in the classroom. In S. Coopersmith (Ed.), *Developing motivation in young children.* San Francisco: Allan.

Csikszentmihalyi, M., & Larson, R. (1984). *Being adolescent.* New York: Basic Books.

Daniels, D., & Plomin, R. (1985). Differential experience of siblings in the same family. *Developmental Psychology, 21,* 747-760.

Davidson, B., Balswick, J. O., & Halverson, C. F. (1980). Factor analysis of self disclosure for adolescents. *Adolescence, 15,* 947-957.

Douvan, E., & Adelson, J. (1966). *The adolescent experience.* New York: John Wiley.

Dunn, J., Stocker, C., & Beardsall, L. (1989, April). *Sibling differences in self esteem.* Paper presented at the biennial meeting for the Society for Research in Child Development, Kansas City.

Dunn, J., & Plomin, R. (1990). *Separate lives: Why siblings are so different.* New York: Basic Books.

Elder, G. H. (1963). Parental power legitimation and its effects on the adolescent. *Sociometry, 26,* 50-65.

Ellis-Schwabe, M., & Thornburg, H. D. (1986). Conflict areas between parents and their adolescents. *Journal of Psychology, 120,* 59-68.

Epstein, N. B., Bishop, D. S., & Levin, S. (1978). The McMaster model of family functioning. *Journal of Marriage and Family Counseling, 4,* 19-31.

Erikson, E. (1959). *Childhood and society.* New York: Norton.

Erikson, E. (1968). *Identity: Youth and crisis.* New York: Norton.

Eskilson, A., Wiley, M. G., Muehlbauer, G., & Dodder, L. (1986). Parental pressure, self-esteem and adolescent reported deviance: Bending the twig too far. *Adolescence, 21,* 501-515.

Eysenck, H. J., & Eysenck, S. B. G. (1975). *Manual of the Eysenck Personality Questionnaire (junior and adult).* Sevenoaks, Kent: Hodder & Stoughton.

Farber, E., & Joseph, J. (1985). The maltreated adolescent: Patterns of physical abuse. *International Journal of Child Abuse and Neglect, 9,* 201-206.

Feeney, J. A., & Noller, P. (1990). Attachment style as a predictor of adult romantic relationships. *Journal of Personality and Social Psychology, 58,* 281-291.

Feeney, J. A. (1991). *The attachment perspective on adult romantic relationships.* Unpublished doctoral dissertation, University of Queensland, Australia.

Feeney, J. A., & Noller, P. (1991). Attachment style and verbal descriptions of romantic partners. *Journal of Social and Personal Relationships, 8,* 187-215.

Feeney, J. A., Noller, P., & Hanrahan, M. (in press). Assessing adult attachment: Developments in the conceptualization of security and insecurity. In M. B. Sperling & W. H. Berman (Eds.), *Attachment in adults: Theory, lifespan developmental and treatment issues.* New York: Guilford.

Fox, G. L. (1980). The mother-daughter relationship as a sexual socialization structure: A research review. *Family Relations, 29,* 21-28.

Fox, G. L., & Inazu, J. K. (1980). Patterns and outcomes of mother-daughter communication upon sexuality. *Journal of Social Issues, 36,* 7-29.

Galambos, N. L., & Dixon, R. A. (1984). Adolescent abuse and the development of personal sense of control. *Child Abuse and Neglect, 8,* 285-293.

Garbarino, J., & Gilliam, G. (1980). *Understanding abusive families.* Lexington, MA: Lexington.

Gebhard, P. H. (1977). The acquisition of basic sex information. *Journal of Sex Research, 13,* 148-169.

Gecas, V., & Schwalbe, M. L. (1986). Parental behavior and adolescent self-esteem. *Journal of Marriage and the Family, 48,* 37-46.

Goldstein, M. J. (1985). Family factors that antedate the onset of schizophrenia and related disorders: The results of a fifteen year prospective longitudinal study. *Acta Psychiatrica Scandinavia, 71,* 7-18.

Goldstein, M. J., & Strachan, A. M. (1987). The family and schizophrenia. In T. Jacob (Ed.), *Family interaction and psychopathology* (pp. 451-508). New York: Plenum.

Grotevant, H. D., & Cooper, C. R. (1985). Patterns of interaction in family relationships and the development of identity exploration in adolescents. *Child Development, 56,* 415-428.

Grotevant, H. D., & Cooper, C. R. (1986). Individuation in family relationships: A perspective on individual differences in the development of identity and role taking in adolescence. *Human Development, 29,* 82-100.

Harris, I. D., & Howard, K. I. (1984). Parental criticism and the adolescent experience. *Journal of Youth and Adolescence, 13,* 113-121.

Hauser, S. T., Powers, S. I., Noam, G. G., Jacobson, A. M., Wiess, B., & Follansbee, D. J. (1984). Familial contexts of adolescent ego development. *Child Development, 55,* 195-213.

Hazan, C., & Shaver, P. R. (1987). Romantic love conceptualized as an attachment process. *Journal of Personality and Social Psychology, 52,* 511-524.

Herrenkohl, R. (1977). Research: Too much too late? In M. Lauderdale, R. Anderson, & S. Cramer (Eds.), *Child abuse and neglect: Issues of innovation and implementation* (pp. 174-184). Washington, DC: U.S. Department of Health and Human Services.

Hetherington, E. M., Stouwie, R., & Ridberg, E. H. (1971). Patterns of family interaction and child rearing attitudes related to three dimensions of juvenile delinquency. *Journal of Abnormal Psychology, 77,* 160-176.

Hoelter, J., & Harper, L. (1987). Structural and interpersonal family influences on adolescent self-conception. *Journal of Marriage and the Family, 49,* 129-139.

Hoffman, M. L. (1980). Moral development in adolescence. In J. Adelson (Ed.), *Handbook of adolescence* (pp. 319-335). New York: John Wiley.

Hunter, F. T., & Youniss, J. (1982). Changes in functions of three relations during adolescence. *Developmental Psychology, 18,* 806-811.

Hunter, F. T. (1985). Individual adolescents' perceptions of interactions with parents and friends. *Journal of Early Adolescence, 5,* 295-305.

Jacob, T. (1974). Patterns of family conflict and dominance as a function of child age and social class. *Developmental Psychology, 10,* 1-12.

Jacob, T. (1975). Family interaction in disturbed and normal families: A methodological and substantive review. *Psychological Review, 82,* 33-65.

Jessop, D. J. (1981). Family relationships as viewed by parents and adolescents: A specification. *Journal of Marriage and the Family, 43,* 95-107.

Jessor, R., & Jessor, S. L. (1977). *Problem behavior and psychosocial development: A longitudinal study of youth.* New York: Academic Press.

Jessor, R., Costa, F., Jessor, S. L., & Donovan, J. E. (1983). Time of first intercourse; A prospective study. *Journal of Personality and Social Psychology, 44,* 608-626.

Jourard, S. M. (1971). *Self-disclosure: An experimental analysis of the transparent self.* New York: John Wiley.

Jurich, A. P., Polson, C. J., Jurich, J. A., & Bates, R. A. (1985). Family factors in the lives of drug users and abusers. *Adolescence, 20,* 143-159.

Jurkovic, G. J., & Prentice, N. M. (1974). Dimensions of moral interaction and moral judgment in delinquent and nondelinquent families. *Journal of Consulting and Clinical Psychology, 42,* 256-262.

Jurkovic, G. J., & Ulrici, D. (1985). Empirical perspectives on adolescents and their families. In L. L'Abate (Ed.), *Handbook of family psychology and therapy* (pp. 215-257). Homewood, IL: Dorsey.

Kahn, S., Zimmerman, G., Csikszentmihalyi, M., & Getzels, J. W. (1985). Relations between identity in young adulthood and intimacy at midlife. *Journal of Personality and Social Psychology, 49,* 1316-1322.

Klein, N. C., Alexander, J. F., & Parsons, B. V. (1977). Impact of family systems intervention on recidivism and sibling-delinquency model of primary prevention and program evaluation. *Journal of Consulting and Clinical Psychology, 45,* 469-474.

Komarovsky, M. (1974). Patterns of self-disclosure of male undergraduates. *Journal of Marriage and the Family, 36,* 677-686.

Levy, M. B., & Davis, K. E. (1988). Lovestyles and attachment styles compared: Their relations to each other and to various relationship characteristics. *Journal of Social and Personal Relationships, 5,* 439-471.

Liem, J. H. (1980). Family studies in schizophrenia: An update and a commentary. *Schizophrenia Bulletin, 6,* 429-459.

Marcia, J. E. (1966). Development and validation of ego identity status. *Journal of Personality and Social Psychology, 3,* 551-558.

Marsh, H. W., Parker, J., & Barnes, J. (1985). Multidimensional adolescent self-concepts: Their relationship to age, sex and academic measures. *American Educational Research Journal, 22,* 422-444.

Martin, M. J., Schumm, W. R., Bugaighis, M. A., Jurich, A. P., & Bollman, S. R. (1987). Family violence and adolescents' perceptions of outcomes of family conflict. *Journal of Marriage and the Family, 49,* 165-171.

McCubbin, H. I., Needle, R. H., & Wilson, M. (1985). Adolescent health risk behaviors: Family stress and adolescent coping as critical factors. *Family Relations, 34,* 51-62.

McLeod, L. (1987). *Battered but not beaten: Preventing wife-battering in Canada.* Ottawa, Ontario: Canadian Advisory Council on Status of Women.

Middleton, R., & Putney, S. (1963). Political expression of adolescent rebellion. *American Journal of Sociology, 67,* 527-537.

Minuchin, S. (1974). *Families and family therapy.* Cambridge, MA: Harvard University Press.

Montemayor, R. (1982). The relationship between parent-adolescent conflict and the amount of time adolescents spend alone and with parents and peers. *Child Development, 53,* 1512-1519.

Montemayor, R. (1983). Parents and adolescents in conflict: All families some of the time and some families most of the time. *Journal of Early Adolescence, 3,* 83-103.

Montemayor, R., & Hanson, E. (1985). A naturalistic view of conflict between adolescents and their parents and siblings. *Journal of Early Adolescence, 5,* 23-30.

Morrison, D. M. (1985). Adolescent contraceptive behavior: A review. *Psychological Bulletin, 98,* 538-568.

Mulcahey, G. A. (1973). Sex differences in patterns of self-disclosure among adolescents: A developmental perspective. *Journal of Youth and Adolescence, 2,* 343-356.

Mussen, P. H., Conger, J. J., & Kagan, J. (1974). *Child development and personality* (4th ed.). New York: Harper & Row.

Newman, B. A., & Murray, C. I. (1983). Identity and family relations in early adolescence. *Journal of Early Adolescence, 3,* 293-303.

Niemi, R. G. (1974). *How family members perceive each other: Political and social attitudes in two generations.* New Haven, CT: Yale University Press.

Noller, P. (1990). *Attachment and personality in a student sample.* Unpublished manuscript, University of Queensland, Australia.

Noller, P., & Bagi, S. (1985). Parent-adolescent communication. *Journal of Adolescence, 8,* 125-144.

Noller, P., & Callan, V. J. (1986). Adolescent and parent perceptions of family cohesion and adaptability. *Journal of Adolescence, 9,* 97-106.

Noller, P., & Callan, V. J. (1988). Understanding parent-adolescent interaction: The perceptions of family members and outsiders. *Developmental Psychology, 24,* 707-714.

Noller, P., & Shum, D. (1988). The Self Esteem Inventory on an adult sample. *Psychological Test Bulletin, 1,* 3-7.

Noller, P., & Callan, V. J. (1990). Adolescents' perceptions of the nature of their communication with parents. *Journal of Youth and Adolescence, 19,* 349-362.

Noller, P., & Callan, V. J. (1991). *The adolescent in the family.* London: Routledge.

Noller, P., Seth-Smith, M., Bouma, R., & Schweitzer, R. (1992). Parent and adolescent perceptions of family functioning: A comparison of clinic and nonclinic families. *Journal of Adolescence, 15,* 101-114.

Norem-Hebeisen, A., Johnson, D. W., Anderson, D., & Johnson, R. (1984). Predictors and concomitants of changes in drug use patterns among teenagers. *Journal of Social Psychology, 124,* 43-50.

Offer, D. (1969). *The psychological world of the teenager.* New York: Basic Books.

Offer, D., & Sabshin, M. (Eds.). (1984). *Normality and the life cycle.* New York: Basic Books.

Olson, D. H., McCubbin, H. I., Barnes, H. L., Larsen, A. S., Muxen, M. J., & Wilson, M. A. (1983). *Families: What makes them work?* Beverly Hills, CA: Sage.

Openshaw, D. K., Thomas, D. L., & Rollins, B. C. (1984). Parental influences on adolescent self-esteem. *Journal of Early Adolescence, 4,* 259-274.

Orlofsky, J. L., Marcia, C. E., & Lesser, I. (1973). Ego identity status and the intimacy versus isolation crisis of young adulthood. *Journal of Personality and Social Psychology, 27,* 211-219.

Pears, J. (1992). *Youth homelessness: Abuse, gender and the process of adjustment to life on the streets.* Unpublished manuscript, University of Queensland, Australia.

Pistole, M. C. (1989). Attachment in adult romantic relationships: Style of conflict resolution and relationship satisfaction. *Journal of Social and Personal Relationships, 6,* 505-510.

Poole, M. E., & Gelder, A. J. (1985). Family cohesiveness and adolescent autonomy in decision making. *Australian Journal of Sex, Marriage and Family, 5,* 65-75.

Roberts, E. J., Kline, D., & Gagnan, J. (1978). *Family life and sexual learning: A study of the role of parents in the sexual learning of the child.* Cambridge: Population Education Inc.

Rodick, J. D., & Henggeler, S. W. (1982). Parent-adolescent interaction and adolescent emancipation. In S. W. Henggeler (Ed.), *Delinquency and adolescent psychopathology: A family ecological systems approach.* Littleman, MA: Wright PSG.

Rollins, B. C., & Thomas, D. L. (1979). Parental support, power and control techniques in the socialization of children. In W. R. Burr, R. Hill, F. I. Nye, & I. L. Reiss (Eds.), *Contemporary theories about the family* (pp. 317-364). New York: Free Press.

Rothenberg, P. B. (1980). Communication about sex and birth control between mothers and their adolescent children. *Population and Environment, 3,* 35-50.

Russell, D., Peplau, L. A., & Cutrona, C. E. (1980). The revised UCLA Loneliness Scale: Concurrent and discriminant validity evidence. *Journal of Personality and Social Psychology, 39,* 472-480.

Sebald, H., & White, B. (1980). Teenagers' divided reference groups: Uneven alignment with parents and peers. *Adolescence, 15,* 979-984.

Sheehan, G., & Noller, P. (1992, December). Effects of siblings' perceptions of differential treatment on family functioning, attachment and adjustment: A twin study. Paper presented at It Runs in the Family Conference. Newcastle, NSW Australia.

Sheppard, M. A., Wright, D., & Goodstadt, M. S. (1985). Peer pressure and drug use—Exploding the myth. *Adolescence, 20,* 949-958.

Smith, T. E. (1970). Foundations of parental influence upon adolescents: An application of social power theory. *American Sociological Review, 35,* 860-873.

Sorenson, R. C. (1973). *Adolescent sexuality in contemporary America.* Cleveland: World.

Spielberger, C., Gorsuch, R., & Lushene, R. (1968). *The State-Trait Anxiety Scale.* Palo Alto, CA: Consulting Psychologists Press.

Stanley, S. (1978). Family education: A means of enhancing the moral atmosphere of the family and the moral development of adolescents. *Journal of Counseling Psychology, 25,* 110-118.

Steinberg, L. D., & Hill, J. P. (1978). Patterns of family interaction as a function of age, the onset of puberty and formal thinking. *Developmental Psychology, 14,* 683-684.

Steinhauer, P. D. (1987). The family as a small group: The process model of family functioning. In T. Jacob (Ed.), *Family interaction and psychopathology: Theories, methods and findings* (pp. 67-115). New York: Plenum.

Walters, J., & Walters, L. H. (1980). Parent-child relationships: A review 1970-1979. *Journal of Marriage and the Family, 42,* 807-822.

Waterman, A. S. (1982). Identity development from adolescence to adulthood: An extension of theory and a review of research. *Developmental Psychology, 18,* 341-358.

Wilks, J. (1986). The relative importance of parents and friends in adolescent decision making. *Journal of Youth and Adolescence, 15,* 323-335.

Youniss, J., & Smollar, J. (1985). *Adolescent relations with mothers, fathers and friends.* Chicago: University of Chicago Press.

4. Cultural Perspectives on Continuity and Change in Adolescents' Relationships

Catherine R. Cooper
University of California at Santa Cruz

The importance of considering stability and change in cultural influences on adolescents' relationships is illustrated in the voices of two individuals. Stability is reflected in the words of a young man in the French town of Aubusson, renowned for its centuries-old tradition of weaving tapestries. When asked how he chose his occupation, he looked surprised. "Why did I become a wool dyer? Because my family has been wool dyers for five generations!" Change is reflected in the words of a Hmong woman, now a college student in California, describing her relationship with her father before and after their experiences as refugees immigrating to the United States. As a child in Laos, she recalls,

> My father would teach me how his medical instruments were used, or he would show me to his patients. . . . I felt so close to him. However, since we came to this country, . . . he began to build walls around us by becoming so overly protective. . . . It was not his fault that he did not know how to be included in our lives. It was just that he didn't know how to get involved with his children. That was why my brothers and sisters and I decided to introduce my father to bowling. It was a little bit foreign for me to be the one teaching my father, and I sensed that Father felt odd, too. But once he got the hang

AUTHOR'S NOTE: I thank my colleagues Margarita Azmitia, Hiroshi Azuma, Cindy Carlson, Gene Garcia, Per Gjerde, Harold Grotevant, Jacquelyne Jackson, Keiko Kashiwagi, Yurio Kosawa, Hiroshi Shimizu, and Otoshi Suzuki for our stimulating and fruitful collaborations, and Robert Cooper for insightful support of my work. The research described in this chapter was supported by grants from the Spencer Foundation of Chicago, National Institute of Child Health and Human Development, Office of Educational Research and Instruction of the United States Department of Education, University of Texas at Austin, University of California at Santa Cruz, and from the Linguistic Minority Research Project and the Pacific Rim Foundation of the University of California System.

of it, he did well. . . . I think it was much more than bowling that Father enjoyed. It was the emotional closeness that he felt with us which made him come back to bowl again. The next time we went bowling, he was teaching the younger children. . . . It occurred to me that this was the beginning of building a bridge across a long-created gap between Dad and his children. (Her, 1990, pp. 194-195)

These examples show how cultural influences can foster both continuity and change in adolescent development, as cultural values are both handed down and renegotiated.

Studies of cultural influences often compare individuals from different national or cultural groups on the basis of global qualities, particularly individualism or collectivism (e.g., Markus & Kitayama, 1991). Such cultural qualities are often portrayed as stable and relatively uniformly held among individuals within each group. Yet members of many cultural groups experience pressures to change in order to adapt to new circumstances such as industrialization or immigration, and historians have challenged views of traditional cultures as ever having been either stable or uniform (Skolnick, 1991).

This chapter begins with an overview of four views of adolescents' relationships commonly encountered in both scholarly and popular discourse, then presents an argument for including considerations of culture in our thinking on these issues. Finally, these four views are reframed in terms of this ecocultural model, with illustrations from recent research.

FOUR TRADITIONAL VIEWS
OF ADOLESCENT DEVELOPMENT

American psychologists have typically held four interrelated views of adolescents and their relationships. First, many developmental psychologists have defined adolescents' maturity in terms of individualistic values of autonomy, distance, and emancipation from parents, and clinical psychologists have considered a family as healthy if they express opinions and disagreements openly and directly (e.g., Feldman & Elliot, 1990; Framo, 1972). A second common view is that socialization between older and younger generations operates as a unilateral process of transmission of values and attitudes or "social capital" from older experts to younger novices. The view of acculturation or "becoming

American" as a process of unilateral conformity to American "culture" also reflects this perspective. A third common theme is that adolescents' identity development functions as a rational process of exploration and choice within a relatively unrestricted set of opportunities. Finally, a fourth common view of adolescents and their relationships is that the different contexts of their relationships operate in competition with one another. This assumption is exemplified by the "cross-pressures" view of the battle for adolescents' loyalty between their relationships with parents and their relationships with peers, and in recent discussions of "cultural incompatibility" of family and school contexts for ethnic minority students.

This chapter will examine how cultural perspectives on adolescents' relationships challenge and reframe each of these familiar views of adolescence: first, by defining the self and identity as inherently part of relational contexts; second, by framing transactive rather than unilateral models of developmental change in individuals and relationships as well as in cultures; third, by understanding the effect of variations in opportunity structures on adolescents' relationships; and fourth, by mapping linkages—both bridges and barriers—across relational contexts of development. We begin by considering a conceptual framework for "unpackaging culture."

"UNPACKAGING CULTURE"

A large body of research views various cultural groups in terms of dichotomized qualities that are assumed to be relatively uniform and static within each group; for example, the United States is regularly considered to be an "individualistic" culture, and Japan and Mexico to be "collectivistic." But increasing numbers of social scientists are challenging this approach. Developmental scholars are grounding their frames of reference in multidimensional contexts, moving from considering children and adolescents in terms of static demographic categories of family structure or ethnic group to viewing individuals, families, community, and culture each as developing through time (Bronfenbrenner, 1988; Skolnick, Baumrind, & Bronson, 1990). "Unpackaging" culture, as proposed by the anthropologist Beatrice Whiting (1976), represents an important alternative to the "comparative" perspective. As Weisner, Gallimore, and Jordan (1988) argue,

> Culture is not a nominal variable to be attached equally to every child, in the same way that age, height, or sex might be. Treating culture in this way assumes that all children in a cultural group have common natal experiences. In many cases, they do not. The assumption of homogeneity of experience of children within cultures, without empirical evidence, is unwarranted. . . . The method error that follows is to measure culture by assigning it as a trait to all children or parents in a group, thus assuming culture has uniform effects on every child. A similar error is to treat national or ethnic status as equivalent to a common cultural experience for individuals. (p. 328)

This chapter argues that to account for adolescent competence and vulnerability, we need to move beyond stereotypic, global, and static features of culture by developing multidimensional descriptions of the ecocultural niches of adolescents and their relationships. Building on the work of Weisner et al. (1988), we consider the qualities of the ecocultural niche of central importance to understanding adolescent development to stem from activity settings in which important cultural information is appropriated. These include (a) key personnel, the configurations and qualities of primary relationships involved in socialization, including siblings, extended kin, fictive kin, and nonkin; (b) scripts, the patterns of interaction and communication (verbal and nonverbal) expressing universal human tasks of guidance, negotiation, planning, and conflict resolution; and (c) the goals and values of socialization. These dimensions do not constitute an exhaustive list of ecocultural features (e.g., Reese et al. 1990); as the ecocultural niche framework is applied to a broader range of problems, the richness of its description will have to expand. Nonetheless, the dimensions examined here are key characteristics of every culture and have proved useful in our own work.

Most work on ecocultural issues has focused on infancy and middle childhood (LeVine, 1988; Tharp & Gallimore, 1988; Weisner, 1986), but scholars interested in diversity in the United States and other countries are beginning to use this work to understand adolescents. Several clarifications should be made. First, the features of the ecocultural niche are interdependent: for example, ecocultural theory underscores the importance of distinctive cultural practices concerning personnel and activity settings. In families of many ethnic traditions in the United States, nonparental adult kin and child caregivers perform functions ascribed to parents in middle-class European-American families, and important close relationships are formed in the process). This occurs for both cultural reasons such as familistic values and socioeconomic reasons such as schedules of parental employment. The full complement of such matrices of relationships may come into play during adolescent identity formation as adolescents consider and constitute their educational and occupational futures and their political, religious, gender, and ethnic identities (Cooper, Jackson, Azmitia, & Lopez, in preparation; Grotevant & Cooper, 1986).

Second, although we can expect to find many differences between cultural groups in features of the ecocultural niches of adolescents and their relationships, the framework is especially useful for investigating within-group variation. For example, recent changes in Japanese culture toward greater dominance of the nuclear family and increased opportunities for women's employment, followed by economic changes reducing women's opportunities for career tracks in Japanese corporations, have relevance for investigating variations in family guidance and negotiation of adolescent sons and daughters' educational and career development (Gjerde & Cooper, 1992).

Third, although it is not functional as a theory in terms of its potential for falsifiability, the ecocultural framework dimensionalizes qualities of individual, relational, and group change that allow us to test hypotheses to account for within-culture variation in both competence and vulnerability during adolescence. It even challenges our interpretation of which is which. For example, an ecocultural perspective forms the basis for Burton's (1990) account of adolescent pregnancy as normative rather than an error in certain African-American communities. Thus a key advantage of this multidimensional model is that it enables us to avoid stereotyping differences between mainstream and minority group adolescents in terms of deficits (McLoyd, 1990), a particular risk because so much research on American minority youth has been driven by the problem orientation of federal criminal justice, drug, and adolescent pregnancy funding initiatives. We now turn to reconsider traditional views of adolescent development with these cultural perspectives.

SELF AND IDENTITY
IN RELATIONAL CONTEXT

A first step in reframing adolescent development in the context of culture has been recent work documenting the adaptiveness of continuing closeness in parent-adolescent attachments and values.

Current research distinguishes aspects of adolescents' development of the self, including identity, ego development, and self-esteem rather than focusing exclusively on autonomy (Feldman & Elliot, 1990). These new approaches conceptualize adolescents as developing in the context of relationships rather than independently of them. As Ryan and Lynch clarify, "Individuation is not something that happens from parents but rather with them" (1989, p. 341).

Compatible with these approaches is the theoretical perspective of our own work, which focuses on the interplay between individuality and connectedness in the ongoing mutual regulation involved in relationships, thus serving as an important mechanism for both individual and relational development (Cooper & Cooper, 1992; Grotevant & Cooper, 1986). Individuality involves processes that reflect the distinctiveness of the self; in language, it is seen in assertions, disclosures, and disagreements with others. Connectedness involves processes that link the self to others, seen in acknowledgment of, respect for, and responsiveness to others. A second proposition of the model is that children's and adolescents' experiences in family relationships regarding the interplay of individuality and connectedness carry over to attitudes, expectations, and skills in self and relational functioning in contexts beyond the family.

Our model draws upon developmental and clinical conceptualizations, including individuation, attachment, and family systems theory, which point to the importance of the continuing interplay between individuality and connectedness within family relationships for the well-being of their members and the long-term consequences of early family experience. This approach is also consistent with work in cognitive development that frames relationships as the content as well as the context of individual development, with parents and children continuously adapting their relationship (Rogoff, 1990).

We began research on this model with middle-class European-American families of early adolescents in sixth grade and high school seniors, and assessed individuality and connectedness in face-to-face interaction so that we could observe these transactive processes in real time. (It is an important theoretical and empirical question as to whether and when individuals may become sufficiently aware of these processes that they can serve as informants concerning their operation, and how family members' shared and nonshared views of their relationships bear upon adolescent competence and vulnerability; see Carlson, Cooper, & Spradling, 1991, for discussion of these issues.) Adolescents and their families were observed in their home with a task designed to stimulate families to express and negotiate their ideas. Individuality and connectedness were assessed in face-to-face conversations so we could observe these transactive processes in real time, and discourse was coded with a system that operationalized the dimensions of individuality and connectedness in relationships.

A central finding of our work with high school seniors is that family members' expressions of their own points of view as well as their disagreements with others appear to be predictive of qualities of adaptive identity exploration and relational skills in their adolescents (Cooper et al., 1983; Grotevant & Cooper, 1985). In such interactions, the adolescent can hear, consider, and integrate differing points of view, and decisions are made through negotiation rather than by the unilateral imposing of a solution. What we see, then, is a co-occurrence of conflict and cohesion, which parallels the finding in cognitive developmental research that in discussions in which friends disagree and express the nature of that disagreement, they make the greatest cognitive gains (Nelson & Aboud, 1985). In our subsequent work, we have examined both developmental changes in such patterns and how individuality and connectedness are expressed and coordinated in families whose traditions prescribe less egalitarian roles for fathers, mothers, and adolescents.

TRANSACTIVE MODELS
OF CHANGE AND CONTINUITY
IN ADOLESCENTS' RELATIONSHIPS

Developmental Change and
Continuity in Family Negotiation

Change and continuity at the level of relationships in the family can be seen in the changing interplay of individuality and connectedness in family negotiation from early to later adolescence (Cooper & Carlson, 1990). When we compared 6th-and 12th-grade European-American adolescents, parents negotiated with older adolescents, both males and females, in a more egalitarian manner, as seen in their expressions of compromises and agreements, than with younger adolescents. In contrast, fathers typically prompted early adolescents' ideas with questions, while mothers provided both task-oriented directives and acknowledgments. Older adolescent girls, compared to younger girls, expressed both more disagreements and more compromises with their fathers, indicating their greater ability to negotiate disagreements by coordinating and integrating perspectives.

Houchins (1991) looked more closely at developmental changes and continuities in the way that guidance was provided by the parents of older and younger adolescents in this task. She found that fathers of younger adolescents elicited their children's suggestions more often than fathers of older adolescents, stated more reasons for their decisions, offered more compromises incorporating their adolescents' suggestions, and rejected their adolescents' suggestions less often than did fathers of older adolescents. Older adolescents were likely to bring greater knowledge and more skills in making their views clear, which prepared them for more independent participation. Mothers' levels of elicitation of their adolescents' ideas were equal at the two age levels. This work demonstrates that change and continuities can both occur within the family system in scripts for guidance and negotiation.

Cultural Perspectives on Intergenerational Continuity and Change in Values and Communication

Psychologists often define maturity in terms of autonomy and initiative, and consider well-functioning families as preparing children for these ideals, yet many cultural traditions place value on familism: norms of collective support, allegiance, and obligation. Here a good child shows support, respect, and reticence in the family, especially toward fathers. Achievement or failure brings pride or shame to the family as a whole rather than signifying autonomy or independence of the individual family member.

Familistic values have been defined by various features, including strong in-group feelings, emphasis on family goals, common property, mutual support, and the desire to perpetuate the family (Bardis, 1959). Familism has been considered a key adaptive strategy for ethnic families of color, especially under conditions of racism, immigration, or poverty (Harrison, Wilson, Pine, Chan, & Buriel, 1990). In comparative studies, Mexican Americans, Central Americans, and Cuban Americans have endorsed norms of mutual family obligation, family support, and use of the family as reference group, with family support being the most stable of these dimensions across generations after immigration to the United States (Sabogal, Marin, Otero-Sabogal, Marin, & Perez-Stable, 1987). Studies of traditional Chinese, Filipino, and Vietnamese culture also emphasize the importance of values regarding family harmony, social etiquette, and face-saving communication among family members, as well as norms of respectful behavior within the family hierarchy, marked by conformity and obedience to those in authority (Hong, 1989; White & Chan, 1983).

In our work, we have been especially interested in the expression of individuality and connectedness within family relationships when traditions emphasize norms of respect and cohesion, and how these powerful traditions can remain dynamic, changing in the process of immigration, acculturation, and economic mobility. Recent work challenges stereotypes of fathers' dominance and documents how marital roles may become more egalitarian with acculturation (Cromwell & Ruiz, 1988). One explanation of these changes may be economic necessity as women increasingly work outside the home and families move outside of ethnic neighborhoods. Davis and Chavez (1985) have described role reversals within Mexican-American families, in which unemployed men assume greater responsibility for household maintenance while their wives work outside the home. In other cases, changing marital roles may reflect adoption of middle-class democratic and egalitarian values.

In a recent study (Cooper, Baker, Polichar, & Welch, in press), we predicted that adolescents of Chinese, Filipino, Mexican, and Vietnamese descent would attribute higher levels of familistic values than adolescents of European descent to their parents and grandparents but not to themselves. We also predicted that when familistic values of respect for the family hierarchy render adolescents' relations with parents more formal, siblings may become more important in accounting for family-peer links, but we also investigated possible complementarity or compensation between adolescents' relationships with parents and peers.

In our northern California college sample, a high proportion of the adolescents who described themselves as being of Chinese, Filipino, Vietnamese, or Mexican descent were themselves immigrants. Parents of the Filipino-descent adolescents were highest in educational level, while the Mexican-descent adolescents in the sample had attained significantly less education than those in other groups. Because we were interested in learning about communicating individuality and connectedness in families where norms of respect might make overt expression of individuality—especially disagreements—rare, we used self-report rather than the observational methods of our previous studies. Throughout our research, we consulted small focus groups of adolescents from each ethnic background studied so that instrument development, data analysis, and interpretations were consistent with their experiences.

Adolescents rated the degree to which they perceived that a set of familistic values were held by themselves, their mothers, their fathers, and their maternal and paternal grandparents. These items, adapted from studies of Hispanic and Asian acculturation (e.g., Sabogal et al., 1987), assess the extent to which families are seen as sources of support and obligation and as a reference group for norms and values (e.g., "Family members should make sacrifices to guarantee a good education for their children," "Older siblings should help directly support other family members economically," "Much of what a son or daughter does in life should be done to please parents," "Families should consult close relatives, e.g., uncles, aunts, concerning what they see as important decisions"). Adolescents also rated their comfort with a variety of expressions of individuality and connectedness with their mothers, fathers, siblings, and friends (e.g., "When I disagree with this person I try to negotiate," "This person communicates openly with me about their feelings," "I discuss my problems with this person"), as well their comfort in discussing topics such as school, careers, sex, and drugs with each person.

Adolescents' differential responses to familism questions demonstrated both similarities and differences between cultural groups. Adolescents from all groups strongly endorsed the statement "Family members should make sacrifices to guarantee a good education for their children." However, European-descent adolescents saw themselves and their parents endorsing a statement reflecting norms of material support, "Older siblings should help directly support other family members economically," significantly less than adolescents from all other groups. Overall, Chinese-, Filipino-, Mexican-, and Vietnamese-descent adolescents saw themselves, their parents, and their grandparents as placing greater value than European-American adolescents on norms of support and the use of family for advice. Our prediction of higher familistic values for parents and grandparents but not adolescents underestimated the stability of familistic values among adolescents in our sample, but evidence of intergenerational change was seen in their endorsing familistic values less than their parents and grandparents did.

Adolescents in all groups reported more communication of individuality and negotiation with their mothers, siblings, and friends than with their fathers, and lower comfort in negotiating differences and discussing problems with fathers. In focus groups held separately for each ethnic group, Mexican-American and Asian-American adolescents confirmed holding the familistic values that they should rely on families for advice in conjunction with experiencing formal relationships with fathers and respect for both parents. They also placed especially high value on friendships as contexts for discussing parents' achievement expectations. For practical and personal topics, the strongest predictors of comfort in communicating with friends were their communication with siblings. For some students, complementarity rather than continuity was evident between fathers and friends. Focus group discussions emphasized the challenges of adolescents developing bicultural adaptations between the feelings of responsibility to their traditional parents and feelings of isolation with friends who did not share their immigration experiences (Hoffman, 1992).

Thus recent portrayals of adolescents as renegotiating asymmetrical patterns of parent-child regulation toward peerlike mutuality may better describe European-American families than more recent immigrants from Asia and Mexico, for whom more formal relationships with parents, especially their fathers, appear more common. Within-group differences in family-peer linkages indicate both continuity and complementarity across contexts of development and suggest similarities and differences among youth in the relations among beliefs, relationships, and development.

OPPORTUNITY STRUCTURES AS
CONTEXTS OF ADOLESCENTS' RELATIONSHIPS

The Role of Poverty in
Parental Goals and Guidance

My colleagues and I have been using the ecocultural model to examine the ecology of family guidance in low-income Mexican-American and European-American families (Azmitia, Cooper, &

Garcia, 1993) as part of a larger investigation of continuities and discontinuities in the linkages from family to school experiences. We were interested in identifying both resources and vulnerabilities for parental guidance toward the educational, vocational, and personal goals that parents hold for their children. The study examined goals and aspirations held by low-income Mexican-American and European-American parents for their children and adolescents as well as parents' guidance in helping them attain these goals.

Mexican Americans are experiencing severe unemployment and poverty, with school dropout rates of Mexican-American youth among the highest of students of color (Garcia, in press). To assess how dimensions of Mexican-American culture may influence family guidance, we focused on immigrant parents whose children were born in the United States. Families' hopes of education as a way out of poverty often motivate their immigrating to the United States so their children can attend American schools (Gibson & Ogbu, 1991). Studies of Mexican immigrants from the state of Michoancan have reported that the families who come to the United States are neither the poorest nor the most wealthy of the area, but members of a "potential middle class" who come to the United States to achieve ambitions for upward mobility (Dienrman, 1982, cited in Martinez, 1986).

Low-income European Americans experience both persistent and temporary poverty for multiple reasons, including divorce, job loss, and lifestyle choice. They constitute the majority of those living in poverty but are often ignored in discussions of poverty, developmental risk, and school failure (McLoyd, 1990). The pessimism of low-income European-American parents regarding education as a way out of their poverty has been proposed as an explanation for why their children do poorly in school (Heath, 1983), yet many questions concerning within-group differences remain regarding the home ecologies of these families.

In our study, we examined variability within both Mexican-American and European-American groups as well as comparisons between them because relying solely on comparisons between groups may foster misperceptions that one is deficient relative to the other (McLoyd, 1990). Most Mexican-American families in our sample were headed by two parents, who were typically employed as farm laborers or in canneries. Most described themselves as literate in Spanish but not in English. Most of the European-American families were headed by a single parent. Parents were employed as skilled manual workers, craftspersons, clerical or sales workers, or menial houseworkers, and all were able to read and write English. Although all families in the study were considered "low income" for purposes of AFDC and free or reduced-price school lunch programs, most parents in the Mexican-American families in the sample had only attended elementary school and had limited English proficiency, whereas most parents in the European-American families in the sample had completed at least high school, and many had attended college. Thus each group had its own unique ecology with regard to personnel, yet interviews with parents revealed both similarities and differences with regard to issues of goals and guidance scripts.

Consistent with Reese, Balzano, Gallimore, and Goldenberg (1991), both groups had high educational aspirations for their children. As one Mexican-American parent said, "We aren't here [in the United States] because we like working here or like to live here. . . . We live better in Mexico. But I make this sacrifice so that I want them to study, to learn English." However, more Mexican-American parents indicated that they would be content for their children to finish high school, whereas more European-American parents expressed hopes that their children would attend graduate school, although they were also more likely to allow their child to choose their level of education—for example:

> I say kind of loosely that she goes to college or junior college, to find out if she is kind of interested. . . . That is something I already suggested to my 13-year-old, that he start out at something like [local community college], cause it's cheap—you can go for next to nothing, and then if he's good, maybe he can win some scholarship or save money and branch from there.

Although parents in both groups saw themselves helping their children attain their occupational aspirations by offering encouragement, help, advice, and tutoring, some Mexican-American parents saw their contribution as providing negative role models, such as not working in the fields or cannery as they did—for example, "anything as long as it isn't in the fields. . . . When I was very young I started to pick strawberries and I wouldn't want him to do that." Most European-American parents said they would allow their children to choose their own career—for example, "I don't want to impose anything on him, but I do tell him he has to study. I don't tell him he has to study such and such because I like it. . . . I just want him to study a short career so that he has a future." Parents in both groups expressed hopes their children would be moral persons, respect others and themselves, and stay away from drugs, gangs, and other "vices," and both provided direct guidance in this domain by advising and tutoring their children. Mexican-American parents more frequently saw themselves as positive role models for personal maturity than for vocational aspirations, and none described themselves as negative models for personal aspirations. Likewise, European-American parents also saw themselves as positive models of personal maturity more than for vocational or educational attainments. Said one Mexican-American parent, "If [my child] comes home and tells me he bought a [toy] car, I have him tell me where he bought it, how much it costs, from whom, and everything, you know. Because you have to teach [them] not to take other's things." A European-American parent commented, "I am helping her by being who I am as a mother. Also by learning for myself to love and to serve people. I talk to her a lot and I am honest with her about what is happening in my life."

These findings suggest that in vocational and educational domains in which low-income Mexican-American parents feel they do not have expertise, they use themselves as negative examples but also broker other resources to help their children; where they feel they do have expertise, they offer it. Families in both Mexican-American and European-American groups showed competence in using the resources they had and in their commitment to helping their children succeed. Most striking was both groups' determination to guide their children to maturity, defined not only in terms of school and occupational achievement but also in moral terms ("buen camino"—the good path; Reese et al., 1991).

However, even though low-income parents hold high aspirations for their children, some parents (especially newly immigrated Mexican-American parents) do not know that their children's vocational goals require a college education, and others who seek college educations for their children are unsure about application and financial aid procedures (Reese et al., 1991). Deeper vulnerabilities of these families are indicated by the fear and ambivalence toward school expressed by both Mexican-American and European-American parents in our sample for their adolescents. Mexican-American parents viewed education as a way out of poverty and wanted their children to be successful, but feared they would be distanced from their families and communities. They especially feared their children attending high school because of the risks of drugs, violence, and pregnancy. Said one parent, "I have seen other people that their children spend years in school and for what? All they learn are vices, and in the end, they no longer feel comfortable in our community and then they aren't comfortable anywhere, at home or at school." We witnessed the attempts of parents to protect their children by buying them Nintendo games to keep them indoors. The threat to which these parents are trying to respond is illustrated by the fact that during the course of our study several drive-by shootings occurred in the community, and the older sister of one of our participating children was assaulted and killed in her schoolyard.

LINKAGES ACROSS CONTEXTS OF DEVELOPMENT: BRIDGES AND BARRIERS

Linkages Between Adolescents' Family and Peer Relationships

Models of the linkages between adolescents' relationships with parents and peers once centered exclusively on their differences: how the two relational systems operate to compensate for one another's deficits, compete with one another for adolescents' loyalty, or contrast in the way power is distributed, with parent-adolescent relationships seen as asymmetrical and peers as egalitarian chums (Cooper & Cooper, 1992). Newer work has probed the nature and extent of continuities as well as discontinuities between family and peer relationships. Drawing on our model of individuality and connectedness, my colleagues and I have tested the proposition that adolescents' experiences of individuality and connectedness in the family affect both individual and interpersonal competence. The model is based on a premise that psychological well-being is defined not simply in terms of autonomy or self-reliance but in terms of the capacity to differentiate a distinctive self while maintaining closeness with others. For this reason, we have assessed how family experiences might offer adolescents the capacity to view themselves as competent individuals with the rights and capacities to express distinctive viewpoints while being able to sustain cohesion in peer relationships.

Our recent work provides evidence that adolescents who experience themselves as relationally competent are those who are able to integrate individuality and connectedness in peer relationships. These data are based on open-ended interviews in which adolescents gave descriptions of actual conflicts with their friends, their ratings of self and relational competence on Harter's measures, and their responses to an analogue of Selman's Interpersonal Negotiation Strategies interview (Spradling, Cooper, & Carlson, 1989, cited in Cooper & Cooper, 1992). We found that those adolescents who saw themselves as competent appeared to be able to integrate individuality and connectedness in a hypothetical dilemma with a peer by using negotiation strategies involving collaboration. For example, those who viewed themselves as competent were more likely to approach negotiating with a peer who wanted them to drink by declining the drink while offering face-saving remarks that retained connectedness with the friend, rather than using the popularized strategy of "just saying no." Those who evaluated themselves in less favorable terms said they would use lower-level, unilateral strategies with the peer that involved either submission or dominance. These findings provide evidence that the linkages between selfesteem and relational competence are expressed in the ability to coordinate self and other in collaborative conflict resolution.

Our observations of these early adolescents' actual negotiations with their parents differed from their negotiations with friends, yet individual differences among the adolescents in their peer interactions could be understood from examining their family negotiation patterns. In our observations, early adolescent boys and girls disagreed more openly with their friends and expressed more connectedness with their parents. In both settings, boys expressed disagreements more than girls, whereas girls expressed more connectedness than boys. Although boys were more likely to disagree in response to their friends' questions, suggestions, and disagreements than when responding to these same expressions from their parents, these boys were also more likely to respond with highly engaging suggestions following disagreements with friends than with their parents. This gives us a picture of boys' arguments with one another as heated exchanges of ideas rather than just conflicts. In parallel findings, girls were also more likely to disagree with their friends' disagreements and questions than to the same expressions from their parents. These patterns are consistent with Piaget and Sullivan's portraits of the egalitarian nature of adolescents' relationships with their peers as compared to parents (Cooper & Cooper, 1992).

Despite these overall patterns, individual differences in adolescents' negotiations with their friends could be predicted by the patterns of family negotiation. Those who coordinated individuality and connectedness with their peers could be seen as experiencing similar patterns in negotiations with their parents, particularly their fathers. These findings suggest that the origins of key competences of peer relationships can be traced to family experience seen in adolescence.

Patterns of Bridging
Between Adolescents' Worlds

Linkages across contexts of development shift between middle childhood and adolescence. Jarrett (1991) observed that African-American families living in conditions of urban poverty who adopted what she termed "community-specific" strategies often took a survival orientation, living in clusters of economically homogeneous families, with more open household boundaries, with survival-oriented use of community institutions such as churches, and with parenting strategies that were inconsistent or ineffective. "Community-specific" families were more likely to be economically dependent and to have children who became unwed mothers and/or school dropouts than "community- bridging" families, who were mobility oriented and more likely to live in areas of greater socioeconomic heterogeneity and geographic dispersal. Community-bridging families experienced their household boundaries as defended and respected, while building links with community institutions such as churches and schools not merely to get food, clothing, and shelter, but to get social and educational benefits. Jarrett noted that the protective community-specific patterns characterized well-functioning families of children in elementary school, but that such unilateral, control-oriented, and ultimately isolating strategies were not sufficient for meeting the developmental needs of adolescents, with their increasing autonomy and mobility.

Phelan, Davidson, and Cao (1991) have described high school students' "multiple worlds" of family, school, and peer relationships and have shown how these adolescents struggle to mediate and integrate their experiences across these worlds with their views of themselves. According to Phelan and Davidson, the term "world" is used to designate "cultural knowledge and behavior found within the boundaries of students' particular families, peer groups, and schools;

we presume that each world contains values and beliefs, expectations, actions, and emotional responses familiar to insiders" (p. 1). Borders between worlds can be defined by psychosocial, sociocultural, socioeconomic, linguistic, or gender-based features. Phelan and her colleagues studied a sample of adolescents varying in gender, ethnicity, achievement level, and immigration history from their first to second year of high school by means of a series of open-ended interviews as well as observations. Four patterns emerged by which high school students "migrate" among school, family, and peer group settings, and clustered their sample into four prototypic groups. Some students experienced congruent worlds and smooth transitions across boundaries; values and normative ways of behaving were compatible across family, school, and peer worlds. Whether high or low achieving, these students experienced congruence between their own goals and expectations and those of parents, friends, and teachers. Although a second group of students occupied different worlds with regard to culture, socioeconomic status, ethnicity, and/or religion, they appeared to find border crossings "manageable," creating conditions of bicultural adaptation (Phinney, Lochner, & Murphy, 1990). These students were able to adapt to mainstream patterns of interaction yet return to home and community patterns when with their peers in social settings, but the risks for those attempting such transcultural identities involved criticism from those in the disparate worlds who expected adherence to the conventions of each. A third group of students seemed to occupy different worlds but found border crossings difficult, and the most vulnerable fourth group experienced themselves as occupying different worlds and found the borders between them impenetrable.

This work shows how adolescents' own tasks of integrating their worlds may be at variance with the perceptions of adults around them, and how even students who look as if they are succeeding in bicultural adaptation and academic achievement may be incurring high costs. We now consider the contribution of academic outreach programs in bridging the cultures of home, school, and university.

Academic Outreach Programs as Bridges
From Home to University

Many adolescents of color, including Mexican-American and African-American and American-Indian youth, experience restricted opportunities for academic success as well as occupational training and choice (Cooper, Jackson, Azmitia, & Lopez, in preparation). With each advancing cohort of students enrolled in junior high school, high school, college, and graduate programs, the percentage of adolescents of color shrinks. As discussed earlier, the families of these students may have high educational and professional aspirations for them, but parents with little formal education may lack specific knowledge about schools and the resources available through them, and those with histories of immigration or ongoing involuntary minority status in the United States may also lose confidence that schooling is accessible or even meaningful to their children (Gibson & Ogbu, 1991). These youth often benefit from both emotional and instrumental support from others who can offer a bridge from family life to schooling and the workplace (Cooper et al., in preparation).

Academic outreach and support programs attempt to capitalize on the fact that minority students are accustomed to a matrix of close nonparental and peer relationships. In our focus groups, African American and Latino adolescents have described adult mentors and peers in their academic outreach programs as sources of both emotional and instrumental support in bridging what can be a bewildering array of goals and expectations across the multiple worlds described by Phelan and her colleagues. One African-American high school senior told us that her mother and grandmother wanted her to be a doctor, her principal and teachers wanted her to be a mathematician and a scientist, the people at her church want her to devote all of her time to church, her student leadership program wanted her to be a politician, and her academic outreach program wanted her to be what she wanted to be and do it well: attend a 4-year institution, go on to graduate or law school, become a congresswoman, and educate her people. It is notable that students spontaneously refer to the programs as like their family, including regarding peers as like siblings.

With more difficult issues of vulnerability, Latino and African-American students have also recounted the value of academic outreach program affiliation. One challenge lies in counteracting the barriers of academic "gatekeeping" (Erickson & Schultz, 1982), in which teachers and counselors discourage them from taking the advanced math and science classes required for university admission and attempt to track them into noncollege courses. Students also feel support in meeting the challenge integrating their multiple worlds, retaining their sense of legitimacy in outreach programs with their goals for academic and career success while retaining ties to friends who may not be in school or be in gangs.

CONCLUSIONS

In sum, recent conceptual and empirical work has reframed our basic ways of thinking about relationships in adolescence. The findings of the studies discussed in this chapter demonstrate how ecocultural analyses of activity settings can help us "unpackage" global characterizations of diverse groups as "communal" or "individualistic" by pointing to useful dimensions of goals, personnel, scripts, and activity settings. Several methodological implications should also be emphasized. The first is the importance of collaboration—among colleagues, students, and research participants with a range of cultural experiences. This is especially important given the danger of using middle-class European-American experience to make claims for models of universal patterns of relational development. Second, self-report, ethnographic, and observational methodologies each make important contributions to cultural research. Discourse analyses provide insight about transactive relational patterns of which individuals may not be aware and hence able to report, and complement survey methods, which are critical for assessing generalizability over the diverse populations for whom we are especially concerned on issues of family-peer-school linkages. Open-ended interviews with individuals and with focus groups are critical for overcoming ethnocentrism and the inevitable limitations of any one investigator's own cultural experiences. Finally, rather than pursuing mythical representative samples, it may be more useful to provide "ballpark" descriptions of parameters of samples linked to key ecocultural dimensions, such as communities of origin, generation and goals of immigration, family structure and membership, and languages spoken (Schofield & Anderson, 1989).

Research on cultural perspectives on adolescence is enriching the study of normative adolescent development by bringing issues of diversity, including gender, family structure, ethnicity, social class, and acculturation, into mainstream developmental theory and by moving beyond examining group differences to linking intragroup variability to normative-developmental markers. Analyses of these features of adolescents' home, school, peer, and community contexts can help us "unpackage" our accounts of cultural transmission within each setting and understand adolescents' bicultural adaptations that allow them to constitute viable identities as maturing young adults.

REFERENCES

Azmitia, M., Cooper, C. R., & Garcia, E. E. (1993). *Mentoring for maturity: Guidance of children and adolescents by low-income Mexican American and European families.* Santa Cruz: University of California, Santa Cruz, Center for Research in Cultural Diversity and Second Language Learning.

Bardis, P. D. (1959). A familism scale. *Marriage and Family Living, 13,* 340-341.

Blos, P. (1979). *The adolescent passage: Developmental issues.* New York: International University Press.

Bowen, M. (1972). Towards the differentiation of self in one's family of origin. In J. Framo (Ed.), *Family interaction: A dialogue between family researchers and family therapists.* New York: Springer.

Brittain, C. V. (1963). Adolescent choices and parent-peer cross pressures. *American Sociological Review, 28,* 385-391.

Bronfenbrenner, U. (1988). Foreword. In A. R. Pence (Ed.), *Ecological research with children and families: From concepts to methodology.* New York: Teachers College Press.

Burton, L. M. (1990). Teenage childbearing as an alternative life-course strategy in multigeneration black families. *Human Nature, 1,* 123-138.

Cooper, C. R., & Baker, H. (1991). *Ethnic perspectives on individuality and connectedness in adolescents' relationships with family and peers.* Paper presented at the meetings of the International Society for the Study of Behavioral Development, Minneapolis.

Cooper, C. R., & Carlson, C. I. (1990). *Shifts in family discourse from early to late adolescence: Age and gender patterns.* Paper presented at the meetings of the NIMH Family Research Consortium, Monterey, CA.

Cooper, C. R., & Cooper, R. G. (1992). Links between adolescents' relationships with their parents and peers: Models, evidence, and mechanisms. In R. D. Parke & G. W. Ladd (Eds.), *Family peer relationships: Models of linkages.* Hillsdale, NJ: Lawrence Erlbaum.

Cooper, C. R., Grotevant, H. D., & Condon, S. M. (1983). Individuality and connectedness in the family as a context for adolescent identity formation and role taking skill. In H. D. Grotevant & C. R. Cooper (Eds.), *Adolescent development in the family: New directions in child development* (pp. 43-59). San Francisco: Jossey-Bass.

Cooper, C. R., Jackson, J. F., Azmitia, M., & Lopez, E. M. (in preparation). Multiple selves, multiple worlds: Ethnically sensitive research on identity, relationships, and opportunity structures in adolescence. In V. McLoyd & L. Steinberg (Eds.), *Conceptual and methodological issues in the study of minority adolescents and their families.*

Cromwell, R. E., & Ruiz, R. Ansi. (1988). The myth of macho dominance in decision making within Mexican and Chicano families. *Hispanic Journal of Behavioral Sciences, 1,* 355-373.

Davis, S. K., & Chavez, V. (1985). Hispanic househusbands. *Hispanic Journal of Behavioral Sciences, 7,* 317-332.

Erickson, R., & Shultz, J. (1982). *The counselor as gatekeeper: Social interaction in interviews.* New York: Academic Press.

Feldman, S., & Elliot, G. R. (Eds.). (1990). *At the threshold: The developing adolescent.* Cambridge, MA: Harvard University Press.

Garcia, E. E. (in press). "Hispanic" children: Theoretical, empirical, and related policy issues. *Educational Psychology Review.*

Gibson, M. A. & Ogbu, J. U. (Eds.). (1991). *Minority status and schooling.* New York: Garland.

Gjerde, P. F., & Cooper, C. R. (1992). *Family influences in Japan and the U.S.: Between and within-cultural analyses of ecocultural niches.* University of California Pacific Rim Foundation.

Grotevant, H. D., & Cooper, C. R. (1986). Individuation in family relationships: A perspective on individual differences in the development of identity and role taking in adolescence. *Human Development, 29,* 82-100.

Harrison, A. O., Wilson, M. N., Pine, C. J., Chan, S. Q., & Buriel, R. (1990). Family ecologies of ethnic minority children. *Child Development, 61,* 347-362.

Heath, S. B. (1983). *Ways with words.* Cambridge, UK: Cambridge University Press.

Her, M. (1990). Bowling to find a lost father. In K. K. Howard (Ed.), *Passages: An anthology of the Southeast Asian refugee experience.* Fresno: California State University, Fresno, Southeast Asian Student Services.

Hong, G. K. (1989). Application of cultural and environmental issues in family therapy with immigrant Chinese Americans. *Journal of Strategic and Systematic Therapies, 8,* 14-21.

Houchins, S. C. (1991). *Parental scaffolding of early adolescents' interpersonal negotiation skills.* Dissertation, University of Texas at Austin.

Jarrett, R. (1991). *Ethnographic contributions to the study of low-income African-American families and children: Past and future directions.* Presentation to the SRCD Pre-Conference on Ethnicity and Diversity: Implications for Research and Policies, Seattle.

Lee, L. C., & Zhan, G. Q. (1991). Political socialization and parental values in the People's Republic of China. *International Journal of Behavioral Development, 14,* 337-373.

Lin, C-Y. C., & Fu, V. R. (1990). A comparison of child-rearing practices among Chinese, immigrant Chinese, and Caucasian-American parents. *Child Development, 61,* 429-433.

Markus, H. R., & Kitayama, S. (1991). Culture and the self: Implications for cognition, emotion, and motivation. *Psychological Review, 98,* 224-253.

Martinez, M. A. (1986). Family socialization among Mexican Americans. *Human Development, 29,* 264-279.

McLoyd, V. C. (1990). Minority children: Introduction to the special issue. *Child Development, 61,* 263-266.

McLoyd, V. C. (1991). What is the study of African American children the study of? In R. J. Jones (Ed.), *Black psychology* (3rd ed.). Berkeley, CA: Cobb & Henry.

McLoyd, V. C., & Flanagan, C. A. (1990). Economic stress: Effects on family life and child development. *New Directions for Child Development, 46.* San Francisco: Jossey-Bass.

Nurmi, J. (1991). How do adolescents see their future: A review of the development of future orientation and planning. *Developmental Review, 11,* 1-59.

Ogbu, J. U. (1989). The individual in collective adaptation: A framework for focusing on academic underperformance and dropping out among involuntary minorities. In L. Weis, E. Farrar, & H. G. Petrie (Eds.), *Dropouts from school: Issues, dilemmas, and solutions.* New York: State University of New York Press.

Phelan, P., Davidson, A. L., & Cao, H. T. (1991). Students' multiple worlds: Navigating the borders of family, peer, and school cultures. In P. Phelan & A. L.

Davidson (Eds.), *Cultural diversity: Implications for education*. New York: Teachers College Press.

Phinney, J. S., Lochner, B. R., & Murphy, R. (1990). Ethnic identity development and psychological adjustment in adolescence. In A. R. Stiffman & L. E. David (Eds.), *Ethnic issues in adolescent mental health*. Newbury Park, CA: Sage.

Reese, L., Balzano, S., Gallimore, R., & Goldenberg, C. (1991, November). *The concept of educacion: Latino family values and American schooling*. Paper presented at the annual meeting of the American Anthropological Association, Chicago.

Reese, L., Goldenberg, C., Loucky, J., & Gallimore, R. (1989). *Ecocultural context, cultural activity, and emergent literacy: Sources of variation in home literacy experiences of Spanish-speaking children*. Paper presented at the annual meeting of the American Anthropological Association, Washington, DC.

Rogoff, B. (1990). *Apprenticeship in thinking: Cognitive development in social context*. New York: Oxford University Press.

Ryan, R. M., & Lynch, J. H. (1989). Emotional autonomy versus detachment: Revisiting the vicissitudes of adolescence and young adulthood. *Child Development, 60*, 340-356.

Sabogal, F., Marin, G., Otero-Sabogal, R., Marin, B. V., & Perez-Stable, E. J. (1987). Hispanic familism and acculturation: What changes and what doesn't? *Hispanic Journal of Behavioral Sciences, 9*, 397-412.

Schofield, J. W., & Anderson, K. (1987). Combining quantitative and qualitative components of research on ethnic identity and intergroup relations. In J. S. Phinney & M. J. Rotheram (Eds.), *Children's ethnic socialization: Pluralism and development*. Newbury Park, CA: Sage.

Skolnick, A. (1991). *Embattled paradise: The American family in an age of uncertainty*. New York: Basic Books.

Skolnick, A., Baumrind, D., & Bronson, W. (1990). *Development in sociocultural contexts*. Unpublished manuscript, University of California at Berkeley.

Spencer, M. B., & Dornbusch, S. M. (1990). Challenges in studying minority youth. In S. S. Feldman & G. R. Elliott (Eds.), *At the threshold: The developing adolescent*. Cambridge, MA: Harvard University Press.

Spradling, V. Y., Ayers-Lopez, S. J., Carlson, C. I., & Cooper, C. R. (1989). *Conflict between friends during early adolescence: Sources, strategies, and outcomes*. Paper presented at the meetings of the American Psychological Association, New Orleans.

Suarez-Orozco, M. M. (1991). Immigrant adaptation to schooling: A Hispanic case. In M. A. Gibson and J. U. Ogbu (Eds.), *Minority status and schooling*. New York: Garland.

Weisner, T. S. (1986). Ecocultural niches of middle childhood: A cross-cultural perspective. In W. A. Collins (Ed.), *Development during middle childhood: The years from six to twelve* (pp. 335-369). Washington, DC: National Academy Press.

Weisner, T. S., Gallimore, R., & Jordan, C. (1988). Unpackaging cultural effects on classroom learning: Native Hawaiian peer assistance and child-generated activity. *Anthropology and Education Quarterly, 19*, 327-351.

White, W. G., & Chan, E. (1983). A comparison of self-concept scores of Chinese and white graduate students and professionals. *Journal of Non-White Concerns in Personnel and Guidance, 11*, 138-141.

Whiting, B. (1976). The problem of the packaged variable. In K. Riegel & J. Meacham (Eds.), *The developing individual in a changing world: Historical and cultural issues (Vol. 1)*. The Netherlands: Mouton.

5. "We're Popular, but We're Not Snobs": Adolescents Describe Their Crowds

James Youniss
The Catholic University of America

Jeffrey A. McLellan
The Catholic University of America

Darcy Strouse
The Catholic University of America

This chapter presents a theoretical perspective on peer culture and offers new empirical data on adolescents' perceptions of their peer group membership insofar as it bears on peer culture. The term *peer culture* is taken from Corsaro (1985), who identified the developmentally changing social systems that are shared by children, have their onset in nursery school settings, and continue to evolve through adolescence. Corsaro's initial insight was based on observations of orderliness in young children's interpersonal and group interactions. Children followed rules in their exchanges and generated meanings that group members shared. The social system of the nursery school thus represented a culture that children understood as their own and that ran parallel to rules and meanings used by children in interactions with teachers and parents. At the same time, Corsaro noted that these two systems were not sealed off from one another; rather, elements that obviously had their origin in one culture often reappeared in another. For instance, emphasis that adults gave to the size or age of children subsequently emerged as focuses in children's relations with peers.

A valuable feature of this view is that peer interactions are studied in their own right rather than as offshoots of or precursors to adult culture. Peer culture becomes primarily a result of children's own interactions and reflective understandings. Children themselves construct the rules by which they interact as well as the procedures through which they reach shared meaning. Children use these rules and procedures to guide conduct, and their practice continuously redefines the culture by sustaining the referential meaning of interactions.

This position is potentially coherent with our previous work on parent and peer interpersonal relationships (Youniss, 1980; Youniss & Smollar, 1985). We proposed that children's social development proceeds through participation in distinct forms of relationship with adults and with peers. Peer relationships are marked by use of symmetrical reciprocity and guided by the overarching principle of cooperation by equals. Children have to codiscover interactive procedures that fit the principle and, through practice, sustain their symmetrical relationship. Relationships with adults, in contrast, are based on reciprocity of complement and structured in terms of unilateral authority. These two forms, then, allow children to experience social life through distinct relationships, each of which makes a unique contribution to understanding social possibilities (see Hartup, 1983; Hinde, 1979; Youniss, 1980). We suggest a possible analogy in which friendship is to peer crowds as parental relationship is to adult culture. Peer crowds and adult culture afford separate but equally important ways of experiencing social life and oneself within a larger cultural context.

PEER CULTURE AND ADOLESCENCE

In a recent elaboration of their position, Corsaro and Eder (1990) addressed the social functioning of adolescents, asking how they sustain membership in peer groups while also acquiring rules and meanings that lead to membership in adult society. Corsaro and Eder proposed that adolescent peer culture is an extension of earlier constructions within a peer system that is continuously open to redefinition. Understandings of peer culture come from reflective feedback on actual interactions with peers as well as with adults. The successive redefinition of peer culture occurs in a series of reorganizations from early childhood through adolescence (Corsaro & Eder, 1990).

In our view, this position redresses the problem of granting priority in socialization to adult society over peer groups. When this is done, socialization through peer groups is no longer judged mainly in a negative or deficit comparison with adult culture. Consequently, peer groups can be studied as social systems in themselves, rather than assessed along scales of dissimilarity to adult society. Such an orientation examines basic principles of socialization that may inhere in peer interactions and allows potentially positive aspects of peer culture to be identified.

Contrasting Peer and Adult Culture

Concern about the negative impact of peer culture that Coleman (1961) stimulated 30 years ago remains of broad interest today. His 1961 study of high school students in the United States documented the emergence of a social system with its own rules and values that seemed distinct from their counterparts in adult society. More recently, Coleman's thinking about the issue has been recast in terms of the distribution and transmission of social capital (Coleman, 1987; Coleman & Hoffer, 1987). Coleman begins with the premise that socialization ultimately leads to membership in adult society, which is structured according to historically grounded norms and values. If adults possess knowledge of the norms and values, adolescents without access to relationships with adults lack access to capital and hence suffer a disadvantage in entering adult society (Youniss, 1989).

Sociologists traditionally viewed adult and peer cultures as separate but parallel in the sense that peer culture tended to duplicate structural features of adult society. For instance, Hollingshead (1949) showed that the variety of peer groups in the local high school reflected the hierarchical class structure that existed among adults in a midwestern town. Coleman's (1961) observations caused a stir because they documented an apparent alteration in these parallel structures. Peer groups seemed to have become uncoupled from adult society and were encapsulated inside a distinct culture with its own values and codes of conduct that adults could not readily penetrate.

In retrospect, the timing of Coleman's (1961) study can be seen as especially opportune. Gilbert (1986) has outlined the emergence of a new public attitude toward peer groups during the 1950s, the decade preceding Coleman's (1961) study. The affluence that followed the end of World War II began to change the economic and social structure of the American population. As families moved to the suburbs, schools became enlarged through consolidation, new forms of work were created, and education began to expand as a segment of the economy. At this time also, adolescents became a new target for marketing in areas of music, clothes, food, and entertainment. When Coleman made his observations, these elements were already being organized by the manufacturing, educational, entertainment, and government sectors of the economy.

It is not surprising that at this time researchers took note of adolescent peer culture and questioned its relation to adult culture. According to Gilbert's analysis, one source of concern was a new mixing of values across what had previously been fairly impermeable social class boundaries (cf. Hollingshead, 1949). In the new consolidated high school, for instance, students from different geographic areas were brought together in one setting, exposing them to cross-class influences. In entertainment, for another instance, urban youth adopted a taste for music that combined "black" and "country" forms, both of which represented a "downward" social class orientation.

One of the first kinds of studies to reflect recognition of a problem was centered on possible cross-pressures between parents and peers (see Hartup, 1970, for a review of the literature). Adults (parents) who were well-functioning members of normative society were assumed to want their children to acquire norms and values that would lead to adult social status. Insofar as youth culture was segregated from adult society, it posed a threat to this desire. Youth who were not yet members of society or not committed to it were apt to construct norms that differed from adult norms and might even be oppositional to them. This argument was abetted by the belief that youth, left to themselves, lacked self-discipline and required adults' supervision (Bronfenbrenner, 1970; Shorter, 1976). When the symbolic implication of lower class functioning was added, peer culture became even more suspect for its antisocietal potential.

Only recently has this oppositional view of parents and peers come to be questioned anew by researchers. First, the methodology of the cross-pressure studies was criticized for having forced disjunctive choices between parents and peers when in reality they might not be in opposition. Second, new studies showed that most adolescents believed their parents and friends had similar views (e.g., Berndt, 1979). Third, observers who tracked findings across decades failed to find a widening historical gap between views held by adolescents' parents and friends (Sebald, 1986). Fourth, a new appreciation of children's ability to cooperate with peers in constructing reality came into the literature. Previously, peers had been characterized as nonadults whose combined impulsivity was liable to create hedonistic chaos. This conception gave way to the view that peers supported one another's positive social development through processes of cooperative social interaction (Damon, 1977; Youniss, 1980; Youniss & Damon, 1992). And fifth, the general idea began to emerge that parents and peers might represent separate but equally important social influences for children's development. Hartup (1983), for example, argued that parents and peers constituted different but overlapping social systems, each of which was legitimate, but with the potential to be integrated with the other.

Peer Culture as Its Own Structure

Corsaro's use of the term *culture* refers to at least three aspects of social interactions he observed in nursery school settings.

1. Children in these settings behave in a rule-like fashion. Their play is organized according to repeatable routines, and deviations from them are occasions for comment and negotiation.
2. Children operate as if they shared meanings for actions and norms for procedures through which they can establish mutual understanding. Interpretation of interaction events is not ad hoc, or moment to moment, but is based on meanings that children carry forward across events, using a shared framework of understanding. Indications of nonmutuality are met with procedures designed to reestablish meaning from which subsequent interaction can then proceed.
3. Activities of members of the group are focused around repeatable themes that all members of the group recognize. These topics are recurrent in discussions and games. Children in the classroom understand these themes and share a store of experiences pertaining to them.

We add a fourth principle of social identity that integrates the individual child into the group. Children believe that the interactions in which they partake are orderly and, in a sense, necessary (Furth & Kane, 1992; Youniss, 1992; Youniss & Damon, 1992). Although children construct interactions and rules for interacting, they believe that the rules are not arbitrary and have a longstanding basis. For instance, in Piaget's (1932) classic monograph on moral judgment, children argued that rules for games were established historically by their forefathers. When asked how he learned rules for a game of marbles, one boy in Piaget's study said he learned them from an older boy, who learned them from his father, who, in turn, learned them from his father, who was a lawyer! This property of children's beliefs helps to clarify the usefulness of the term *culture*. Children do not think that anyone can simply begin to interact as he or she sees fit. Rather, there should be regularities that give interactions an orderliness without which there could be no mutual understanding. When order is respected, children can enter interactions with the ability to achieve intentional outcomes, adjusting as new intentions come in or recognizing when there has been miscommunication. This belief helps children identify with the social order and work toward sustaining mutual understanding among their peers with whom they share this culture. By using shared procedures, children attend to immediate needs while they sustain the larger structure, duplicating its elemental roots. As Corsaro and Eder (1990) have noted, "The structural properties of social systems are both medium and outcome of the practices they recursively organize" (cited in Giddens, 1984, p. 25).

Peer and Adult Culture

An attractive feature of this approach is that peer and adult cultures are not construed as arising from separate starting points that are conflictual or need to be reconciled. Both are open to continuous redefinition, and each can be penetrated by the other. With this latter feature, properties from one culture can be brought into the other and made a part of it. Corsaro uses the example of ranking according to age as a characteristic that probably comes from adults and older children but is integrated into the peer system. The salience of size and intelligence are examples of other features that might also have their origins outside peer culture.

Corsaro adds an additional point that brings focus back to interactions. Many procedures that children construct for operating in their own culture are not so unique as to be inapplicable to interactions with adults. Consider basic operations such as establishing shared understanding or trying to resolve differences of opinion. These functions may be served by asking questions of the other person, explaining one's viewpoint, or justifying one's action with reference to an assumed prior agreement (Corsaro & Rizzo, 1988; Youniss, 1980). Specific actions that mediate such procedures may differ in execution between the cultures; children may argue more symmetrically with peers but in a more complementary fashion with parents or teachers. Nevertheless, the procedures used in the one system are potentially translatable into the other.

The work of Goffman (1967, 1974) has been invoked by sociologists studying the peer culture of childhood as a tool for analyzing what takes place between children in play settings (Corsaro, 1985; Fine, 1981). For Goffman, these settings are organized in the interaction order, which differs from the formalized, legalistic rules that govern what people do in institutionalized contexts such as workplaces. This interaction order applies in situations of "copresence" as persons encounter one another in face-to-face situations. One of the remarkable things about these situations is the knowledge of how to "go on" that people commonly display in them. The ease with which people can deal with others with whom they share no interaction history suggests the existence of tacit rules for ordering such situations.

Brown (1990) discusses the utility of high school peer groups in helping give structure to the adolescent interaction order. He notes that even among interactants who are not well known to one another, "crowd" membership can provide valuable clues for managing encounters: "Developing a categorization scheme for peer crowds or peer cultures helps one to negotiate relationships with peers who remain acquaintances or strangers" (p. 181). For any social encounter, there are several perspectives that could be brought to the question of "what is going on." However, adolescents seem quite able to handle the issue by quickly coordinating perspectives and proceeding toward intended goals. Clearly, more is happening than on-the-spot construction through interactional trial and error. The shared knowledge adolescents bring to interactions allows them to proceed in an orderly and efficient manner. It is reasonable to assume that a portion of this orderliness resides in awareness of relevant dimensions of social functioning and discrimination among types or groups of adolescents.

Goffman (1961) notes that adults distinguish among potential interactants in terms of those who may be relied upon to sustain an encounter versus those who are not bound to abide by a common code of conduct. Knowledge of crowd membership may serve a similar function for adolescents. The usual sense in which adolescent crowd designations make their way into the literature is with reference to the status "pecking order" that obtains among them. Thus members of high-status groups may avoid or refuse to interact with members of low-status groups. Clearly, issues of superior versus inferior status are dealt with by adolescents through crowd membership, but crowds can also serve in the management of interests, orientation toward adult institutions, and friendship expectations (Eckert, 1989).

In *The Adolescent Society,* Coleman drew attention to some of the organizing principles of adolescent peer groups. Thereafter, several ethnographic studies documented life in adolescent peer groups, mainly in school settings (e.g., Eckert, 1989; Varenne, 1982). These studies reveal a peer culture with a high level of complexity and sophistication, albeit one that varies from the dominant adult culture in certain ways. Examples include the preeminence of concern with athletic accomplishment and popularity (Friesen, 1968) and the adoption of cultural accoutrements peculiar to a "youth subculture"—e.g., "punk," or "freak" peer groups (Brake, 1985).

In summary, the combination of interaction order and peer culture makes the social domain of peer interaction worth studying in its own right as a positive source of social development. Some prior work has been limited to outward appearances that make peer functioning seem simple and inevitably distant from adult norms and values. Ethnographic work, however, suggests that peer culture is more complex than outward signs suggest. The present study is designed to add to these ethnographic depictions by having adolescents give insider accounts of the peer culture and the groups or crowds they distinguish within it.

THE PRESENT STUDY

We will now present empirical data that consist in adolescents' descriptions of the peer crowds to which they belong. Our goal is to learn about the categorization schemes adolescents use to define the peer world. Categorization of crowds is considered basic to knowing what is going on and how to achieve one's goals with other peers. We hope to learn how adolescents discriminate among types of crowds and whether females and males use similar schemes.

The present study reports crowd assignments and descriptions from 905 adolescents. The data were originally collected by Kahn (1989), who studied middle-class, white adolescents from four private and two public high schools in Atlanta, Georgia. A section of her questionnaire asked questions about peer groups. Students were given a list of names of crowds and told to check the one or more groups to which they belonged. The list was taken from reports in the literature (e.g., Brown & Lohr, 1987; Brown, Lohr, & Trujillo, 1990) and contained the names *Jocks, Populars, Brains, Loners, Druggies, Normals, Toughs, Outcasts,* and *Other.* Once students checked the crowds to which they belonged, they wrote in "the main characteristics of the crowds" they had checked. If they checked *Other,* they were to give the appropriate name with a description.

Students generated 1,833 scorable statements about their groups. We will now present the findings in four sections. First, we describe the 19 categories that were extracted from the students' written characteristics of their crowds. These data provide an insider's account of the main dimensions by which adolescents discriminate among types of groups in their schools. Second, we discuss the most frequently used categories for each crowd. Third, we report data on multiple group membership because one third of the students said they belonged to two or more groups. These results provide new evidence on individual placement within the peer culture, suggesting that many adolescents view themselves as fitting into more than one particular group. And, fourth, results are reviewed to show ways females and males differentially organize peer culture.

Descriptions of Main Characteristics

Written characteristics for each crowd were initially submitted to a content analysis. Two of the authors read statements from a sample of 100 students and developed a coding scheme consisting of 30 themes. The three authors then discussed the themes and agreed to a reduction to 19 categories. Reliability was checked with a sample of 250 students and yielded a Cohen's Kappa of .83. We then scored all 1,833 statements according to these categories. We note that the categories were generated from statements that were intended to depict particular crowds; therefore most of the categories correspond to a "definitive" characteristic of a specific crowd. For example, there is a code called *partying/going to social events* that was generated mainly by students who designated themselves as belonging to the Popular crowd. It is noted, however, that these seeming crowd-specific statements were generated by students belonging to various crowds. For instance, statements in the *partying/going to social events* category were given by students in six of the crowds. Table 5.1 shows the 19 categories and lists examples of statements for each. Table 5.2 shows the most commonly used categories for each group as generated by the 603 students from the total sample who said they belonged to a single group. We will now describe each group in turn. Because only five students checked the Toughs crowd, we combined their data with the Druggies, to whom they were most similar.

Populars

Four categories accounted for 74% of all statements given by the 123 students in the Popular group. The categories were *having many friends/being well known, principled sociality, partying/going to social events,* and *having fun/being cool/looking good.* The general orientation to sociality shown by these Popular students diverges into three emphases. Getting along well with and being friendly to many peers was one emphasis. Respecting and caring for peers was another emphasis. And a third was having fun and enjoying peer associations. The first emphasis represents a political type of orientation, the second an ethical approach, and the third a fun-loving attitude. It may be concluded that the Popular group is not composed of a single social type, but rather is composed of variations in kinds of sociality that adolescents acknowledge.

That Popularity carries a complex connotation is seen by the additional finding that 34 of the statements from Popular students brought up negative characteristics that were associated with being popular. These statements fell into two categories. In *stating crowd problems,* students gave negative descriptors of their crowd as being "snobbish" or "superficial." In *denying crowd problems or negative behavior,* students gave statements such as "We're not snobs." These reflective statements are congruent with Eder's (1985) report on popular adolescent females. Cheerleaders who had achieved choice positions within the peer hierarchy acknowledged difficulty in holding onto their popular status and in dealing with jealousy from other females. The implied dynamic is that elite groups within the school are necessarily exclusive and that persons who are excluded can develop antipathy toward the "in-group." Many adolescents in our study signified their recognition of an inherent duality of belonging to the popular crowd. They did so by acknowledging others' negative perceptions or by denying these negative perceptions. Hence being popular is not a

Table 5.1 Crowd Statement Coding Scheme and Example Statements

Code Category	Example Statements
1. Having many friends or being well known	"Populars have lots of friends and get along well with people in all grades." "Being known by everyone."
2. Getting along well with peers	"We get along well with everyone." "We all get along well."
3. Partying/going to social events	"We go to parties and like social events." "We go out on the weekends."
4. Having fun/being cool/looking good	"Being cool and sociable." "Good dressers, we wear the styles."
5. Principled sociality	"Help people and show compassion." "Nice, sharing, and caring."
6. Liking sports	"Like sports." "Athletic."
7. Participating in physical activities	"Play basketball, football, and soccer." "Work out (with weights)."
8. Being average	"We're average." "Not real popular, but not an outcast."
9. Normal	"A normal person who does normal things." "Normal everyday student."
10. Academic ability/high grades	"Good grades; honors courses." "Grades are important."
11. Being smart	"Smart, creative." "Smarter than the average person."
12. Fighting/physical aggression	"We're big; not pushed around." "Start fights."
13. Using drugs or alcohol	"We get drunk a lot." "Do drugs."
14. Nonconformity	"Don't conform." "Independent."
15. Lack of acceptance	"People think you're nerds." "Rejected because you're not cool."
16. Feeling alone/belonging to a tiny group	"On the outside." "Having no boyfriends."
17. Stating crowd problems	"People think you're nerds." "We're snobbish."
18. Denying crowd problems or negative behavior	"We're not snobs." "We're rejected because we're not cool."
19. Particularity/group trait	"Angels: Party, but don't drink." "Jew crew: Jewish kids who hang out. I guess because of our religion." "Headbangers: Like to listen to music."

Table 5.2   Most Frequent Crowd Descriptors, by Crowd

Crowd	% of Statements
Populars (n = 366)	
Having many friends or being well known	32
Partying/going to social events	19
Having fun/being cool/looking good	18
Principled sociality	05
Jocks (n = 278)	
Liking sports	54
Participating in physical activities	17
Brains (n = 162)	
Academic ability/high grades	49
Being smart	27
Normals (n = 614)	
Normal	13
Being average	11
Having fun/being cool/looking good	11
Denying crowd problems or negative behavior	11
Partying/going to social events	10
Loners (n = 87)	
Feeling alone/belonging to tiny group	37
Nonconformity	20
Lack of acceptance	15
Druggie/Toughs (n = 68)	
Using drugs or alcohol	29
Fighting/physical aggression	21

NOTE: n = number of statements made by students within a specific crowd.

simple status in that it may require balancing gains in prestige with negative feelings from others who seek to displace you.

Jocks

Two categories accounted for 71% of the all statements given by 57 students in this crowd. The dominant categories were *liking sports* and *participating in physical activities.* This group seemed to be simpler than the Populars in its basic constitution. However, as will be shown, several other adolescents who called themselves Jocks also assigned themselves to one or more additional crowds.

Brains

Two categories accounted for 76% of all statements given by the 51 students who placed themselves solely in the Brain category. The categories were *academic ability/high grades* and *being smart/intelligent.* As with the Populars, students in this group gave reflective statements that acknowledged possible negative perceptions that were associated with membership. Twelve students mentioned *crowd problems:* "social rejection," "lack of opposite-sex relationship," and "the stigma" that can come from being a member of the Brains.

Normals

This crowd was the single group name for 247 students. The five main categories, accounting for 56% of all statements, were *normal, being average, having fun/being cool/looking good, partying/going to social events,* and *denying crowd problems or negative behavior.* Students using the last category said they "didn't drink," took "no drugs," or were "not nerds." It seems that even the elemental identification of being average may include a reflective dimension such as not being deviant.

Loners

Only 33 students embraced the Loner group. Fifty-seven percent of the statements came from the categories of *feeling alone or belonging to a tiny group* or *being nonconforming.* Fifteen percent were reflective statements that emphasized a *lack of acceptance* on the part of other students.

Druggies and Toughs

Fifty percent of the statements from the 36 students calling themselves Druggies or Toughs referred to *using drugs or alcohol* or *fighting/physical aggression.* Of all the groups, Druggies and Toughs seem to be the simplest in composition, with focus on specific salient behaviors.

Others

Of the 61 students who checked Other rather than a group name we had offered, 43% specified an explicit group name that defined their primary identification. Examples include "Headbangers," "The Jew crew," "Preps," "Angels," "Goody-goodies," and "SMAKS" ("anarchists"). These data suggest that students in some schools may use alternate names for discriminating among groups.

Before proceeding to the next analysis, we note that these categories suggest a complexity we had not expected. The list of discriminating features is long. Moreover, most features apply across crowds and appear to be combinable so as to add finer discrimination than single terms can provide. This kind of complexity has been suggested by ethnographic researchers who have participated in high schools over periods of time (e.g., Kinney, 1990). Consider the categories pertaining to Popularity. Some students are oriented to *having many friends or being well known* and *getting along well with peers.* Others exaggerate the somewhat hedonistic direction of *having fun/being cool/looking good* or *partying/going to social events.* Still others, however, emphasize *principled sociality* with an orientation to concern, caring, and respect for peers.

Another argument for complexity can be made by noting the reflective comments in which students acknowledged the negative side of membership in groups. Negative characteristics were either directly named or explicitly denied. Adolescents appeared to be pointing to possible misunderstandings others might have of members of selected groups. Their mention accompanied positive statements of the features the groups had. This coupling, which integrates self-definition with a view of others' perception of the crowd, offers insight into the refined scheme adolescents use in organizing their peer domain.

A final point that merits consideration is that some students took note of being rejected by or being on the fringe of the major crowds. These statements help to verify that criteria for crowd membership are shared widely among adolescents in a school, in that even students not in crowds know the characteristics crowd members should have. Students who know but do not possess the required characteristics either call themselves outcasts or claim to be consciously nonconformists.

Multigroup Membership

In this section we report data on the number of groups in which adolescents claimed membership. It is noted that some reports in the literature imply that any crowd represents a single type of adolescent and that each adolescent can be assigned to a particular group. It is therefore important to inspect the present findings that show that many adolescents assigned themselves to more than one group. Of the 905 adolescents, 603 (67%) checked one group name, but 209 (23%) checked two names, and 93 (10%) checked three or more names. The number of claims for membership in more than one group extends the finding on organizational complexity discussed above.

Irrespective of the group name with which it was coupled, Popular was the most common name used for group combinations; it accounted for 72% of two- and three-group combinations. The main couplings were Populars-Jocks, Populars-Brains, and Populars-Jocks-Toughs. This result further supports Eder's (1985) insight that being popular is double-edged in that it brings the obvious reward of prestige, but also jealousy and admonition from others who would displace you. One way of managing this difficult position is to additionally assign oneself to another group whose status would counter the negative connotations of popularity. For example, in the present sample, some adolescents said they belonged to the Populars and the Brains. Such a combination might help to counter criticism that popular kids are superficial and lack seriousness.

Gender

In this section we will review results that indicate differences between females' and males' ways of organizing the peer culture. A chi-square test was used to assess gender differences in category usage. The omnibus result was significant—$\chi^2 (18) = 112.53, p < .0001$. Nine of 19 categories showed gender effects according to Haberman's (1978) adjusted residual statistic. More females than males gave statements that appeared in the categories of *having fun/being cool/looking good, principled sociality, academic ability, nonconformity,* and *denying crowd problems or negative behavior.* Males gave more statements than females in the categories of *liking sports, participating in physical activities, fighting/physical aggression,* and *using drugs or alcohol.*

Table 5.3 reports percentages of females and males who assigned themselves to the various single and multiple groups. A chi-square test of independence (χ^2 (5) = 29.28, $p < .001$) indicates an association between gender and group membership. The proportion of females to males differed in all groups except Brains. More females than males called themselves Populars, Normals, and Loners; more males than females called themselves Jocks and Druggies.

Figures 5.1 and 5.2 display proportions of group membership for both genders. The most common assignment for females (32%) and for males (22%) was to the Normal group. The second most common crowd for females was Populars (19%) and for males was Jock-Popular (18%). This fits reports in the literature (e.g., Coleman, 1961; Friesen, 1968) that males gain popularity through athletic participation. Where our findings differ from other studies is that the third most common crowd assignment for females was the Jock-Popular combination (7%), suggesting that in the 1980s more female students may have been able to pursue popularity through the traditional male avenue of athletics.

Nevertheless, on the whole, females appeared more "expressive" than males, with greater emphasis on being pleasant and caring in interactions. They were also more sensitive to appearances, especially in offering reflective denials of negative aspects of peer group reputations. This may also be taken as evidence of a greater female attunement to the interactional sphere in general. For instance, females more than males indicated conscious and deliberate nonconformity and independence.

Males, on the other hand, were more likely to use categories involving sports and manifesting deviance—drug and alcohol use and aggression. Also, males were less likely than females to mention academic achievement. These findings are in keeping with greater male athletic participation and higher levels of male delinquency found in the literature.

The present findings on gender support an emerging picture of differential organization of peer culture by females and males (Coleman, 1961; Eder, 1985; Eder & Halinan, 1978). Females seem highly invested in popularity and the social perceptions that it entails, whereas males seem more occupied with physical prowess and deviance. However, present results do not show us how the organizations of

Table 5.3 Most Common Single Crowd Assignments, by Gender

Crowd	n	% Female	% Male
Populars	123	72*	28
Normals	247	61*	39
Jocks	57	35	65*
Brains	51	52	48
Loners	33	61*	39
Druggies	31	39	61*

NOTE: Gender effects were determined using Haberman's (1973) adjusted residual (ri) statistic to identify cells with counts significantly higher or lower than expected if group assignment was independent of gender.
*$p < .05$.

crowds by females and males might be related in a complementary manner. For instance, Holland and Eisenhart (1990) suggest that college-age females organize their relations with other females in great part in order to attract and be attracted to males. We cannot know the degree to which the descriptions given here reflect cross-gender dynamics, except when emphasis was placed on good looks and appealing appearance.

CONCLUSIONS

Our findings lead to four general conclusions. First, adolescents claim membership in a multiplicity of crowd types. This shows that the organization of peer culture entails a refined discrimination among groups. Numerous researchers have reported distinctive groups in the peer context: for example, Eckert (1989) found differences between "jocks" and "burnouts," and Buff (1970) found differences among "greasers," "dupers," and "hippies." The present results confirm and extend the reality of a multifaceted adolescent culture.

The second general conclusion flows from the nature of the descriptions given by the students for the crowds they endorsed. We found that categories of statements that seemed to depict specific crowds also recurred across crowds. For example, the category of *getting along well with peers* was identified in scoring the statements of students in the Popular crowd. However, the same category comprised a substantial proportion of statements given also by Jocks

118

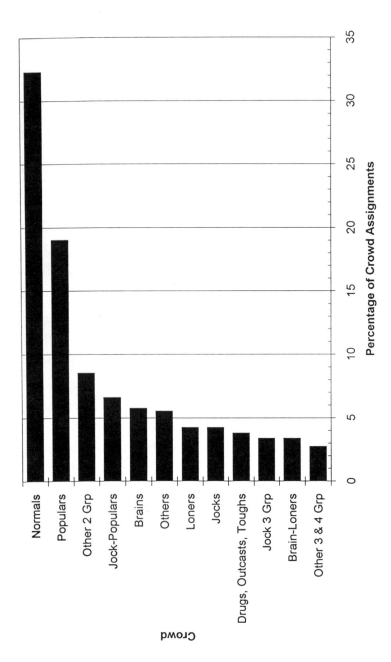

Figure 5.1 Distribution of Female Adolescents' Crowd Assignments

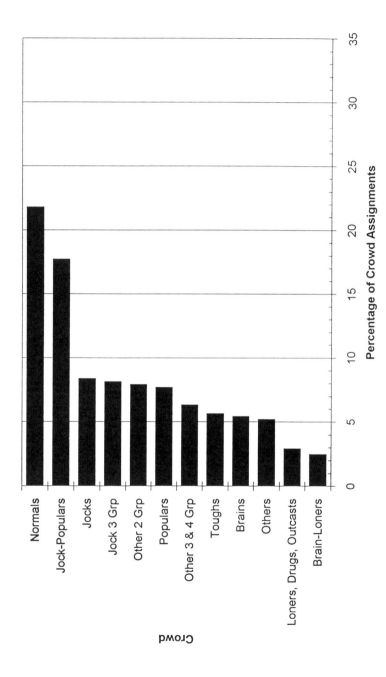

Figure 5.2 Distribution of Male Adolescents' Crowd Assignments

119

and Normals. Other researchers have also noted similarities across group boundaries. For instance, Friesen (1968) observed that some students were either "academic" or "athletic," but that other students could not be placed solely in one of these types because they had characteristics of both. In a different vein, Kinney (1990) observed that some students belonged to more than one crowd and changed membership flexibly, especially during the latter years of high school. This breaking down of boundaries was associated with the recognition of shared interests and concerns by members of different crowds.

Third, present data lend little support to the view that the peer culture is organized mainly in opposition to adult society. The peer culture does not seem to be an immature, less differentiated version of adult values. Rather, it ranges in scope from Druggies and Toughs, who are deviant, sensation seeking, and antinomian, to Brains, who are as school oriented as any traditional principal or parent could wish.

Fourth, the gender arrangements in this culture can be said to reflect gender arrangements that obtain in adult society. Females showed a expressive orientation whereas males were more activity centered. This is somewhat surprising, given that high school students are not yet constrained by marital or career roles. Nonetheless, females in this sample were more concerned with matters of interpersonal sensitivity and attractiveness, whereas males were more concerned with physical activities and athletic prowess. These distinctions are strong enough to warrant pursuit of their developmental forerunners in preadolescence (e.g., Lever, 1978). They are also interesting enough to suggest further study of their consequences during the college years (Holland & Eisenhart, 1990).

In summary, even among such a homogeneous, largely middle-class and white group of adolescents, there arises a complex order of interaction that admits of a multiplicity of styles within a widely shared value system. The adolescents in this study contribute to the growing picture that high school students in the United States generate a complexly structured culture that is as differentiated as adult social institutions.

REFERENCES

Berndt, T. J. (1979). Developmental changes in conformity to peers and parents. *Developmental Psychology, 15*, 608-616.
Brake, M. (1985). *Comparative youth culture*. London: Routledge & Kegan Paul.

Bronfenbrenner, U. (1970). *Two worlds of childhood: U.S. and U.S.S.R.* New York: Russell Sage Foundation.

Brown, B. B., & Lohr, M. J. (1987). Peer group affiliation and adolescent self esteem: An integration of ego-identity and symbolic interaction theories. *Journal of Personality and Social Psychology, 52,* 47-55.

Brown, B. B. (1990). Peer groups and peer cultures. In S. S. Feldman & G. R. Elliott (Eds.), *At the threshold: The developing adolescent* (pp. 171-196). Cambridge, MA: Harvard University Press.

Brown, B. B., Lohr, M., & Trujillo, C. (1990). Multiple crowds and multiple lifestyles: Adolescents' perceptions of peer group characteristics. In R. E. Muss (Ed.), *Adolescent behavior and society: A book of readings* (pp. 30-36). New York: Random House.

Buff, S. (1970). Greasers, dupers and hippies: Three responses to the adult world. In L. Howe (Ed.), *The white majority* (pp. 60-70). New York: Random House.

Coleman, J. S. (1961). *The adolescent society.* New York: Free Press.

Coleman, J. S. (1987). Families and schools. *Educational Researcher, 16,* 32-38.

Coleman, J. S., & Hoffer, T. B. (1987). *Public and private schools: The impact of communities.* New York: Basic Books.

Corsaro, W. A. (1985). *Friendship and peer culture in the early years.* Norwood, NJ: Ablex.

Corsaro, W. A., & Eder, D. (1990). Children's peer cultures. *Annual Review of Sociology, 16,* 197-220.

Corsaro, W. A., & Rizzo, T. A. (1988). Discussione and friendship: Socialization processes in the peer culture of an Italian nursery school. *American Sociological Review, 53,* 879-894.

Damon, W. (1977). *The social world of the child.* San Francisco: Jossey-Bass.

Eckert, P. (1989). *Jocks and burnouts: Social categories and identity in the high school.* New York: Teachers College Press.

Eder, D. (1985). The cycle of popularity: Interpersonal relations among female adolescents. *Sociology of Education, 58,* 154-165.

Eder, D., & Hallinan, M. T. (1978). Sex differences in children's friendships. *American Sociological Review, 43,* 237-250.

Fine, G. A. (1981). Friends, impression management, and preadolescent behavior. In S. Asher & J. Gottman (Eds.), *The development of children's friendships* (pp. 29-52). Cambridge, UK: Cambridge University Press.

Friesen, (1968). Academic-athletic-popularity syndrome in the Canadian high school society. *Adolescence, 3,* 39-52.

Furth, H. G., & Kane, S. (1992). Children constructing society: A new perspective on children at play. In H. McGurk (Ed.), *Childhood social development: Contemporary perspectives* (pp. 149-173). Hove, UK: Lawrence Erlbaum.

Giddens, A. (1984). *The constitution of society.* Berkeley: University of California Press.

Gilbert, J. (1986). *A cycle of outrage: America's reaction to juvenile delinquency in the 1950's.* New York: Oxford University Press.

Goffman, E. (1961). *Encounters: Two studies in the sociology of interaction.* Indianapolis: Bobbs Merrill.

Goffman, E. (1967). *Interaction ritual: Essays on face-to-face behavior.* Garden City, NY: Doubleday.

Goffman, E. (1974). *Frame analysis: An essay on the organization of experience.* New York: Harper & Row.

Haberman, S. J. (1978). *Analysis of qualitative data* (Vol. 1). New York: Academic Press.

Hartup, W. W. (1970). Peer interaction and social organization. In P. Mussen (Ed.), *Carmichael's manual of child psychology* (Vol. 2, pp. 361-456). New York: John Wiley.

Hartup, W. W. (1983). Peer relations. In E. M. Hetherington (Ed.), *Handbook of child psychology: Vol. 4. Socialization, personality and social development* (pp. 103-196). New York: John Wiley.

Hinde, R. A. (1979). *Toward understanding relationships*. London: Academic Press.

Holland, D., & Eisenhart, M. (1990). *Educated in romance: Women, achievement, and college culture*. Chicago: University of Chicago Press.

Hollingshead, A. B. (1949). *Elmtown's youth*. New York: John Wiley.

Kahn, C. M. (1989). *Family relationships and friendships in adolescence: Continuities and discontinuities*. Unpublished doctoral dissertation, Department of Psychology, The Catholic University of America.

Kinney, D. (1990). Dweebs, headbangers, and trendies: Adolescent identity formation and change within sociocultural contexts. Unpublished doctoral dissertation, Department of Sociology, Indiana University.

Lever, J. (1978). Sex differences in the complexity of children's play and games. *American Sociological Review, 43,* 471-483.

Piaget, J. (1932). *The moral judgment of the child*. London: Routledge & Kegan Paul.

Sebald, H. (1986). Adolescents' shifting orientation toward parents and peers: A curvilinear trend over recent decades. *Journal of Marriage and the Family, 48,* 5-13.

Shorter, E. (1976). *The making of the modern family*. New York: Basic Books.

Varenne, H. (1982). Jocks and freaks: The symbolic structure of the expression of social interaction among American senior high school students. In G. Spindler (Ed.), *Doing the ethnography of schooling* (pp. 213-235). New York: Holt, Rinehart & Winston.

Youniss, J. (1980). *Parents and peers in social development*. Chicago: University of Chicago Press.

Youniss, J. (1989). Parent-adolescent relationships. In W. Damon (Ed.), *Child development today and tomorrow* (pp. 379-392). San Francisco: Jossey-Bass.

Youniss, J. (1992). Parent and peer relations in the emergence of cultural competence. In H. McGurk (Ed.), *Childhood social development: Contemporary perspectives* (pp. 131-147). Hove, UK: Lawrence Erlbaum.

Youniss, J., & Damon, W. (1992). Social construction in Piaget's theory. In H. Beilin & P. Pufall (Eds.), *Piaget's theory, its past and its future* (pp. 267-286). Hillsdale, NJ: Lawrence Erlbaum.

Youniss, J., & Smollar, J. (1985). *Adolescent relations with mothers, fathers, friends*. Chicago: University of Chicago Press.

6. Casting Adolescent Crowds in a Relational Perspective: Caricature, Channel, and Context

B. Bradford Brown
University of Wisconsin-Madison

Margaret S. Mory
University of Wisconsin-Madison

David Kinney
Research for Better Schools, Inc.

For most individuals in our society, the transition from childhood to adolescence, often heralded by entry into middle school or junior high school, is accompanied by major transformations in peer relationships. Not only does the new school feature a much larger population of peers (by combining students from several elementary schools), but the daily routine of moving from class to class brings students into contact with a greater number of peers than they typically saw in the self-contained classrooms of elementary school. What is more, youngsters soon discover that the adolescent social world is a heterosexual world, so that opposite-sex peers, who have been largely ignored in middle childhood (Hartup, 1983), must become part of their social network—and they must become proficient at interacting with both sexes. At the same time, adult supervision of peer relationships recedes, leaving the young person to negotiate this expanded peer context with its new relational demands without the guiding or controlling hand that adults provided in earlier years.

Such momentous transformations in the peer social system could easily overwhelm a young person if programs, institutions, and cultural forms did not evolve to help adolescents adjust to them. One such "evolution" is the emergence of peer "crowds." Crowds refer to collections of adolescents identified by the interests, attitudes, abilities, and/or personal characteristics they have in common. They differ from other groupings of adolescents, such as friendship groups or "cliques," in that they are based on a person's reputation rather than interaction patterns (Brown, 1990). A crowd defines what a person is like more than who she or he "hangs around with." Of course, because "birds of a feather flock together" it is common for adolescents to interact with peers from the same crowd and avoid relationships with peers from other crowds with markedly different reputations. Yet such interaction patterns are not a prerequisite of crowd affiliation.

For many decades, social scientists have debated the functions that crowds serve without reaching clear consensus. From our perspective, however, crowds have two major functions: They foster individuals' development of identity or self-concept, and they structure social interactions. In this chapter we are concerned primarily with the second function, the ways in which crowds serve to regulate social relationships among adolescents. Some investigators have regarded this as the major organizing principle of adolescent crowds. For example, several authors have argued that high school crowds cluster adolescents into the socioeconomic strata (Buff, 1970; Eckert, 1989; Hollingshead, 1949) or the racial and ethnic groupings (Ianni, 1989; Matute-Bianchi, 1986) that structure social interactions in the surrounding (adult) community. Others have portrayed crowds as a major mechanism for socializing young people into adult social roles. The most classic example is Dunphy's (1963) portrait of how crowds evolve across adolescence to facilitate heterosexual orientations and dating patterns.

In much of this work, authors cast their depictions of crowds in relational perspective: How do various crowds get along with each other? What is the quality of relationships within each crowd? Rarely, however, are these relational issues the focus of analysis. Rather, they are a mechanism by which researchers can address the larger sociological or social psychological issues with which they are concerned: socioeconomic stratification, generational conflict, socialization into adult roles, and so on. As a result, our understanding of adolescent crowds from a relational perspective is rather fragmented.

Our intent in this chapter is to provide a more systematic analysis of how relational principles reveal the structure and function of adolescent crowds. We perceive three major ways in which crowds may be cast in relational perspective. First, adolescents construct an image, or *caricature*, of each crowd that reflects their perceptions of the typical or stereotypical traits of its members. These caricatures trace the symbolic relationships that exist among crowds: How crowds are different from one another and how well crowds get along with each other. This helps teenagers to understand the alternative "social identities" that are available, as well as to appreciate the norms governing relationships and peer interactions within their social milieu. Second, in a more concrete fashion, crowd affiliation serves to *channel* teenagers toward forming relationships with certain peers rather than others. Crowds are arranged in "social space" in such a way that relationships between teenagers in different crowds are facilitated in some cases and inhibited in others. Finally, crowds serve as *contexts* for peer relationships in which systematic variations in the quality of relationships can be observed as a function of the group's norms, orientations, and status position. Thus whereas adolescents in one crowd may form lasting and caring friendships, adolescents in another crowd may display superficial and competitive relationships.

In the sections that follow, we will sketch out the relational issues that emerge when one approaches crowds as caricatures, channels, and contexts. Empirical evidence will be cited that seems to illustrate each of these perspectives. Yet it is important to acknowledge that this is a relatively new approach to adolescent crowds; research evidence that bears upon this approach is still quite limited. Our commentary is intended to be more suggestive and provocative than definitive. Before embarking on this relational analysis, it seems wise to clarify our perspective on the nature or essence of adolescent crowds.

THE NATURE OF ADOLESCENT CROWDS

From ethnographic depictions one often gets the impression that adolescent crowds are very concrete entities (e.g., Cusick, 1973; Eckert, 1989; Eder, 1985). They have widely acknowledged labels and readily identifiable memberships. They lay claim to a particular hangout at school or in the neighborhood—a lunchroom table or hallway or street corner. They have implicit control of certain school activities: The politicos preside over the student council, while the burnouts dominate the auto shop. To be sure, such depictions reflect a concrete and visible reality in most American high schools, namely, cliques that embody the attitudes, behaviors, and lifestyles that define a particular crowd.

Yet such depictions have perplexed other ethnographers, who witness blatant contradictions between the spoken norms of a crowd and crowd members' observable behavior. Varenne (1982), for example, was bemused that members of two crowds routinely depicted as archrivals could often be observed interacting with each other, or that a student widely regarded as a member of the popular crowd, known for its trendy style of dress, often came to school in blue jeans and a work shirt—the signature apparel of a very different crowd. Such contradictions led Varenne to propose that crowds seemed to exist much more "in teenagers' heads" than in reality.

How visible and distinctive are adolescent crowds? Certainly, individuals or cliques that are widely acknowledged representatives of a particular crowd can be easily located in most schools. They also can easily become the target of ethnographic or participant observer studies. But to a certain degree, adolescent crowds exist more profoundly at the cultural and symbolic level than at the level of definitive individual behaviors (Lesko, 1988). Crowds stipulate (in stereotypic ways) a set of alternative value systems, lifestyles, and behavioral repertoires that are readily recognizable within the adolescent social system. In other words, each crowd represents a different prescriptive identity or identity prototype. Thus teenagers may feel quite comfortable characterizing jocks as individuals who are "out for" sports teams, out for a good time on the weekend, into the latest styles, and only moderately concerned with academic achievement, even though they recognize that several peers associated with the jock crowd do not manifest all of these characteristics.

In fact, a teenager's *actual* attitudes and behaviors are unlikely to jibe perfectly with the normative image of *any* single crowd in his or her social milieu. If a teenager's characteristics are highly similar to the prototypic attitudes and behaviors of a specific crowd, he or she is likely to be associated with that crowd by most peers. But for many, if not most, adolescents, the fit between personal attitudes and behaviors and the prototypic characteristics of a given crowd is an imperfect one. As a result, a certain teenager may be viewed as a member of crowd X by some peers, a member of crowd Y by other peers, and a member of *both* crowds by still other peers. In other words, although some adolescents fit neatly into a specific crowd, many others seem to have multiple or partial crowd affiliations, often of varying intensities.

This helps to define adolescent crowds as distinctive in several ways from most other groups that social scientists study. In the first place, membership in adolescent crowds is not as obvious and exclusive. By occupation, one is a lawyer or a hairdresser or a physician or a construction worker or whatever. By religious affiliation, one is an Orthodox Jew or an Episcopalian or a Roman Catholic or an atheist, and so on. But by crowd, an adolescent can easily be both a "jock" and a "Mexican." Second, exclusive membership in a particular crowd is readily disavowed by adolescents. Few adults would deny their occupation or their neighborhood of residence. They might "waffle" a bit about their political party affiliation or their socioeconomic status. Rarely, however, do social scientists encounter the sort of reluctance or denial that we and others (Lesko, 1988; Varenne, 1982) have observed when asking adolescents, "What crowd do *you* belong to?" "I really don't belong to any crowd" or "I mix with several crowds" are common responses. There are several reasons for such responses. One is that students are reluctant to appear close-minded and exclusionary, as if they only interact with peers in one particular crowd. Another is that because they mix with several crowds during the school day (even if they tend to hang out with one specific group after school or on weekends) it is difficult for them to see themselves as belonging to just one crowd. What's more, because crowds are meant to depict one's global identity, or basic reputation with peers, rather than just one facet of self (as occupation or religious affiliation or political party membership do for adults), being "typecast" too rigidly into one crowd violates the American emphasis on individuality, autonomy, and personal uniqueness.

Finally, some crowds are legitimate, meaningful categories but are—almost by definition—unobservable. The "loners," for example, comprise a crowd of adolescents who are described as having no friends, no hangouts, no group activities; yet they possess (in the minds of adolescents) as clear a prototypic identity as any other group (Brown, Lohr, & Trujillo, 1990).

Such characteristics give teenage crowds a different dynamic than other groupings of adolescents or adults. They also affect the effort to examine and understand the relational characteristics of crowds. For one thing, they encourage analyses on a symbolic as well as a behavioral level. That is, researchers must attend to adolescents' "social construction" of peer crowds, to the way that teenagers employ crowd labels, and to crowd characterizations to explain and understand their social world. It is to this symbolic level that we now turn attention.

CROWDS AS CARICATURES

Those who have studied teenage crowds have found most adolescents to be willing if not eager to characterize the crowds that dominate their social milieu. From our own interviews with teenagers come these portrayals of various crowds: "Oh, yeah; they all wear these tight-fitting jeans and sit around the commons in between classes like they own the place!" "You'd be crazy to walk down the B-wing by yourself because the headbangers, they, like, attack you." "They all wear glasses and 'kiss up' to teachers, and after school they all tromp uptown to the library, or they go over to somebody's house and play some stupid computer game until 9:00 at night—and then they go right to bed 'cause their mommies make 'em!" Such depictions appear to be more elaborated and animated when elicited from dyads or groups of teenagers rather than from individuals.

What are teenagers attempting to accomplish with these pronouncements? Are these earnest attempts at accurate depictions of various crowds, or whimsically oriented exaggerations of reality? The answer depends in part on one's perspective on how individuals make sense of the world around them—an issue that has bred considerable controversy over the years (Gergen, 1984). Rather than aligning with either the logical positivists, who contend that knowledge accurately maps the realities of the world, or the phenomenologists, who counter that human beings fit reality into the categories they have created to make sense of the world, we prefer an alternative perspective derived from symbolic interactionist theory. It suggests that meaning emanates from the process of interactions between people, such that individuals construct reality (or come to an understanding of reality) through interactions with each other (Berger & Luckman, 1967; Blumer, 1969). Youniss (1980) describes how young people collaborate with peers in consensual validation of their interpersonal world. At adolescence, this would include building an understanding of crowds. Thus one's image of a crowd is honed not simply through personal observation and interpretation of crowd members' attitudes and activities, but also through conversations about and evaluations of the crowd with friends. The result is an image of a crowd that is not entirely subjective (personally unique), nor so objective that it is widely shared. In short, through social interactions, teenagers construct *caricatures* of crowds, somewhat distorted but consensually validated images of groups that serve to structure social interactions and facilitate identity development.[1]

How can teenagers maintain an image of crowds that is avowedly inaccurate? Why would a caricature of crowds (including their own group) serve their developmental agenda better than accurate portrayals of peer groups? To answer these questions we draw upon principles of social identity theory (Tajfel, 1981). This theory was crafted by European social psychologists to explain principles of group formation and intergroup or intragroup interaction. Among its major tenets are that once group membership has been established, individuals will tend to (a) accentuate differences between one's own group and other groups, (b) overstate the positive characteristics of one's own group, and (c) overstate the negative characteristics of other groups. The exaggerated images of the "in-group's" strengths and the "out-group's" shortcomings are worked out and reinforced through in-group interactions; that is, they are consensually validated. Their expression reaffirms group membership and builds the solidarity of the group as a whole.

We can easily observe these principles at work. Consider, for example, how sports fans celebrate a goal or touchdown with the enthusiastic chant, "We're number one!" even when their team is far from first place in league standings or experts' ratings. A more classic example concerning children's peer group interactions comes from the "Robbers' Cave" experiments (Sherif, Harvey, White, Hood, & Sherif, 1961). In this study, a sample of preadolescents in a summer camp was assigned to groups that competed with each other for desirable rewards. Soon after group assignments the investigators observed remarkable changes in social interaction patterns within the sample. Each group coalesced into a relatively cohesive unit, began denigrating the other group with inaccurate or exaggerated portrayals of their shortcomings (caricatures), and spurned social interaction with the other group's members. Only by creating a situation in which the groups had to work together to achieve a desired reward were the investigators able to overcome the intergroup rivalries and reestablish friendly social relationships across group membership lines.

Ethnographic accounts of interrelationships among adolescent crowds offer additional support for the tenets of social identity theory. Willis (1977) detailed the unflattering terms by which one working-class crowd of youth, the "lads," described their working-class peers who were more school oriented and compliant with adult authority. Even the name that the lads gave to this group, the "ear 'oles," reflected their disdain for their rivals. Similarly, both Eckert (1989) and Lesko (1988) underscored the rather hostile relationship between a high-status, school-oriented crowd (jocks or populars) and a more alienated, deviantly oriented group (burnouts) with reference to the derogatory caricatures that members of each crowd drew of the other crowd. In each case the authors argued that the unduly negative image of the out-group exacerbated tensions and hostility between the rival crowds. Yet it was also an especially effective means of affirming the credibility and superiority of one's own crowd. As Tajfel (1972, pp. 293-294) notes, "The characteristics of one's group acquire their significance only in relation to their perceived differences from other groups and the evaluation of these differences."

To be sure, these ethnographic accounts are intriguing and revealing. Yet by focusing narrowly on rather cohesive cliques of teenagers they may oversimplify the nature of symbolic relationships among adolescent crowds, thus overstating the degree to which such crowds fit the group dynamics described by social identity theory. As stated earlier, many teenagers maintain multiple crowd affiliations or avoid being associated with any crowd at all. Thus, rather than being clearly differentiable clusters of individuals, crowds exist as identity prototypes whose memberships are nonexclusive and partially overlapping. With divided group loyalties, teenagers may not so readily manifest patterns of "in-group" favoritism and "out-group" denigration. Instead, the nature of one group's caricaturing of another should be moderated by the degree of affinity the crowds have for each other.

These more complicated patterns are revealed in two survey studies of peer group stereotyping. Brown, et al. (1990) asked junior and senior high school students in one Midwestern community to name the major crowds in the school, then describe each crowd on six behavioral and interpersonal traits (dress and grooming, orientation toward achievement, sociability, extracurricular participation, school hangouts, and weekend activities) by indicating which of several descriptors fit the crowd the best (e.g., would a crowd's dress and grooming style be best described as following the latest styles, casual/athletic, neat and clean, tough or messy, or outdated or in poor taste?). Although each of six crowd types that were examined had a unique profile on these traits, consensus on the specific traits of each crowd was not overwhelming. For only 15 of the 36 distributions examined (six traits for each of six crowd types) did at least two thirds of respondents select the same descriptor for the crowd.

In a recent reanalysis of the high school portion of this data set, Mory (1992) helped to explain the lack of consensus. Using another item in the questionnaire (self-professed crowd affiliation), Mory divided the sample into four comparison groups: elites (members of the jock or popular crowd, which enjoyed high status among peers), druggies, normals (the undifferentiated mass of average students who don't stand out on any trait), and others. Comparisons of the way that each group characterized its own and other crowds revealed two notable patterns. First, confirming a basic tenet of social identity theory, members of a given crowd tended to portray their own crowd in a more positive light than nonmembers. Of course, this diluted consensus on each crowd's characteristics. More interesting, however, was the rather complicated set of dynamics governing out-group stereotyping. For example, Mory examined how each of the comparison groups described the elites and the druggies. On every trait, elites and normals held a remarkably similar image of the druggies. By contrast, druggies and normals had more discrepant images of the elites, and in most cases the normals tended to be more inclined than either the druggies or miscellaneous others to adopt the elites' own impression of the elite crowd. For example, elites portrayed themselves as having a generally (but not excessively) positive orientation toward school and described the druggies as hating school. Druggies saw themselves as being lukewarm or moderately positive about school achievement, and the elites as being *very* achievement oriented. Normals concurred with elites: Druggies hated school and elites were generally positive about achievement. In more general terms, out-groups sometimes shared a very common image of a particular crowd, but in other cases the image of a particular crowd differed noticeably among out-groups.

Mory interpreted this as evidence that normals were more closely aligned with elites than with druggies, perhaps because of greater overlap in crowd membership between elites and normals than between normals and druggies. It could also be, however, that many teens in the normal crowd emulated the elites in an effort to gain membership in that crowd (Kinney, 1993). In either case, the implication is that social identity theory principles bear some modification when applied to the stereotyping or caricaturing of adolescent crowds. The inclination to overstate the positive characteristics of one's own group is extended to crowds with whom one feels some affinity or partial affiliation. The inclination to denigrate out-groups is reserved for crowds with whom one feels no affinity or partial affiliation.

To be sure, there are several good reasons for adolescents to appraise crowds objectively and strive for consensus on each crowd's characteristics. Crowds stipulate the range of identities or identity prototypes that are readily recognized by peers. They indicate how one's attitudes and behaviors would have to change in order to shift from one social identity to another. And by providing a system for categorizing unknown peers into social types with predictable characteristics, they allow teenagers to anticipate the sort of relationship that would develop if one were to engage a particular unknown peer in social interaction. Yet these reasons for accurate appraisals of crowds are offset by the need to cast one's own group (which is often tantamount to one's own provisional identity) in a positive light and the need to understand the relationships among crowds from the perspective of one's own group. In other words, adolescents' depictions of each crowd are filtered through the biases of their own personal and social identity. The result is a set of caricatures that sketch out the *symbolic relationships* that exist among crowds. They serve as an abstract "road map" of the interrelationships among crowds in the system, based on one's own place within the system.

It is worth emphasizing that crowd caricaturing is an inherently relational activity: First, it occurs *within social relationships*. That is, adolescents do not form their impressions of crowds independently and autonomously; they coconstruct caricatures with peers who share their crowd affiliation. Thus caricatures make sense only with reference to the crowd from which they emerge; and one often observes that individuals from disparate crowds will construct very different caricatures of a given group. Second, caricaturing is often *predicated on relational statements*. DesChamps (1982, p. 87) proclaims that "groups exist within a system of mutual dependence; they acquire a reality which is defined in and through their interdependence." Crowds are often described not in absolute terms but in relation to characteristics of other crowds. For example, "The partyers goof off a lot more than the jocks do, but they don't come to school stoned like the burnouts do." Third, caricatures are frequently *explicit about intergroup affinities and hostilities*: "The Asians get along real well with the brains and the normals, but not so much with the jocks and definitely not with the Mexicans!"

In sum, we propose that adolescents' caricatures of crowds serve a variety of functions. They clarify the alternative identity prototypes that exist in the social system; they bolster the identity prototype that one has selected (at least tentatively) for oneself; they demarcate probable friends and foes, collaborators and competitors in social interactions; and they predict the relative ease or difficulty of switching identities or forming friendships across crowds. They encode a great deal of subjective information about the teenage social system. That is, they trace the symbolic relationships that exist among crowds. But these symbolic relationships, in turn, affect actual relationships an adolescent has with agemates. In large measure, they do so through their capacity to channel adolescents toward interacting with certain peers and not others, an issue to which we now turn our attention.

CROWDS AS CHANNELS

Although caricatures sketch out symbolic rather than literal relationships between crowds, they are by no means divorced from reality. They may provide overgeneralizations that flatter one's own crowd and other groups with whom one bears some affinity, but they are basically accurate portrayals of relationships among individuals in the social milieu. For example, it may not always have been true, as students in one school we studied maintained, that populars would only date fellow populars, or maybe a jock (their neighbors in the social status hierarchy). Yet, generally speaking, if you weren't in the popular or jock crowds, you just weren't on a popular kid's date list. The general accuracy of caricatures is what makes them useful road maps to adolescent relationships. Crowds do indeed help structure social interactions for teenagers. One of the major means of doing so is to *channel* adolescents into relationships with certain peers and away from interactions with others.

The combined activities of recognizing and caricaturing crowds and then sorting peers into these groupings help adolescents predict whether a given peer will be open or hostile to interpersonal overtures and whether one's friends are likely to encourage or protest one's association with a particular peer. This is accomplished by encoding three key features into crowd caricatures: the degree to which persons from a particular crowd have much in common (attitudes, interests, activities) with members of one's own group, the degree to which that crowd is receptive to association with one's own crowd (or any other crowd), and the degree to which it would be socially desirable to be associated with that crowd or its members. In other words, crowd affiliations direct adolescents toward associations with peers whose crowds are *proximal, permeable,* and *desirable.* This section will explain and illustrate these three major principles by which crowd affiliations channel adolescents into or away from associations with particular peers.

Evidence of Channeling

Before considering each principle, it would seem wise to ascertain that channeling does indeed occur. Evidence of channeling is admittedly paltry, but is sufficient to lend credence to this relational feature of crowd affiliation and to give guidance to our discussion of the operation of channeling principles.

Eder (1985) traced the roots of channeling to the emergence of the popular crowd in middle school. Girls who made it into this crowd found themselves highly sought after by classmates, so much so that it was practically impossible to respond to all the overtures for friendship. What is more, the popular girls worried that befriending certain classmates would endanger their stature in the popular crowd because of the negative opinions fellow populars had of these classmates. As a result, most popular girls became very selective in cultivating friends, preferring to confine most relationships to girls in their own crowd. As they began ignoring outsiders or shunning friendship overtures, they earned a reputation as snobs, and their "popularity" (likability) among classmates declined. In time, many girls began snubbing the populars, partly, Eder concluded, to avoid the rejection that their friendship overtures were likely to engender. In short, girls who achieved membership in the popular crowd became very selective in their friendships, limiting their social network to a manageable set of relationships, mostly with peers in their own crowd. Girls who aspired to membership in the popular crowd attempted to use friendships with populars as a point of entry, but as their overtures met with rejection they lowered their opinion of populars and channeled their efforts at forging friendships toward peers in other crowds. It is quite likely that similar dynamics underlay the tendency of popular girls to ignore African-American peers in the middle school that Schofield (1981) studied.[2]

Eckert (1989) also argued that the channeling function of crowds emerged in middle school or junior high school, but in her study it was more the result of the bifurcation of the student body into two basic crowds: jocks (similar to Eder's populars) and burnouts, who constituted the more rebellious and alienated students in the school. According to Eckert, as students entered junior high school they had the opportunity to become affiliated with the jocks or the burnouts, or to remain in the amorphous and rather anonymous middle ground between these two crowds. Eckert (1989, p. 86) observed that "many friendships broke up over [crowd] affiliation, as those who did not want to get into trouble moved away or were left behind by their more daring Burnout friends."

Like most ethnographies, Eder's and Eckert's accounts offer a constrained view of the ways in which crowd affiliation channels relationships because of their emphasis on one or two of the more diverse array of crowds that typically exist in secondary schools. To broaden this perspective, Clasen and Brown examined the friendship patterns of students in a wider array of crowds in one junior high school. Each student in this school was asked to list his or her closest friends at the school ("the students you hang around with most often"); students could list as many friends as they wished. In a separate portion of the study, all students were classified into crowds according to a revised version of Schwendinger and Schwendinger's (1985) "Social Type Rating" procedure (Brown, 1989a). Clasen and Brown then examined how students in each of the school's five major crowds—preppies (individuals who enjoyed high peer status and exhibited a "yuppie" lifestyle), brains (bright students who focused on school achievement), dirtballs (teens who were alienated from school and "into" drug use and deviant behavior), outcasts (whose shyness, poor social skills, or "out of vogue" interests earned them reputations as loners or nerds), and normals (average students who were not distinctive on any characteristic)—

distributed their friendship nominations among members of various crowds. The crowds also were compared to students classified as hybrids (whose reputation among peers was split between two crowds), floaters (who were not consistently associated with any particular crowd), or outsiders (who were not known well enough by peers to be placed in any crowd; see Brown, 1989b).

In this school, the crowds differed dramatically in size: Twenty-four percent of the student body was associated with the preppie crowd, compared to only 3% who were classified as brains. To adjust for these differences, we converted friendship nominations to percentage scores (the percentage of friends each respondent nominated who were members of each major crowd), then divided these scores by the percentage of the student body affiliated with that crowd. The resulting figures indicate whether the proportion of one's friends who come from a particular crowd is above (numbers greater than 1.00) or below (numbers less than 1.00) what would be expected by chance. Results are reported in Table 6.1. Except for the normals, students drew their friends disproportionately from within their own crowd. What is more, friends outside of one's own crowd were not drawn evenly from other crowds, nor were they distributed in a similar manner for members of different crowds. For example, normals were overrepresented in the friendship networks of brains and outcasts but underrepresented in the networks of preppies and dirtballs. The uneven and inconsistent distribution of friendships across crowds also characterized the networks of floaters, hybrids, and outsiders.

Because these results come from just one school, their generalizability is uncertain at best. Yet they clearly confirm ethnographic observations that crowd affiliation does channel friendship selection, and they give us a more elaborated view of the connections between crowd affiliation and friendship choice by which to consider the effects of major principles of channeling. In other words, the question is how proximity, permeability, and desirability might explain the crowd differences that we observed in this school—or that ethnographers have reported in their studies—in the distribution of friendships among peers in particular crowds.

Proximity: Mapping "Social Distance" Among Crowds

To be sure, one of the key ingredients in the formation of friendships is physical proximity: Two people are more likely to become

Table 6.1   Crowd Differences in the Proportionate Share of One's
Friendship Network Drawn From Each Major Crowd

R's Crowd Classification	Proportionate Share of Close Friends Who Were				
	Preps	Normals	Brains	Dirtballs	Outcasts
Preppies	3.04	0.50	0.33	0.17	0.00
Normals	0.83	1.50	1.67	0.67	0.75
Brains	0.67	1.44	6.67	0.17	0.50
Dirtballs	0.21	0.83	0.00	4.67	0.50
Outcasts	0.17	1.11	0.67	0.67	3.00
Floaters	0.71	1.17	0.00	0.67	0.87
Hybrids	0.83	1.11	0.67	0.83	1.12
Unknowns	0.46	0.89	0.67	0.83	1.25

friends if they live near each other or work near each other—or, for adolescents, if they attend the same school or occupy the same classroom (Newcomb, 1961; Priest & Sawyer, 1967). We would argue that this principle can be extended to peer groups: Two teenagers are more likely to be friends if they are part of proximal crowds (or better yet, the *same* crowd). In this case, however, proximity is not measured in terms of physical distance but "social distance." That is, crowds are arranged in what might be termed "symbolic social space." Adolescents who enter a social system complex enough to feature crowds must not only construct an image of each crowd (through the caricaturing described earlier) but also locate each crowd in social space. The closer two crowds are on this social map, the more compatible their memberships will be, and thus the more receptive members of one crowd should be to forging relationships with peers in the other crowd. It is not entirely clear, however, just how adolescents construct these social maps. What are the key dimensions by which teenagers determine the proximity of two crowds in symbolic social space?

Some investigators have argued for a unidimensional arrangement of adolescent crowds, ordering groups in terms of peer social status (e.g., Coleman, 1961) or adult socioeconomic status (e.g., Hollingshead, 1949). Eckert (1989) even attempted to synthesize these two by characterizing the peer group system in the high school she observed as anchored at one end by the high-status jocks, who reflected a middle-class values orientation, and at the other end by the burnouts, whose working-class roots seemed to contribute to their low prestige among peers. Regrettably, Eckert essentially ignored the several crowds between these two extremes, largely because she regarded them simply as offshoots of the two "anchor" groups. Because of their oppositional relationship, it was very difficult for members of the jocks and burnouts to befriend each other, but Eckert did not provide information on the ease of striking up a friendship with a member of a more proximal crowd.

Not all investigators have been satisfied with a unidimensional scheme. Rigsby and McDill (1975) suggested that there are actually two distinct reward structures to which students in American high schools must attend: the formal reward system that emphasizes academic achievement and compliance to adult authority and the informal reward system that emphasizes conformity to the "teen culture" as formulated by Coleman (1961). From these two dimensions they derived four student types: the "well rounded," who were high on both dimensions; the "studious," who were strongly oriented toward the formal reward system but weakly oriented toward the informal reward system; the "fun culture," who showed the opposite orientation; and the "uninvolved," who were low on both dimensions. Though conceptually derived, these types seem quite similar to the basic image of common adolescent crowds. In fact, in exploratory data derived from high school students in a community quite similar to the one from which our friendship network data were derived (Table 6.1), we attempted to map the school's major crowds onto Rigsby and McDill's schemes by asking students how respected and well liked by teachers each crowd was and how much status and prestige each crowd enjoyed among peers. The resulting map, depicted in the left half of Figure 6.1, placed most crowds in what appeared to be the appropriate quadrant of Rigsby and McDill's model.

Of course, all of these arrangements of adolescent crowds in social space have been conceptually rather than empirically driven. Indeed, authors have been less concerned with the structural arrangement of crowds than with a specific conceptual issue: the transmission of class-oriented culture across generations (Eckert, Hollingshead), the success of social elites in subverting academic objectives in high schools (Coleman), or the consequences of coping with two distinct value systems in secondary schools (Rigsby and McDill). It would be wise to complement these approaches with a

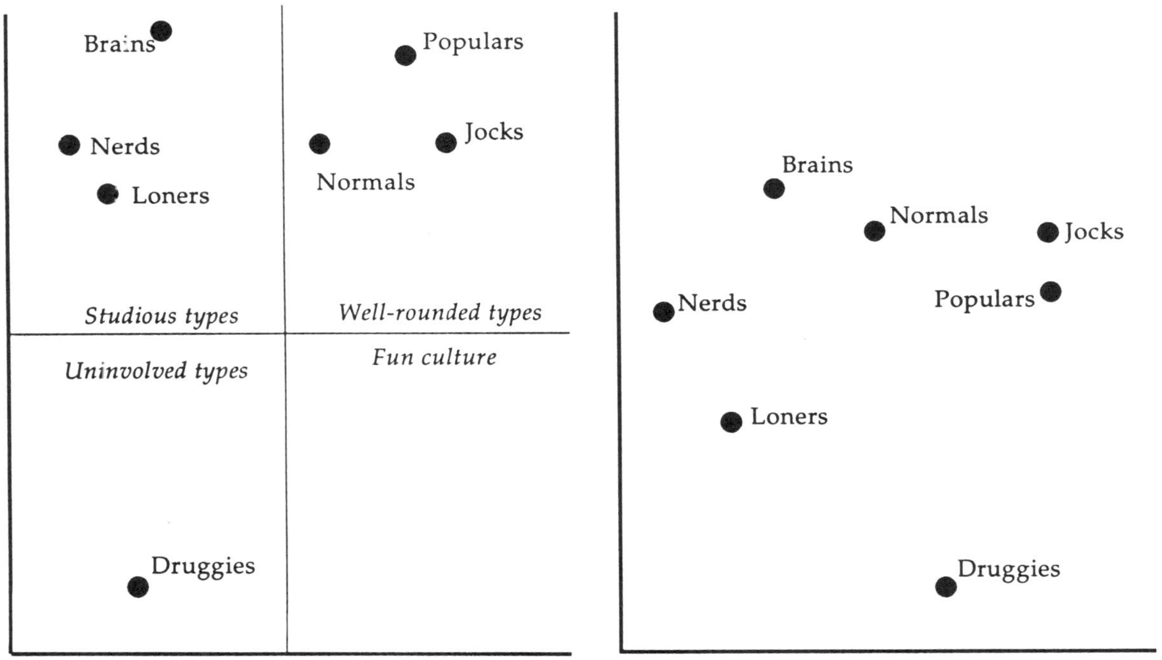

Figure 6.1 Two-Dimensional Social Maps of Adolescent Crowds. On the left is a map according to Rigsby and McDill's (1975) conceptual scheme; on the right is the result of MDS analyses of college sample data.

more empirical effort to capture teenagers' own perceptions. As a modest step in that direction, we asked a sample of 108 college undergraduates to recall the relationships among crowds in their high schools. After identifying eight major crowd types common to most of the diverse array of high schools the sample had attended, we asked respondents to rate the similarity of each possible pair of crowd types. Data analyses using multidimensional scaling techniques revealed a two-dimensional solution that fit the data fairly well; it is presented in the right half of Figure 6.1. It is strikingly similar to the two-dimensional scheme reflecting Rigsby and McDill's conceptual scheme, except for the shift in quadrant location for the druggies.

The question remains, however, as to whether the proximity of two crowds in symbolic social space affects the likelihood of relationships between the crowds' members. To illustrate the type of work that needs to be done in this area, we can examine how the various social maps proposed above compare to the pattern of friendship selection in the junior high school described earlier (see Table 6.1). Assuming that proximity is the key to friendship selection, then a rank ordering of crowds by their proximity to the target crowd ought to correspond to the rank ordering of crowds by their relative contribution to one's friendship network.

We were able to construct unidimensional maps of the arrangement of crowds, based on students' assessments of the status ranking of each crowd (peer status) and on crowd members' description of their parents' occupation and education (socioeconomic status). We could also "plug" the school's crowds into the two-dimensional maps derived conceptually from Rigsby and McDill's model, or empirically from the college student multidimensional scaling data (Figure 6.1). We expected that the largest share of the junior high students' friends would come from their own crowd, the next largest share would come from the most proximal crowd (based on Euclidian distance in the case of two-dimensional maps), the next largest from the next most proximal crowd, and so on. Transforming the data in Table 6.1 to these rank orderings, we assessed how the actual ordering of crowds (by their contribution to the friendship network of students in a particular crowd) compared to the rank ordering predicted by each mapping scheme: the one-dimensional orderings of crowds by peer status or family socioeconomic status, the location of crowds along Rigsby and McDill's two dimensions, and the two-dimensional array empirically derived by multidimensional scaling. None of the conceptual mapping schemes consistently matched the observed rank orderings. The one-dimensional schemes were particularly unimpressive, even though they were based on data from the same school as the friendship data. Interestingly, however, although the multidimensional scaling model was derived from a very different sample (college students), it accurately predicted the rank ordering for two crowds (preppies and normals) and came close for a third crowd (brains). Rigsby and McDill's model, also derived from a different sample, came close to the appropriate ordering for four of the five crowds but consistently misplaced the outcasts (see Table 6.2).

It is likely that the social maps that teenagers construct—and consequently the proximities or "social distances" between crowds—differ from one context (school or neighborhood) to the next; they may also change across age groups in one context (e.g., grade differences in one school). Thus it is not surprising that the two-dimensional schemes that were "imported" for these analyses did not fit the junior high school data perfectly. Yet their ability to supersede the fit of one-dimensional models leads us to recommend that investigators consider multidimensional social maps in future, more rigorous analyses of the effects of proximity among crowds on the channeling of peer relationships.

In sum, just as physical proximity affects the likelihood that two individuals will initiate an interpersonal relationship, "reputational" proximity—the comparative similarity of two crowds—appears to channel adolescents into relationships with peers from certain crowds more so than others. Most adolescents are predisposed to select close friends from within their own crowd; when they venture beyond this group it is more often to peers in neighboring crowds than peers in crowds that bear little similarity to their own group. Yet social distance is not the only facet of crowds to affect friendship selection. Even among neighboring crowds, teenagers must be able to cross the boundaries between their groups in order to strike up a friendship.

Permeability: The Receptiveness of Crowds to Outsiders

One of the consequences of the "in-group favoritism" and "out-group denigration" that, according to social identity theory, characterizes

Table 6.2   Each Crowd's Observed Ordering of Other Crowds by
Their Proportionate Contribution to Members' Friendship
Networks, as Compared to the Ordering Predicted by
Various Social Maps

Crowd	Rank Ordering of Crowds From Which Friendships Are Drawn			
Mapping Model	1	2	3	4
Preppies				
Observed	Normal	Brain	Dirt	Outcast
Rigsby & McDill	Normal	Brain	Outcast	Dirt
MDS model	Normal	Brain	Dirt	Outcast
Normal				
Observed	Brain	Preppie	Outcast	Dirt
Rigsby & McDill	Preppie	Brain	Outcast	Dirt
MDS model	Brain	Preppie	Outcast	Dirt
Brain				
Observed	Normal	Preppie	Outcast	Dirt
Rigsby & McDill	Normal	Outcast	Preppie	Dirt
MDS model	Normal	Outcast	Preppie	Dirt
Dirtball				
Observed	Normal	Outcast	Preppie	Brain
Rigsby & McDill	Outcast	Normal	Preppie	Brain
MDS model	Preppie	Normal	Brain	Outcast
Outcast				
Observed	Normal	Brain/ Dirtbag	Brain/ Dirtbag	Preppie
Rigsby & McDill	Brain	Normal	Preppie	Dirtbag
MDS model	Brain	Normal	Preppie	Dirtbag

relationships between groups is the tendency of group members to
"close their doors" to outsiders. This raises the expectation that
adolescent crowds would be equally impermeable. Forging relationships across crowds should be a formidable task. Yet as we have
already mentioned, the ambiguous, dynamic, and nonexclusive nature
of crowd affiliations forces some modifications in the principles of this
theory. This raises questions about how rigidly boundaries are maintained across crowds. Perhaps adolescents tend not to befriend peers in

proximal crowds, choosing instead peers in groups that, although more distant, are more receptive to intercrowd associations.

Interestingly, ethnographers disagree about the permeability of adolescent crowds, and their contrasting portrayals seem to be as much a function of their conceptual focus as the reality of intercrowd relationships. Those who have focused on two groups that engage in antagonistic relationships or display markedly different normative attitudes and behaviors emphasize impermeability. Cusick (1973) contrasted the lifestyle of a male clique from the jock crowd with one from a more alienated crowd of underachievers; according to Cusick, the two crowds were hostile, exclusive, and impermeable. Schofield (1981) emphasized the barrier that European-American girls in the popular crowd constructed to cross-racial associations; African-American girls were systematically ignored by the popular crowd, contributing sharply to the de facto segregation that existed within this ostensibly integrated school. Eder (1985) regarded the construction of boundaries between the populars and the normals as a mechanism for popular girls to contend with the overload of friendship overtures and a mechanism for normals to respond to the rejection they encountered in attempting to befriend populars.

On the other hand, ethnographers who have considered a wider array of crowds provide a more complex portrait of permeability. Larkin (1979), for example, found a fair amount of intermingling among members of the three crowds that formed the social elite of the high school he observed, but he also noted that these groups were rather unreceptive to interactions with peers in crowds at the other end of the status hierarchy: the greasers and the blacks. In fact, when out of earshot of black students, elite crowd members frequently made remarks that revealed their racial prejudices.

Thus although it is possible to conceive of crowd permeability in absolute terms—all crowds are equally impermeable, or some crowds are open to outsiders while others remain rather impermeable—it is likely that permeability operates in a more relative fashion: A given crowd is open to interactions with members of certain crowds but not receptive to relationships with members of other crowds. The most compelling evidence for this perspective comes from Kinney's (1993) recent efforts to trace the evolution of the peer group structure and the interrelationships among crowds in one Midwestern community. Based on conversations with and observations of adolescents in a variety of crowds in the community's high school,

Kinney formulated a composite map of the crowd structure that effectively integrates the principles of proximity and permeability. He found that the structural arrangement of crowds evolved through three phases from students' middle school to late high school years (see Figure 6.2).

In middle school, the crowd system consisted simply of two crowds: The high-status and relatively small group of "trendies," and the balance of the student body, known as "dweebs." A clear and stringent boundary was drawn between these two crowds. The transition to high school, with its more elaborated social structure and broader range of extracurricular activities, gave dweebs an opportunity to gain admission to one of a variety of new crowds: "normals," "headbangers," "grits," and "punkers." Headbangers began to vie with trendies for top social status, while the grits and punkers drifted to the bottom of the status hierarchy. Each group remained rather impermeable although the boundaries between trendies, normals, and headbangers were not as strong as between these groups and the grits or punkers. By the end of high school, peer status played a less prominent role in differentiating crowds, leading Kinney to depict the crowd structure in a more "flattened" egg shape (compared to the tall pyramid of middle school). Headbangers were essentially equal in status to the trendies, and normals had made inroads to higher status as well. Although the normals remained effectively isolated from the headbanger crowd, the boundaries between each of these groups and the trendies became more permeable. The boundary between grits and headbangers effectively disappeared with the emergence of a hybrid group known as the "grit-headbangers." What is more, a number of individuals actually transferred crowd affiliations (as indicated by the arrows between crowds in Figure 6.2), which further served to break down barriers between crowds. Yet such barriers did not disappear completely; boundaries between the grits and both the trendies and the punkers, for example, remained rather impenetrable.

The important lesson to be learned from this study is that only through the joint consideration of proximity and permeability among crowds can one account for the pattern of social relationships that is observed among teenagers in a given social context. Crowds must not only be similar to each other but also open to each other for adolescents from different crowds to easily negotiate a friendship (or, probably, a romantic relationship).

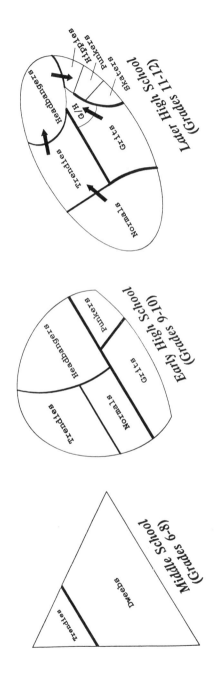

Figure 6.2 Developmental Changes in Crowd Structure. This is a composite view, combining the perspectives of students from a variety of crowds. Line widths represent degree of impermeability between crowds. Vertical location indicates each crowd's position in the school's peer status hierarchy. "G/H" = Grit-Headbangers.

Desirability

However powerful the principles of proximity and permeability are in channeling adolescents to relationships with peers in particular crowds, teenagers' befriending behavior still seems to frequently defy these principles. A boy will conscientiously court a girl from a crowd that is not only very dissimilar to his own but also unreceptive to associations with members of his crowd (a standard plot line in films about teenage romance; e.g., "Say Anything," "Stand By Me," "Grease"). A girl will studiously avoid associations with members of a crowd that is both proximal and permeable. How can one account for these apparently aberrant relational behaviors? A third principle, desirability, seems to be a key factor. Sometimes, affiliation with a certain crowd is so desirable that an adolescent is willing to ignore the great social distance between the crowd and his or her own group and risk rebuffs from the crowd's cliquish membership. Other times, membership is so undesirable that a teenager will pass up associations with a crowd that is open and close at hand.

To understand the role of desirability, it helps to bear in mind the tentativeness and uncertainty of crowd affiliation in adolescence and the power of social relationships to establish or validate one's location in the crowd system. Unlike other group memberships, crowd affiliation is not obvious, indisputable, and immutable. There is always the possibility that by changing one's attitudes, activities, or associates, one will be recognized as a member of a different crowd. Befriending, or being befriended by, members of another crowd is one of the primary mechanisms by which such shifts in crowd affiliation occur. In Eder's (1985) study, for example, the primary motive for normal girls' efforts to make friends with popular girls was to achieve recognition as a member of the popular crowd. A major reason that these overtures were usually rebuffed was popular girls' concerns that by associating with normals they would lose stature among fellow populars and be perceived as "dropping" or defecting into the normal crowd.

To be sure, desirability is related to status: The higher a crowd is on the status hierarchy, the more desirable it is (Coleman, 1961; Eckert, 1989; Eder, 1985). Eder (1985), for example, noted that although ignoring peers was a common feature of interpersonal relations in the junior high school she observed, she only heard complaints from girls about being ignored by members of the popular crowd—a subtle affirmation of the high-status popular crowd's desirability. Yet we sense there is more to the principle of desirability than status strivings. An additional dimension is suggested by ethnographic observations of how adolescents avoid associations with a certain crowd because of its *undesirability*. Fordham and Ogbu (1986) found that students in one inner-city high school, attended primarily by economically disadvantaged African-American youth, conscientiously avoided behavior and friendship patterns that would tie them to the "brainiacs." This crowd was derided by peers as weak and effeminate, as well as supercilious in their efforts to "act white." Although Fordham and Ogbu did not really entertain the concept of crowds in their work, their depiction of brainiacs suggested it was a low-status group. Thus students' efforts to avoid association with its members could be interpreted as more evidence that desirability simply reflects peer status.

We, however, have noted a similar disinclination to be labeled a brain among European-American students (Brown, 1989c). In such populations the brain crowd is *not* a low-status group; in fact, it consistently occupies a middle position in the peer status hierarchy (Brown, 1989b). What is more, the brains are commonly caricatured with a mixture of positive and negative traits (Brown et al., 1990). According to our conversations with adolescents, the reluctance to associate with brains (or to be labeled a brain) stems not from reservations about the brain crowd per se but from its close proximity to another crowd that *is* at or near the bottom of the peer status hierarchy: the nerds. More specifically, students worry that by being associated with the brain crowd they will be misperceived as nerds. Their worries seem well founded. In both two-dimensional renditions of the symbolic social map of crowds, brains and nerds emerge as fairly close neighbors (see Figure 6.1). In fact, in our pilot study with college students who were reflecting back on the crowd structure of their high school, the brains were rated as more similar to the nerds (6.82 on a scale from 1 to 10) than any other crowd. The pair's similarity rating was surpassed only by perceived similarity among populars, jocks, and partyers, and between nerds and loners. As a result, brains may scrupulously avoid contact with nerds for fear of being misperceived as part of a less desirable, neighboring crowd. What is more, many students may avoid contact with brains because of their close proximity to the low-status nerd crowd. Thus in this instance, associations with a very proximal and permeable crowd (nerds) is avoided (by brains) because of the undesirability of that crowd.

The more complicated dynamics of desirability are also illustrated in data we gathered from middle and high school students in two Midwest communities. A group of students who had been classified by peers as members of major crowds in their school was given a questionnaire that asked them to rate how willing they would be (from 1 = "no way" to 5 = "definitely willing") to be members of each major crowd in their school. The desirability of major crowd types varied somewhat by sex (girls were more willing than boys to be normals and populars but less willing to be jocks) and grade level (from Grades 7 through 12 the desirability of nerds traced a u-shaped pattern, whereas the desirability of populars and jocks followed an inverted u-shaped pattern). Of greater interest to this discussion, however, are how ratings of the desirability of a given crowd differed among respondents associated with various crowds. Table 6.3 summarizes these results.

Desirability did not follow the peer status hierarchy. Normals had the highest and druggies the lowest desirability ratings, despite the fact that both groups occupied middle positions in the status hierarchy. Also, with one exception (outcasts), a given crowd's highest rating came from the crowd's own members; this served to validate the classification of respondents into crowds because, by principles of cognitive dissonance theory (Festinger, 1957), one would expect that current members would have the strongest attraction to a given group. In some cases, the disaffection between crowds appears to be mutual: The brains were less willing to be druggies, and the druggies were less willing to be brains, than were members of any other crowd. In other cases, mutuality was lacking: The lowest desirability rating for populars came from druggies, but populars gave the druggie crowd a higher rating than any group except druggies themselves.

The curious relationship between brains and nerds is also reflected in these data. Loners and nerds are generally regarded as very similar, proximal crowds. Here, however, brains gave loners a higher rating than any other crowd, but they gave nerds the lowest desirability rating of any group.

The data in Table 6.3 are just a modest first step toward understanding how desirability of crowds affects adolescents' friendship choices, but they reaffirm that desirability does not operate in an absolute manner (e.g., according to a crowd's position on the peer status hierarchy). Instead, it varies according to an adolescent's own crowd affiliation. Matute-Bianchi (1986) found something similar in

Table 6.3 Differences Among Students Associated With Various
Crowds in the Mean Desirability Rating Given to Each Crowd
Type

	Mean Desirability Rating Given to:						
R's Crowd	Brains	Druggies	Jocks	Loners	Nerds	Normals	Populars
Total	3.01	1.44	3.22	1.91	1.52	3.46	3.45
Brains	3.80	1.09	3.27	2.13	1.15	3.41	3.50
Druggies	2.54	1.91	2.68	1.78	1.71	3.03	3.19
Jocks	3.21	1.26	4.23	1.77	1.51	3.55	3.59
Outcasts[a]	2.95	1.39	2.99	2.05	1.62	3.81	3.32
Populars	2.95	1.45	3.52	1.88	1.46	3.23	3.97
Others	2.80	1.41	3.02	1.88	1.49	3.52	3.30

NOTE: Ratings indicate how willing Rs would be to be a member of the crowd in question (1.00
= "no way!"; 5.00 = "very willing").
[a]Classifications of Rs into crowds are based on peer ratings. The outcasts includes Rs classified
as loners or nerds.

her study of various crowds of Mexican-descendent youth. For
those in the "Mexican-oriented" crowd, terms such as *cholo* and
homeboy were considered derogatory; friendships with peers who
personified these labels were scrupulously avoided. Chicano crowd
members, however, were happy to associate with cholos and home-
boys because they considered these terms to be complimentary.

Summary

Empirical evidence is too limited for researchers to stipulate in a clear
and concise fashion just how crowd affiliation channels adolescents
into or away from relationships with particular peers. The data are
clear enough to indicate that channeling does indeed occur, but at
this point still only suggestive of the complex interplay of factors
that account for channeling. In highlighting the effects of proximity,
permeability, and desirability, we hope to have provided some
direction for the more comprehensive studies in this area that can
be expected in the future. In such efforts it would be prudent for
investigators to be sensitive to contextual factors that can alter
channeling mechanisms.

For example, researchers have been intrigued but perplexed by
the developmental pattern in cross-race relationships from child-

hood through adolescence. Studies indicate that the incidence of cross-race relationships declines across the elementary school years, then remains low through the middle and high school years—even in the face of increasing diversity in friendship networks on other background variables, such as age and sex (Hallinan & Williams, 1989; Shrum, Cheek, & Hunter, 1988). We suspect that the coalescence of crowds at the outset of adolescence helps explain these patterns. In multiethnic schools, ethnicity can emerge as a major variable by which crowds are defined (Brown & Mounts, 1989; Ianni, 1989), accentuating differences between races through caricatures that seem to place each group at some distance from the other on adolescents' maps of symbolic social space. Normative pressures to affirm the primacy of one's own ethnic heritage, and normative sanctions in various minority groups against "acting white," may diminish the permeability between these crowds and those dominated by European Americans. They may also diminish the desirability of provisional identities dominated by another ethnic group, making individuals less receptive to friendship overtures from members of crowds that symbolize these "other-ethnic" identities. In such a scenario, proximity, permeability, and desirability could easily combine to solidify the disinclination toward cross-race friendships that develops through the elementary school years.

Yet such forces are undoubtedly contingent on characteristics of the immediate context. Rival gangs may heighten the social distance between ethnically defined crowds; joint participation in extracurricular activities may diminish it.

CROWDS AS CONTEXTS
FOR SOCIAL RELATIONSHIPS

The relational feature of crowds that has attracted the most attention from researchers—primarily ethnographers—is the manner in which crowds provide a context for peer interactions. Ethnographers are fond of contrasting the quality and character of relationships that are displayed by members of different crowds. They have considered relationships with adults (particularly school personnel) as well as peers, and relationships with members outside one's crowd as well as with fellow crowd members. Indeed, the implicit message of these studies often has been that it is through probing members' *relationships* that one can come to understand the motivations and behavior patterns that typify a crowd.

As we have already mentioned, many ethnographies have been organized to contrast two rival crowds in a school—usually a group high in peer status that draws from the ranks of the middle class or upper middle class in the community, and a lower status crowd that is often populated by students from lower socioeconomic strata. These studies have spanned more than a decade and have addressed adolescents in a variety of communities. The labels ascribed to the high- and low-status crowds are not consistent across studies. Yet descriptions of the quality of relationships within each crowd have been surprisingly similar.

Within the high-status group—populars, jocks, trendies, preppies, politicos, and so on—relationships are usually characterized as superficial and competitive, more "instrumental" than "expressive." Adolescents in this crowd often use friendships to establish and maintain their social position, which means that one must be prepared to cast aside friends (or be cast aside as a friend) when a better candidate comes along. Eder (1985) found populars to be rather wary in their friendships, especially with peers outside their own crowd. They were conscious of and concerned about how associations would affect their image and standing in the popular crowd. Lesko (1988) noted that populars were so status conscious that they even jockeyed for position within their own crowd, which made for unstable friendships. Our own interviews with adolescents reflect this instrumental orientation. One boy explained that to be popular one must "learn how to score points with every group." The objective is to develop a large network of friendships across crowds that can be exploited to extend or maintain one's status—an interesting twist on Granovetter's (1973) conception of the "strength of weak ties." Such an orientation discourages relationships based on loyalty, trust, and self-disclosure.

What accounts for the superficial nature of peer relationships among members of the elite crowd? Eckert (1989) linked it to their socialization into middle-class culture. Parents and teachers, she argued, had trained these youth to adopt a hierarchical, corporate orientation to relationships—an awareness of power and status differentials among interactants. One must be aware of who is above and below oneself in the corporate hierarchy and how these individuals should be treated to enhance one's own success in the corporate structure. In effect, interpersonal relationships were to be viewed as a social means to personal ends. Friendships were secondary to students' academic or extracurricular objectives, so it was reasonable to keep them superficial. Yet it is also possible that the superficiality that ethnographers have observed is a response to the intense relational pressures that confront youth in high-status crowds (Eder, 1985). Perhaps the only rational way—or at least the most expedient way—to cope with the steady barrage of friendship overtures is to settle for short-term, superficial relationships that allow one to be wary of one's partner's motives.

Whatever the reason is for the superficial quality of populars' peer relationships, they are a stark contrast to ethnographers' impressions of friendships among the "contrast" crowd—greasers, burnouts, headbangers, druggies, or whatever. In these crowd contexts, relationships are usually characterized by depth, stability, loyalty, commitment, and honesty. Lesko (1988) portrayed burnouts' peer relationships as blunt and undiplomatic, but egalitarian and enduring. These students did not cultivate a large network of friends and usually drew friendships exclusively from within their own crowd.

Eckert (1989), again, found an explanation for these friendship patterns in the class culture of the lower status crowd. The emotionally distant relationships that working-class parents cultivate with their teenage offspring encourage young people to rely more upon peers than family for emotional and instrumental support and gratification. As a result there is a strong sense of solidarity with peers and an inclination to pool resources within the friendship group. One's friendship network becomes a surrogate family, linking individuals across grade levels and even across schools to a much greater extent than is observed among members of high-status crowds. This familial organization of peer networks is reminiscent of relational styles in deviant gangs (e.g., Campbell, 1984), which, of course, draw a considerable portion of their membership from these lower status crowds.

In sum, ethnographers have argued that crowds at different ends of the status hierarchy provide sharply different contexts for peer relationships, contexts that tend to foster friendships of markedly different character. The different relational styles that typify youth in these two contexts are partly the result of the demands or expectations of their status position and partly the consequence of family interaction patterns or socialization strategies.

We suspect, however, that the different styles also stem from discrepancies in the level of social skills that characterize one crowd or another, discrepancies that may actually be nurtured by the structure of elementary school education. Schwartz (1981) observed classroom interactions in several elementary and junior high schools that "tracked" students into academic ability groups. She noted that students could be differentiated not only by their academic behaviors (their ability, concentration, motivation to do well in school, etc.) but also by their styles of interacting with peers. High-ability students had the capacity to remain "on task" and to appear to be attentive to and compliant with the teacher even when engaging in secretive interactions with peers. They also worked effectively in groups and carried their work-group identity into noninstructional time. Low-ability students, on the other hand, were openly noncompliant, if not hostile, to teachers and squandered much of the class time reserved for individual or group work by socializing with peers. During free time, they displayed an antagonistic interaction style with peers, in which they belittled classmates' academic abilities or efforts and exaggerated their own aptitude and skills (academic or otherwise). The separation of these students into ability groups served to isolate low ability students from peers who might otherwise have served as role models of more effective social skills. This helped reinforce the social interaction patterns that teachers obviously attended to in making tracking assignments. By adolescence, the different ability groups had developed incompatible interactional styles, creating as much of a social as an intellectual chasm between groups.

Although Schwartz did not follow her samples into adolescent crowds, the low ability students that she observed seem to have much in common with the greasers and burnouts that Eckert (1989) and others have described—except in terms of their social skills. Schwartz, however, provides a much less flattering portrait of this group than Eckert does.

Others who have observed the emergence of deviantly oriented peer groups in preadolescence have noted relational skill deficits among members of this group. Cairns et al. (1988), for example, found a tendency for aggressive youngsters who are low in peer status (classified as "rejected" by sociometric ratings) to coalesce into cliques that are characterized not only by deviant activity but also by unstable and antagonistic relationships among group members.

Giordano, Cernkovich, & Pugh (1986) found that both deviant and nondeviant youth manifest a number of positive features in their friendships, but these are complemented by negative characteristics only among deviant youth. Dishion (1993) confirmed this distinction, but also found that the positive features of deviant youths' friendships were often in the service of negative behaviors. That is, delinquents are most cordial and accepting, in conversations with their friend, when the friend is discussing deviant behavior! Discourse focusing on pro-social behaviors goes unrewarded by the dyad.

In any event, the roots of the contrasting interactional styles that characterize different adolescent crowds seem to lie in the social skills and interpersonal orientations that crowd members develop well before adolescence. This helps explain why some adolescents will actually "defect" from a particular crowd when its interactional norms become too onerous to the individual's own sensibilities. Kinney (1992) traced several such defectors in his ethnographic study. He describes one group of females who became disenchanted with the pressures of being a trendy—the need to "look perfect every day and have the right friends" (Kinney, 1992, p. 16). They were attracted to the headbangers (similar to Eckert's burnouts) because of the loyalty, intimacy, and trust that seemed to characterize their friendships. But they became disaffected by the crowd's negative attitudes toward outsiders and disaffection from academics. So, they developed a new crowd, based on the "hippie" culture of the 1960s, which featured a genuine openness to individuals in all crowds. In this context, and with support of the prototypic hippie identity ("do your own thing," etc.), they were able to nurture a different sort of friendship relationship than they found possible to pursue in other crowds in their school.

Certainly, these studies provide fascinating accounts of the different patterns of peer and adult relationships that characterize adolescents from different crowds. But our understanding of crowds as contexts for interpersonal relationships is constrained by the restricted range of crowds and relationships that they have considered. In this regard, three factors are especially worrisome. First, in most cases, investigators have focused on members of the most socially prominent crowd in a school (populars, jocks, etc.) and their alienated and deviantly oriented counterparts at the other end of the status hierarchy (burnouts, headbangers, greasers, and so on). In such studies, comparisons of crowds are confounded (often rather intentionally) by the distinctive class cultures from which the crowds draw, and this serves to obscure the contribution that crowds make to teenagers' interpersonal orientations. Like Larkin (1979) and Kinney (1992), investigators need to consider the broader array of crowds that exist in most schools. Researchers also need to venture into multiethnic schools to discover how crowd affiliation and ethnicity interact to shape the relational styles that adolescents display.

Second, researchers have relied upon relatively small samples of students—one or two prominent cliques from each crowd—to form their impression of the crowd. A well-established and widely recognized clique of populars may not truly reflect the norms and interactional styles of the broader membership of the popular crowd. We have found, for example, that students often view the popular crowd as consisting of two factions: "stuck-ups" or "snobs," who form the sort of tight-knit cliques on which ethnographies tend to focus, and the "nice populars," who remain friendly, approachable, and relatively humble for their high station. It would be wise, then, to complement ethnographic work with methodologies that can reach a broader representation of crowd members.

Finally, few investigators have ventured beyond the study of intracrowd friendships and what might be called intercrowd "acquaintanceships" (the treatment of outsiders); other types of relationships, most notably romantic relationships, have been virtually ignored. Because crowds have been proposed as the primary socializing agent of adolescent heterosexual relationships (Dunphy, 1963), this is a glaring deficiency for future research to address.

As a modest step in this direction, we offer findings from our own self-report survey of a sample of over 800 adolescents (Grades 7-12) in two midwestern communities. The sample was drawn primarily from five of the most prominent crowds in these schools: brains, druggies, jocks, populars, and outcasts (a combination of loners and nerds); participants' crowd affiliations were ascertained by peer ratings (Brown, 1989a). The survey included several basic questions about best friends and romantic (boyfriend/girlfriend) relationships. It also contained scales to assess the importance that respondents attached to socializing with peers, the amount of peer pressure they felt to socialize with peers, and the degree to which they actually engaged in socializing behaviors (going out with friends, conversing with friends on the phone, attending school dances and sporting events, etc.). Respondents also indicated, on a 4-point

Likert scale (1 = none; 4 = a great deal), how much time on weekends they spent with different categories of associates. Finally, they noted how often in the past month they had gone out with someone of the opposite sex, both in the company of other peers and just as a couple; scores on these items ranged from 1 (never) to 5 (almost every day). Whereas ethnographers have highlighted the different relational styles of groups that in our schools were called populars and druggies, we found these crowds to be strikingly similar on the questions we asked. We found the most consistent differences between populars and druggies on the one hand and brains and outcasts on the other. Crowd members did not differ significantly in whether they had a best friend (80% to 90% of each crowd did) or how long this person had been their best friend (from 3 to 3.5 years), but there were significant differences in time spent with one's best friend. The average for druggies (13 hours per week) was over 50% higher than that for brains (8 hours); the other groups averaged between 9.5 and 11 hours per week.

The contrast was even sharper with regard to romantic relationships (see Table 6.4). Nearly two thirds of the druggies claimed to have a boyfriend or girlfriend at the time of the survey, compared to just over one quarter of the brains. Among those with a boyfriend or girlfriend, the relationship had lasted twice as long for druggies as for brains, and occupied considerably more of druggies' free time each week. The incidence of dating, whether with a group of peers or just as a couple, was considerably higher for among druggies than brains. On all of these items, responses of brains and outcasts did not differ significantly, nor did the responses of druggies and populars. The only indications of superficiality in the relationships of elites was in the slightly (but nonsignificantly) lower duration of best friendships among jocks and populars (just over 3 years, compared to at least 3⅓ years in other crowds).

These contrasts carried over to respondents' allocation of time among social network members on weekends (Table 6.5). Brains and outcasts appeared to balance their time more evenly between family and peers (lovers and close friends), whereas druggies and populars tipped the balance more clearly in favor of peers. In the scale scores, although brains accorded comparatively low importance to peer interactions and reported a low incidence of socializing with peers, the pressure they felt from friends to spend time with peers was relatively high. On these scales, outcasts reflected their image as social isolates,

Table 6.4   Crowd Differences in Self-Reported Characteristics of
                 Romantic Relationships

Characteristic	Brains	Druggies	Jocks	Outcasts	Populars	Others
% who have had a boy/ girlfriend this year	58	94	84	60	88	73
% who currently have a boy/girlfriend	28	64	46	33	55	40
Duration of relationship (in months)	5	10	7	6	8	5
Hours per week spent with boy/girlfriend	8.85	13.64	9.23	11.03	13.58	10.78
Frequency of dating:						
with a group	1.86	2.97	2.57	1.97	2.90	2.44
just as a couple	1.63	2.89	2.36	1.91	2.49	2.17

reporting comparatively little pressure from friends to socialize
with peers and a lower incidence of peer social activities than other
groups. It also appeared as if jocks were more oriented toward group
relationships than other crowds. Unlike other respondents with a boyfriend or girlfriend, jocks devoted almost as much time on weekends to
their friendship group as their romantic relationship.

Of course, these data lack the depth of insight that is provided by
ethnographic work. Yet they broaden the perspective of ethnographies
to indicate that each crowd has a distinct profile of characteristics
in peer relationships. These distinctions undoubtedly affect the ease
with which adolescents can move among crowds. A teenager whose
lack of interest in romantic relationships caused little concern among
fellow brains would probably feel very uncomfortable amidst the more
intense dating pressures of the druggies or populars. A loner, accustomed to focusing interaction on a few close friends, might find
membership in the jock crowd, with its emphasis on group interactions, to be a major adjustment. If future studies can integrate the more
qualitative relational focus of ethnography with the broader sampling
of survey research, they can provide a more comprehensive portrait of
the distinctive contexts for social relationships that are inherent in
the peer group system within a particular community.

In sum, we are beginning to understand how adolescent crowds
nurture different patterns of social relationships among their members.

Table 6.5 Crowd Differences in Allocation of Weekend Time and Peer Socializing Scale Scores

Item or Scale Score	Brains	Druggies	Jocks	Outcasts	Populars	Others
Time on weekend spent with:						
Closest friends	2.78	3.09	2.91	2.61	2.97	2.78
Boyfriend/girlfriend	2.73	3.20	2.82	2.81	3.01	2.85
Friendship group	2.20	2.66	2.71	2.21	2.67	2.31
Peer crowd	1.64	2.30	1.99	1.76	2.20	1.95
Family members	2.71	2.22	2.46	2.63	2.36	2.50
Alone	2.38	2.03	2.11	2.29	2.03	2.20
Scale scores:						
Importance of socializing	3.61	4.04	3.84	3.70	3.95	3.81
Peer pressure to socialize	2.10	1.85	2.10	1.87	2.00	1.93
Peer socializing behavior	2.64	3.06	3.04	2.58	3.16	2.84

NOTE: Scores for items reflecting time on weekends spent with various portions of the social network ranged from 1.00 ("none") to 4.00 ("a whole lot"). Scale scores ranged from 1.00 ("not at all important") to 5.00 ("extremely important") for the importance of socializing with peers, 1.00 ("no pressure from friends") to 4.00 ("strong pressure") for peer pressure, and 1.00 ("never") to 5.00 ("almost every day") for peer socializing behavior.

These differences are not simply a function of crowd norms, but a consequence of a variety of factors: the level of social skills and socializing interests of crowd members, the expectations and orientations of other members of their social network (especially family members), the attractiveness of crowd members as partners in relationships, and so on. We have barely begun to explore the factors that shape the nature of social relationships in the diverse array of crowds that comprise adolescents' social system. It is clear, however, that crowd affiliation is a significant factor in the quality of adolescents' social relationships. It would be difficult to fully appreciate the nature of adolescents' relationships with peers and adults without taking their crowd affiliation into consideration.

THE DYNAMIC NATURE OF CROWDS

One of the special challenges for those who study adolescent crowds is that they are chasing a moving target. Crowds are a dynamic, not a stable and static feature of adolescence. The structure of the crowd system and an individual's place within it change from one year to the next, especially, it seems, when individuals make the transition from one school to another. Few investigators have taken a dynamic perspective on crowds; fewer still have attempted longitudinal studies. Yet the data from these few, along with findings from cross-sectional and retrospective analyses, are sufficient to give us some understanding of the dynamic features of crowds. In particular, four such features should be borne in mind by those attempting a relational analysis of adolescent crowds.

First, *peer group structures change* across adolescence. One of us (Kinney, 1993), for example, discovered a marked transformation in the crowd structure between middle school and high school in one midwestern community. From a two-crowd system in middle school (the populars and the dweebs), the structure blossomed into a more diverse array of crowds in high school: normals, punkers, headbangers, grits, and so on. This permitted those who had not "made it" into the popular crowd in early adolescence to find a more self-enhancing crowd identification than their default middle school classification as dweebs. One consequence of the broadening array of crowds was that over time the popular crowd lost exclusive rights to the top rung of the status hierarchy. By senior year, the status differential between populars, normals, and headbangers was barely noticeable (see Figure 6.2).

There are too few studies of the structure of crowds across middle school and high school to determine how common this sort of diversification really is. In other middle schools we have studied, students seem to be aware of a more diverse set of crowds. Yet we have also found that the number of crowds students name increases across adolescence. Also, the proportion of crowds named that fit into what might be called "major" crowds (groups that are common to a number of studies: populars, jocks, brains, drug-oriented youth, and so on) peaks around eighth or ninth grade, the point of transition between junior and senior high school (Brown & Clasen, 1986). Thus there seem to be changes across adolescence in the number and types of crowds that are available to adolescence—or at least in the salience of these groups in the minds of teenagers—as well as in the status ranking of crowds.

A second dynamic feature that investigators have described involves *changes in relational characteristics* of crowds. We have already noted shifts in the status hierarchy (Brown & Clasen, 1986; Kinney,

1993). Yet even during middle school, when populars retain undisputed possession of top rung on the status ladder, individuals' feelings toward and treatment of the populars seems to change (Eder, 1985; Schofield, 1981). Envy and ingratiation turn to resentment and avoidance as young people become disenchanted with populars' snobbery and cliquishness.

Several researchers have noted an increase with age in the permeability of crowds. As one of Larkin's (1979) high school respondents explained:

> It's not so tight that you feel uncomfortable when you go into somebody else's group if you know someone there. You know, there are floaters—people who go around to just any particular group they feel like that particular day. And you just go in and you start talking and it doesn't matter. Nobody really cares. I think that's really good. It's quite an improvement over junior high. (p. 88)

Gavin and Furman (1989), who examined students' perceptions of same-sex cliques between Grades 7 and 12, attributed this to the fact that, with age, adolescents tended to treat "out-group" members in a more positive fashion. This is also reflected in sociometric data suggesting that the tightly bounded cliques of early adolescence give way to a looser pattern of interaction, with more individuals acting as "liaisons" between several friendship groups (Shrum & Cheek, 1987). Kinney (1992), however, cautioned that the increasing permeability may be selective; the boundaries between certain crowds (e.g., populars and headbangers in his study) may start to diminish while the boundaries between other crowds (e.g., punkers and "grits") remain strong.

These structural and relational changes in the crowd system are accompanied by developmental changes in adolescents' orientations toward crowds. One of these (the third dynamic feature) is a *shift in the salience of crowd affiliation*. Both Coleman (1974) and Brown, Eicher and Petrie (1986) found an age-related decline in the importance of belonging to a crowd. According to Brown et al. (1986), early adolescents found reassurance in a crowd's norms and conformity demands, whereas older adolescents felt that crowds frustrated their efforts to express their own personal attitudes and interests. Such a drive toward individuality helps explain the age-related decline in conformity pressures from peers that Clasen and Brown (1985) reported.

Finally, *crowd affiliation itself changes*, that is, it appears as if individuals do not remain attached to the same crowd across adolescence. In one recent longitudinal study (Brown, Freeman, Huang, & Mounts, 1992), over half of a sample of 7th- through 12th-graders changed the crowd with which they claimed affiliation over a two-year period. Interestingly, the likelihood of changing crowds not only varied substantially by initial crowd affiliation but also diminished steadily across grade levels. Perhaps this was because, as crowd boundaries became more permeable, older youth felt less of a need to change affiliations in order to broaden their circle of associates or express an identity that commingled the norms of several crowds.

Developmental analyses are still very much the exception rather than the rule in studies of adolescent peer groups. Yet the need to approach relational features of crowds from a developmental perspective is absolutely clear. Generalizing to adolescence as a whole on the basis of a study of middle school students or, worse yet, high school seniors, is simply not tenable. What is more, the dynamic nature of crowd structures and crowd affiliations is one of the strongest indicators of the relational nature of adolescent peer groups. Just as dyadic relationships evolve over time, so does the adolescent crowd system.

CONCLUSIONS

Some people regard adolescent crowds as a curiously amusing feature of the rather obscure world of American teenagers. Others consider them to be a potent and dangerous force, mandating conformity to teen culture at a time when individuals should be striving for an autonomous identity and integration into adult society. From our perspective, crowds are an important and usually very effective mechanism by which teenagers structure social interactions and forge meaningful social relationships within the new and sometimes confusing social system of adolescence. There are, we believe, four important lessons to be learned from the review that we have undertaken in this chapter.

First, *crowds are an inherently relational construct*. In defining crowds as reputation- rather than interaction-based entities, we seem to be distancing ourselves from a relational perspective. We argue that crowds categorize adolescents by *individual* interests, abilities, attitudes, or ethnic heritage—*not* by social interaction patterns. Yet the label applied to a crowd and the caricatures that accompany it take on meaning only when compared to another crowd. A jock or a druggie or a Korean is not someone with a rigid and absolute set of characteristics, but someone with more of this and less of that than members of some other crowd. What is more, adolescents come to understand crowds through social interaction; crowd images are crafted through mutual consensus, not individual insights. As Lesko (1988, p. 74) has remarked, "Through groups, that is, through associations with people similar to oneself and those who are different, personal and social identities are wrestled with and visualized." Adolescents perceive crowds in relational terms, so for researchers and practitioners to understand the function of crowds, a relational perspective must be adopted.

This brings us to the second lesson, that *adolescents use crowds to construct a symbolic road map of prototypic peer relationships.* Most teenagers recognize the limitations of responding to peers simply as crowd caricatures rather than as unique individuals. Yet they find that the crowd system gives them a language by which to understand and express the complicated and sometimes confusing patterns of social relationships with peers (Schwartz & Merten, 1967; Varenne, 1982). Crowds create abstract models of peer relationships that can provide order and predictability—and therefore a sense of personal control—to actual interactions with friends, acquaintances, and strangers. The symbolic road map of crowds stipulates the ease or difficulty of interacting with certain peers, and what is risked, gained, or lost by nurturing particular peer relationships. These are valuable commodities among individuals whose world is filled with uncertainties. Thus whereas adults may decry the tendency of crowds to compel conformity, reinforce prejudices, and restrict exploration in social interaction patterns, teenagers seem to find that crowds nurture social skills and foster satisfying peer relationships.

A third lesson is that, despite their abstract nature, crowds do affect teenagers' actual social relationships. That is, *a teenager's crowd affiliation and understanding of the crowd system affect the choice of peer associates and the features of peer relationships.* Particularly in the early adolescent years, one's allegiance to or interest in a particular crowd and one's awareness of the social distance among crowds effectively channel a teenager toward particular peers and away from others as candidates for friendship and romance. Teenagers use their symbolic road map of crowds not only to understand peer relationships in general, but also to help decide which peers to pursue for relationships, and which offers of affiliation to accept or ignore. We pointed to proximity, permeability, and desirability as three factors by which adolescents use the crowd system to make choices about peer associates.

What is more, crowd affiliation affects the quality or character of social relationships. The distinguishing features of friendship and romance—and even relationships with adults—are not consistent across adolescents, but contingent upon the norms and social pressures within their crowd. Friendships may be superficial or intense and enduring. Romantic attachments may be instrumental or altruistic. Such variability can be explained, in large measure, by the context that one's crowd affiliation(s) supplies for social relationships.

A final lesson is that crowds are not universal and enduring features of adolescents. Rather, *the crowd system is a dynamic phenomenon that is sensitive to contextual features of a social milieu.* The structure and interrelationships of crowds can change dramatically across the adolescent years. So, too, can a particular teenager's pattern of affiliation with crowds. For example, an adolescent may negotiate middle school as a dedicated member of the populars, become disaffected in early high school and transfer affiliation to the druggies, then drift toward the end of high school into marginal memberships with several groups. The forces that prompt a teenager to remain loyal to a particular crowd or to be constantly seeking new affiliations are not well understood. Yet the flexibility of crowd affiliation and the developmental nature of crowd structure are undoubtedly essential to the capacity of crowds to nurture teenagers' social skills and social relationships (see, e.g., Dunphy, 1963).

By the same token, crowds are sensitive to their social and historical milieu. Coleman (1961) found substantial variation among communities in the capacity of academic achievement to propel someone into or away from membership in the popular crowd. Larkin (1979) reported a remarkable transformation in the character of the politicos that corresponded to historical shifts in the American political climate across a 10-year period. Brown and Mounts (1989) discovered significant differences across communities in adolescents' descriptions of the number, types, and size of crowds in their school. There are even contexts in which adolescent crowds simply do not exist: small, stable, rural populations, for example, in which classmates have grown up together and know each other so well that crowds are unnecessary. Certainly, such contextual variation should make researchers cautious about generalizing from observations of crowds in one particular school or community, just as the developmental nature of crowds limits generalizations from studies of one age group.

For most teenagers, crowds are an important component of negotiating the social world of adolescence. They transform strangers and acquaintances into recognizable types. They channel individuals toward engaging certain peers in social relationships and not others. They provide a context that influences the quality and character of these relationships. They change developmentally and respond to contextual cues in ways that, hopefully, better nurture teenagers' relational skills and interpersonal experiences. Approaching crowds from this relational perspective will not only help researchers to understand the place of crowds in adolescent development, but also provide insights about the character of young people's social relationships.

NOTES

1. We use the term *caricature* because it brings to mind a portrait that exaggerates prominent characteristics in a humorous if not unflattering way. This fits the typical depiction of crowds other than one's own, based on social identity theory principles that are explained in the next paragraph. Admittedly, however, portrayals of one's own crowd are likely to exaggerate characteristics in a flattering way. Still, caricature seems more descriptive than alternatives such as *characterization*, which implies a more objective portrayal, or *stereotype*, which is commonly understood as a naive or simplistic overgeneralization.

2. Some may suspect that the large number of friendship overtures that popular crowd members receive is a function of their superior social skills rather than their location in a particular crowd. This would be an appealing alternative explanation for what Eder observed, were it not for evidence (detailed later) that the quality of popular girls' friendships was not necessarily superlative.

REFERENCES

Berger, P., & Luckman, T. (1967). *The social construction of reality*. Garden City, NY: Doubleday.

Blumer, H. (1969). *Social interactionism: Perspective and method*. Englewood Cliffs, NJ: Prentice Hall.

Brown, B. B. (1989a). *Social type rating manual*. Madison, WI: University of Wisconsin-Madison, National Center on Effective Secondary Schools.

Brown, B. B. (1989b, March). Can nerds and druggies be friends?: Mapping "social distance" between adolescent peer groups. In G. Ladd (Chair), *Peer relationships and school adjustment*. Symposium presented at the annual meetings of the American Educational Research Association, San Francisco.

Brown, B. B. (1989c, March). Skirting the "brain-nerd" connection": How high achievers save face among peers. In J. Braddock (Chair), *The ecology of student achievement in high schools: Noninstructional influences*. Symposium presented at the annual meetings of the American Educational Research Association, San Francisco.

Brown, B. B. (1990). Peer groups and peer cultures. In S. S. Feldman and G. R. Elliott (Eds.), *At the threshold: The developing adolescent* (pp. 171-196). Cambridge, MA: Harvard University Press.

Brown, B. B., & Clasen, D. R. (1986, March). *Developmental changes in adolescents' conceptions of peer groups*. Paper presented at the biennial meetings of the Society for Research in Adolescence, Madison, WI.

Brown, B. B., Eicher, S. A., & Petrie, S. (1986). The importance of peer group ("crowd") affiliation in adolescence. *Journal of Adolescence, 9*, 73-96.

Brown, B. B., Freeman, H., Huang, B. H., & Mounts, N. S. (1992, March). *"Crowd hopping": Incidents, correlates, and consequences of change in crowd affiliation during adolescence*. Paper presented at the biennial meeting of the Society for Research in Adolescence, Washington, DC.

Brown, B. B., Lohr, M. J., & Trujillo, C. M. (1990). Multiple crowds and multiple lifestyles: Adolescents' perceptions of peer group characteristics. In R. E. Muss (Ed.), *Adolescent behavior and society: A book of readings* (pp. 30-36). New York: Random House.

Brown, B. B., & Mounts, N. (1989, April). *Peer group structures in single versus multi-ethnic high schools*. Paper presented at the biennial meetings of the Society for Research in Child Development, Kansas City.

Buff, S. A. (1970). Greasers, dupers, and hippies: Three responses to the adult world. In L. Howe (Ed.), *The white majority* (pp. 60-77). New York: Random House.

Cairns, R. B., Cairns, B. D., Neckerman, H. J., Gest, S. D., & Gariepy, J. L. (1988). Social networks and aggressive behavior: Peer support or peer rejection? *Developmental Psychology, 24*, 815-823.

Campbell, A. (1984). *The girls in the gang*. New York: Basil Blackwell.

Clasen, D. R., & Brown, B. B. (1985). The multidimensionality of peer pressure in adolescence. *Journal of Youth and Adolescence, 14*, 451-468.

Coleman, J. C. (1974). *Relationships in adolescence*. Boston: Routledge & Kegan Paul.

Coleman, J. S. (1961). *The adolescent society*. New York: Free Press.

Cusick, P. A. (1973). *Inside high school*. New York: Holt, Rinehart & Winston.

DesChamps, J-C. (1982). Social identity and relations of power between groups. In H. Tajfel (Ed.), *Social identity and intergroup relations* (pp. 85-98). Cambridge, UK: Cambridge University Press.

Dishion, T. J. (1993, March). Boys' close friendships and early adolescent problem behavior: Geographic and parenting contexts. In L. Steinberg (Chair), *Interactive influences of parents and peers on adolescent misbehavior*. Symposium conducted at the biennial meetings of the Society for Research in Child Development, New Orleans.

Dunphy, D. (1963). The social structure of urban adolescent peer groups. *Sociometry, 26,* 230-246.

Eckert, P. (1989). *Jocks and burnouts: Social categories and identity in the high school.* New York: Teachers College Press.

Eder, D. (1985). The cycle of popularity: Interpersonal relations among female adolescents. *Sociology of Education, 58,* 154-165.

Festinger, L. (1957). *A theory of cognitive dissonance.* Evanston, IL: Row Peterson.

Fordham, S., & Ogbu, J. U. (1986). Black students' school success: Coping with the burden of "acting white." *Urban Review, 18,* 176-206.

Gavin, L. A., & Furman, W. (1989). Age differences in adolescents' perceptions of their peer groups. *Developmental Psychology, 25,* 827-834.

Gergen, K. (1984). Theory of the self: Impasse and evolution. *Advances in Experimental Social Psychology, 17,* 49-115.

Giordano, P. C., Cernkovich, S. A., & Pugh, M. D. (1986). Friendships and delinquency. *American Journal of Sociology, 91,* 1170-1202.

Granovetter, M. (1973). The strength of weak ties. *American Journal of Sociology, 78,* 1360-1381.

Hallinan, M. T., & Williams, R. A. (1989). Interracial friendship choices in secondary schools. *American Sociological Review, 54,* 67-78.

Hartup, W. W. (1983). Peer relations. In P. H. Mussen (Ed.), *Handbook of child psychology: Vol 4. Socialization, personality and social development* (pp. 103-196). New York: John Wiley.

Hollingshead, A. B. (1949). *Elmtown's youth.* New York: John Wiley.

Ianni, F. A. J. (1989). *The search for structure.* New York: Free Press.

Kinney, D. A. (1992, March). Coming together and going your own way: Delineating diversity and change in adolescent crowd associations. In B. Brown (Chair), *Stability and change in adolescent peer relations: Characteristics and consequences.* Symposium conducted at the biennial meetings of the Society for Research in Adolescence, Washington, DC.

Kinney, D. A. (1993). From "nerds" to "normals": Adolescent identity recovery within a changing social system. *Sociology of Education, 66,* 21-40.

Larkin, R. W. (1979). *Suburban youth in cultural crisis.* New York: Oxford University Press.

Lesko, N. (1988). *Symbolizing society: Stories, rites, and structure in a Catholic high school.* Philadelphia: Falmer.

Matute-Bianchi, M. E. (1986). Ethnic identities and patterns of school success and failure among Mexican-descent and Japanese-American students in a California high school: An ethnographic analysis. *American Journal of Education, 95,* 233-255.

Mory, M. S. (1992, March). *"Love the ones you're with: Conflict and consensus in adolescent peer group stereotypes.* Paper presented at the biennial meetings of the Society for Research on Adolescence, Washington, DC.

Newcomb, T. (1961). *The acquaintance process.* New York: Holt, Rinehart & Winston.

Priest, R., & Sawyer, J. (1967). Proximity and peership: Bases of balance in interpersonal attraction. *American Journal of Sociology, 72,* 633-649.

Rigsby, L. C., & McDill, E. L. (1975). Value orientations of high school students. In H. R. Stub (Ed.), *The sociology of education: A sourcebook* (pp. 53-75). Homewood, IL: Dorsey.

Schofield, J. W. (1981). *Black and white in school: Trust, tension, or tolerance?* New York: Praeger.

Schwartz, F. (1981). Supporting or subverting learning: Peer group patterns in four tracked schools. *Anthropology and Education Quarterly, 12,* 99-121.

Schwartz, G., & Merten, D. (1967). The language of adolescence: An anthropological approach to youth culture. *American Journal of Sociology, 72,* 453-468.

Schwendinger, H., & Schwendinger, J. S. (1985). *Adolescent subcultures and delinquency.* New York: Praeger.

Sherif, M., Harvey, O. J., White, B.J., Hood, W. R., & Sherif, C. R. (1961). *Intergroup conflict and cooperation: The Robber's Cave experiment.* Norman, OK: University of Oklahoma, Institute of Group Relations.

Shrum, W., & Cheek, N. H. (1987). Social structure during the school years: Onset of the degrouping process. *American Sociological Review, 52,* 218-223.

Shrum, W., Cheek, N. H., & Hunter, S. M. (1988). Friendship in school: Gender and racial homophily. *Sociology of Education, 61,* 227-239.

Tajfel, H. (1972). La categorization sociale. In S. Moscovici (Ed.), *Introduction a la psychologie sociale* (Vol. 1, pp. 272-302). Paris: Larousse.

Tajfel, H. (1981). *Human groups and social categories: Studies in social psychology.* Cambridge, UK: Cambridge University Press.

Varenne, H. (1982). Jocks and freaks: The symbolic structure of the expression of social interaction among American senior high school students. In G. Spindler (Ed.), *Doing the ethnography of schooling* (pp. 213-235). New York: Holt, Rinehart & Winston.

Willis, P. (1977). *Learning to labor.* London: Columbia University Press.

Youniss, J. (1980). *Parents and peers in social development.* Chicago: University of Chicago Press.

7. Romantic Views: Toward a Theory of Adolescent Romantic Relationships

Wyndol Furman
University of Denver

Elizabeth A. Wehner
University of Denver

> ROMEO: But soft, what light through yonder window breaks?
> It is the east, and Juliet is the sun.
> Arise, fair sun, and kill the envious moon,
> who is already sick and pale with grief
> that thou, her maid, art far more fair than she.
> Be not her maid, since she is envious.
> Her vestal livery is but sick and green,
> And none but fools do wear it; cast it off.
> It is my lady! O, it is my love!
> O that she knew she were!
>
> *Romeo and Juliet*, Act II, Scene 2

Even before the time of Shakespeare, playwrights and poets wrote of adolescent love. Today many of us can still remember the name of our first boyfriend or girlfriend. Although we may now feel that these early romantic relationships were merely crushes, they were central in our social lives and emotional experiences as adolescents. For example, the quality of romantic relationships has been found to be associated with socioemotional adjustment during times of stress and nonstress (Furman, 1987). Moreover, these early romantic experiences are believed to play a pivotal role in both identity and intimacy development (Erikson, 1968) and may

AUTHORS' NOTE: Portions of this chapter were presented at the meetings of the Society for Research in Adolescence, Washington, DC, March 1992. Appreciation is expressed to James P. Connell, Candice Feiring, and William Graziano for their comments on earlier drafts.

shape the course of subsequent romantic relationships and marriages in adulthood (Erikson, 1968; Sullivan, 1953). Certainly, the rising problems of teenage pregnancy, date rape, sexually transmitted diseases, and AIDS underscore the importance of understanding early romance and sexual behavior. Despite the seeming importance of romantic life in early and middle adolescence, scientific research on the topic is surprisingly limited. The extant work primarily consists of demographic studies of dating patterns—many done a decade or two ago (e.g., Hansen, 1977; Wright, 1982). Surprisingly little research exists on the characteristics or development of romantic relationships during early and middle adolescence (vs. late adolescence or adulthood). Some investigators have studied opposite-sex friendships (Blyth, Hill, & Thiel, 1982; Sharabany, Gershoni, & Hoffman, 1981), but they did not distinguish between platonic and romantic ones. Similarly, other investigators have used the quality of romantic relationships as one of several indices of intimacy or identity status, but they did not focus on the romantic relationship per se (Orlofsky, Marcia, & Lesser, 1973; Paul & White, 1990).

Certainly, much important work has been done recently on adolescents' sexual behavior (see Miller & Moore, 1990), but this work cannot substitute for research on romantic relationships. Some adolescents are not sexually active, and for those who are, their relationships involve more than sex. Certainly, parents of adolescents hope so! Thus we know how often different adolescents date and have intercourse, but we don't know what their encounters or relationships are like.

Particularly absent is a theoretical framework to guide research on adolescent romantic relationships. In this paper we outline a behavioral systems conceptualization of romantic relationships that we believe is an important step toward such a goal. Our focus is on heterosexual relationships, but we believe that most of the ideas are applicable to gay and lesbian relationships as well.

ROMANTIC ATTACHMENT THEORY

Our theoretical framework was strongly influenced by attachment conceptualizations of love relationships (Ainsworth, 1989; Shaver & Hazan, 1988). An important shift in the nature of the attachment relationship to the parent is hypothesized to take place in adolescence, due to the hormonal changes brought on by puberty (Ainsworth, 1989). These changes push the adolescent to search for a peer, usually of the opposite sex, with whom to establish a relationship. This partner is assumed to become the new principal attachment figure, replacing the parental attachment figure as uppermost in the attachment hierarchy. Drawing from evolutionary theory, Shaver and Hazan viewed romantic love as an adaptive biological process that facilitates attachment between adult sexual partners, resulting in parenthood and reliable care of the infant (Shaver & Hazan, 1988; Shaver, Hazan, & Bradshaw, 1988). They recognized, however, that adult romantic attachments differ from infant attachments. First, adult romantic attachments are reciprocal, with each partner being attached to the other and serving as an attachment figure to the other. Second, they involve sex. To accommodate these features, Shaver and Hazan hypothesized that romantic love involves the integration of the attachment, caregiving, and sexual/reproductive behavioral systems.

Following Bowlby (1979), Shaver and Hazan argue that there is a strong causal relation between an individual's experience with parents and later capacity to make affectional bonds. They argue that individual differences in how romantic love is experienced and manifested are due to differences in past attachment history. In particular, they propose that three main types of love relationships exist that parallel the three main infant attachment classifications: secure, ambivalent, and avoidant.

More recently, Bartholomew (1990) extended Shaver and Hazan's (1988) and Main, Kaplan, and Cassidy's (1985) ideas and proposed four adult romantic attachment types. She suggested that people develop positive or negative models of others and positive or negative models of themselves. Those with positive models of others and of themselves are secure individuals who are comfortable with intimacy and autonomy. Those with positive models of others but negative models of themselves are described as preoccupied, a category equivalent to Hazan and Shaver's ambivalent. Those with positive models of themselves and negative models of others are called dismissing individuals in that they minimize the importance of needing others. Finally, fearful individuals have negative models of both themselves and others and hence avoid intimacy. Bartholomew suggested that the fearful category was similar to

Shaver and Hazan's avoidant group, whereas the dismissing category was similar to Main et al.'s dismissing group.

Romantic attachment researchers believe that the attachment system lays the foundation for the caretaking and reproductive systems because it is the first socially relevant system to emerge (Shaver & Hazan, 1988). Thus variation in the functioning of the caregiving and reproductive systems can be attributed to variation in the attachment system. The mechanisms for the continuity of relationship character across relationships are the internal working models of self, other, and relationships built up during childhood.

This approach has a number of conceptually appealing features. First, romantic relationships are placed within an evolutionary perspective so that the adaptive nature of the relationships can be understood. Second, when conceptualized as attachments, love relationships can be classified and the origins of differences in love relationships explained. Third, this approach accommodates both healthy and unhealthy love relationships in a single conceptual framework. The attachment approach has received some encouraging empirical support (Bartholomew, 1991; Brennan, Shaver, & Tobey, 1991; Collins & Read, 1990; Feeney & Noller, 1990; Hazan & Shaver, 1987; Simpson, 1990), but is limited in several respects.

First, although both are appealing, traditional attachment theory and adult romantic attachment theory are not identical, conceptually or empirically. For example, dismissing or avoidant individuals were originally conceptualized as individuals who have insecure, negative models of self, but who may present themselves positively as a defensive strategy (Cassidy & Kobak, 1988; Main et al., 1985). Bartholomew (1990), however, argues that dismissing individuals have positive models of self. Moreover, Bowlby would expect a high degree of concordance between models of self and models of others, but Bartholomew's framework suggests that the two types of models are quite distinct from one another, if not oppositional. In fact, approximately one third of the individuals in a college sample had discrepant self and other models on a self-report measure of Bartholomew's classification system (Brennan et al., 1991). Similarly, sex differences are not commonly found in infant attachment types, but they are found with Bartholomew's system (Brennan et al., 1991). Finally, the traditional attachment classifications and adult romantic attachment classifications do not correspond completely. For example, Brennan et al. (1991) suggested that fearfuls may be conceptually akin to Main's disorganized "D" category, but the percentages of such individuals (32% male, 43% female) seem too high for this to be the case. Moreover, Bartholomew's fearful individuals have organized working models in which the self and others are seen negatively, whereas "D" infants have disorganized attachment strategies that may stem from frightened or frightening parental behavior (Main & Hesse, 1990). Similarly, the "U" or unresolved category derived from coding the Adult Attachment Interview reflects unresolved, disorganized, or disoriented states of mind with respect to experiences of loss or trauma (Main, DeMoss, & Hesse, 1989). Thus as these examples illustrate, traditional attachment theory and romantic attachment theory cannot be completely equated.

Second, the comparative literature suggests that the attachment system is not the sole basis for adult pair bonding (MacDonald, 1992). Attachment is ubiquitous in primates, but only 17% of these species have monogamous pair bonding arrangements (Hardy, 1981). Promiscuity or polygamy are more common reproductive strategies than monogamy.

A third limitation is that romantic attachment theory has not fully taken into account the fact that romantic relationships are egalitarian ones that originally develop within the context of the peer group. Characteristics such as collaboration, affiliation, and symmetrical interchanges are central features of romantic relationships that cannot be readily explained in terms of attachment and caretaking. Even when attachment and caretaking are reciprocated between individuals, the interactions that reflect the activation of these systems are asymmetrical in nature; that is, in most specific interactions, one person serves as the caretaker or secure base for the other person who is seeking care. At other times the roles may be reversed, but the particular interaction will still be asymmetrical.

In a related vein, attachment theorists clearly recognize the significance of other relationships to development (Sroufe, 1988), but they have only focused on the continuity between parent-child relationships and love relationships and have not given much attention to the potential impact that friendships or other peer relationships may have on the development of romantic relationships. Ainsworth (1989) has stated that positive relationships with peers are evolutionarily adaptive, functioning to provide members of the social system with additional protection and increasing the success of some endeavors like hunting, but it appears that she and other attachment theorists believe that the individual's capacity to form intimate relationships is primarily affected by the parent-child attachment relationship. We believe that parent-child relationships lay the basic foundation for the ability to be close to and intimate with another, but we will argue that peer relationships, particularly friendships, also make a critical contribution. Specifically in friendships, children develop the ability to be intimate in a reciprocal and mutual fashion.

Finally, adult love relationships are the endpoint of a developmental process. Full-blown attachments to romantic partners do not just appear overnight. Unfortunately, little has been said about how particular relationships may develop into attachment bonds or how past romantic experiences in adolescence or early adulthood may affect the development of such bonds. As Waters, Kondo-Ikemura, Posada, and Richters (1991) so aptly put it, we have "a theory of infant attachment, a theory of adult attachment, and a great deal in between left to the imagination" (p. 227). What is needed is a broader theoretical perspective on social development that takes into account the developmental tasks of childhood and their impact on development. Wedding Sullivan's (1953) theory of social-personality development with attachment theory provides such a theoretical framework.

SULLIVAN'S THEORY

Basic to Sullivan's (1953) theory is the notion of social needs. He felt there were five basic social needs that motivate people to bring about certain types of interpersonal situations that once obtained, decrease unpleasant affective tensions and promote positive emotional states. These needs are (a) tenderness, (b) companionship, (c) acceptance, (d) intimacy, and (e) sexuality. According to Sullivan, development progresses through six stages (see Figure 7.1). At all but the last stage a new social need emerges that is added to the existing needs. Sullivan also felt that at each stage there is a key relationship that is crucial for the fulfillment of the stage's need.

The first stage in Sullivan's theory extends through the infancy period, from birth to about 2 years of age. The need of this stage is for tenderness. If provided, feelings of security occur; if not provided, the infant feels distressed and fearful. The need of this stage and the resulting feelings are very similar to those conceptualized in attachment theory.

In the childhood stage, ages 2 to 5 or 6, "the need for adult participation is added—that is, a need for the interest and participation of a

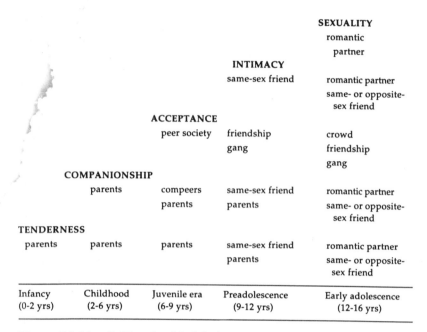

TENDERNESS	COMPANIONSHIP	ACCEPTANCE	INTIMACY	SEXUALITY
				romantic partner
			same-sex friend	romantic partner
				same- or opposite-sex friend
		peer society	friendship	crowd
			gang	friendship
				gang
	parents	compeers	same-sex friend	romantic partner
		parents	parents	same- or opposite-sex friend
parents	parents	parents	same-sex friend	romantic partner
			parents	same- or opposite-sex friend
Infancy (0-2 yrs)	Childhood (2-6 yrs)	Juvenile era (6-9 yrs)	Preadolescence (9-12 yrs)	Early adolescence (12-16 yrs)

Figure 7.1 Neo-Sullivanian Model of Emerging Social Needs and Key Relationships

SOURCE: From Buhrmester, D., & Furman, W. (1986). The changing functions of friends in childhood: A neo-Sullivanian perspective. In V. J. Derlega & B. A. Winstead (Eds.), *Friendship and social interaction* (pp. 41-62). New York: Springer-Verlag. Copyright 1986 by Springer-Verlag New York Publishers. Reprinted with permission.

significant adult in the child's play" (Sullivan, 1953, pp. 290-291). It h-as been argued that this need continues through the life span as the need for companionship (Buhrmester & Furman, 1986). This social need may also be equivalent to the "need" or set goal underlying the affiliative behavioral system of attachment theory. Thus Sullivan believed that early parent-child relationships served two main functions for children—the provision of security and the opportunity for companionship.

The third stage, the juvenile era, begins with the entrance into school and involves two changes from the previous stage. First, the transition between these stages involves a shift in the primary object of the companionship need from parents to peers. The ability to play successfully with other children demands that the child master egalitarian exchange relationships. Second, as children move into the peer world they become aware of the differences among them, and these differences are used to determine the desirability of children as companions. Thus the emerging need of this stage is for acceptance by one's peers in order to avoid feelings of ostracism and exclusion.

The fourth stage, preadolescence, extends from about 9 years of age to puberty. Here, the need for intimate exchange emerges motivated by the desire to experience love and avoid loneliness. The need for intimate exchange results in the establishment of a new type of relationship, a "chumship." A chumship is a collaborative relationship; that is, it involves "clearly formulated adjustments of one's behavior to the expressed needs of the other person in the pursuit of increasingly identical—that is, more and more mutual—satisfactions" (p. 246). Such relationships are based on extensive self-disclosure and consensual validation of personal worth. They are also seen as the prototype of adult friendships and as a foundation for romantic and marital relationships (Berndt, 1982; Buhrmester & Furman, 1986).

The last two stages of Sullivan's theory cover the entire adolescent period, extending from puberty through young adulthood. Early adolescence, which begins with puberty, sees the emergence of true genital interest or lust. There is also a change in the object of the need for intimacy. That is, there is a growing interest in the possibility of achieving intimacy with a sexual partner that is similar to that of the intimacy of preadolescent chumships.

Once this shift has been made, the task of early adolescence becomes one of discovering one's sexual identity and preferred way of relating to a romantic partner. Sullivan sees this as a trial and error process but says little else about it. This task is complicated by the fact that the three main needs of this stage, the needs for security, intimacy, and lustful satisfaction, must be coordinated to negotiate this stage successfully, and yet they often are in opposition. For example, sexual experimentation can result in feelings of embarrassment, which conflict with the need for security. The balancing of needs can also be viewed as the coordination of the newly emerging sexual/reproductive behavioral system with the attachment and affiliative behavioral systems.

The final stage is that of late adolescence, which begins when a pattern of preferred genital activity is established. The task of this final stage is to establish a network of mature interpersonal relationships, one of which is a committed love relationship.

Sullivan's theory has several appealing features. Specifically, it provides a developmental framework for conceptualizing the emergence of social needs and the impact that such changes may have on relationships. Although he only focuses on key relationships in different stages, his theory explicitly recognizes the contributions of both parent-child and peer relationships. On the other hand, Sullivan's descriptions of the stages of development in late adolescence and adulthood are more sketchy. In fact, the theory is generally not presented very systematically, and some topics, such as the origins of caretaking, receive little attention. Moreover, although the theory is frequently mentioned by investigators, it has received remarkably little empirical attention.

A BEHAVIORAL SYSTEMS
CONCEPTUALIZATION

We believe that the insights of adult romantic attachment theory, traditional attachment theory, and neo-Sullivanian theory can be integrated into a behavioral systems conceptualization of romantic relationships. We believe that such a conceptualization can avoid some of the limitations of particular theories and provide a promising framework for understanding some of the central aspects of romantic relationships.

In the sections that follow, we will outline a series of key points in this conceptualization. Specifically, we will propose that the affiliative behavioral system, as well as the attachment, caretaking, and sexual/reproductive systems, is central to romantic relationships. Then we will describe our conceptualization of romantic views, which are conscious and unconscious perceptions of particular romantic relationships. Next we will discuss the links among different relationships. Finally, we will outline a series of hypothesized developmental changes in these relationships.

Four Behavioral Systems

Central to our conceptualization is the idea of a behavioral system, which is a goal-corrected system that functions to maintain a relatively steady state between the individual and his/her environment (Bretherton, 1985). A behavioral system includes an appraisal process that indicates if the set goal of the system is being met or not, emotions elicited by this process when the set goal is met or not, and emotion-related actions and action-tendencies that correct the system when the set goal is not met (Shaver & Hazan, 1988). For example, the set goal of the attachment system is to maintain some degree of proximity to an attachment figure (Bowlby, 1969). Individuals have only one behavioral system of each type (e.g., attachment, sexual/reproductive, affiliative, and so on), but the operation of a particular system may entail interactions with different people in their social networks. For example, one may develop a hierarchy of attachment figures to be turned to at times of distress.

Our first key idea is that romantic partners become major figures in the functioning of the attachment, caregiving, affiliative, and sexual/reproductive behavioral systems. The attachment and caretaking systems have received considerable theoretical and empirical attention, but the affiliative system has only been periodically alluded to by attachment researchers (Ainsworth, 1989; Bretherton & Ainsworth, 1974). We believe that initially parents are the key affiliative figures, but that peers, particularly close friends, become the key figures for most of the course of development. Early on, the behaviors relevant to the affiliative system may simply consist of play with others. However, in egalitarian relationships with peers, the affiliative system evolves into a complex behavioral system that entails more than play behavior. In particular, we believe that the affiliative system may underlie the collaboration, cooperation, reciprocity, and coconstruction that Sullivan described as characteristic of preadolescent chumships.

Thus prior to adolescence, parents and peers are the key figures for the attachment, caregiving, and affiliative systems. As romantic relationships develop and become more central, however, romantic partners become key figures for these different systems as well as for the sexual/reproductive system with its emergence in adolescence.

A Biological Perspective

The present model proposes that romantic relationships are biologically based in part. That is, the four behavioral systems are thought to have evolved because they increased survival during the course of evolution. The proposition that there are underlying biological processes may seem incongruent with the evidence of marked cultural variability in romantic relationships, but we think not. Traditionally, anthropologists and historians had thought that romantic love was an invention of relatively recent Western society, but recent evidence suggests otherwise. Jankowiak and Fischer (1992) report finding evidence of romantic love in at least 88% of the 166 cultures they surveyed, including many cultures where prearranged marriages are the rule. Of course, marked cultural differences exist in the specific nature of these relationships, but contemporary sociobiological theories not only acknowledge but explicitly incorporate cultural factors in their formulations (MacDonald, 1988, 1989). That is, the specific manifestations of biological processes vary as a function of environmental or cultural factors. A biological perspective provides an explanation of the ultimate cause of behavior in our evolutionary past, but does not deny that there are simultaneously many proximate causes of those behaviors (Buss, 1988).

Affiliation, attachment, caretaking, and reproduction are hypothesized to be discrete or independent systems. In contemporary Western society, romantic partners are key figures for all four behavioral systems, but in other cultures different individuals may be involved in the functioning of the different systems. For example, it appears that in classical Grecian society, males turned to their wives for the purposes of reproduction, but were more likely to turn to other males or upper class prostitutes (hetaira) for affiliation (Pomeroy, 1975).

Views

A second key concept in our model is that of views. By *views* we mean conscious and unconscious perceptions of a particular relationship, the self in that type of relationship, and the partner in that relationship. Views of a particular relationship are shaped by the nature of interactions and experiences in that relationship, by past experiences in similar relationships, and finally by past experiences in other relationships. This conceptualization of views resembles attachment theory's concept of working models, but it differs in several important respects.

First, attachment theorists have talked about a general working model of relationships, or at least attachment relationships, but we believe that individuals have distinct views for each relationship. Views are thought to be influenced by experiences in other relationships, but views of different relationships are not expected to be identical because they are strongly influenced by experiences with a particular person. For example, if you had been repeatedly rejected or mistreated in a romantic relationship, it seems likely that you would develop insecure views about this relationship even if you had secure relationships with parents and friends.

At the same time, people do not enter each new relationship as a tabula rasa. Instead, they enter with some preconceptions or expectations of what the relationships is apt to be like, based on their past experiences in similar types of relationships and secondarily on their experiences in other types of relationships. For example, if one has been able to turn to romantic partners at times of distress in the past, one is likely to enter a new relationship with some expectations of being able to turn to the new partner. Such expectations will shape one's perceptions and behavior and thus may lead to a self-fulfillment of expectations (Snyder, Tanke, & Berscheid, 1977). On the other hand, if the expectations are not met, the expectations may gradually be altered.

One important issue is the degree of consistency in views of different specific relationships. An impressive body of longitudinal studies has documented links between early attachment status and competence in subsequent relationships with other adults, peers, and friends (see Elicker, Englund, & Sroufe, 1992). These findings suggest that as a result of early interactions with primary caretakers, a child develops a general working model of relationships that guides subsequent interactions with others.

Yet little consistency has been found in attachment status with different figures. For example, Fox, Kimmerly, and Schafer's (1991) meta-analysis of 11 studies revealed only a modest degree of concordance in the security of attachments to mothers and fathers (60% agreement vs. 55% chance, kappa = .12; 3% of variance accounted for). Similarly, relatively little or no concordance has been found between attachment status with a parent and that with either a day-care center teacher (Goosens & van IJzendoorn, 1990; Howes & Hamilton, 1992) or a kibbutz metapelet (Sagi et al., 1985). The low concordance has been appropriately interpreted as evidence that the Strange Situation or other attachment measures assess the quality of a relationship rather than temperamental or other characteristics of the child. The low concordance also suggests that a child develops different working models for different relationships because these models are expected to be based upon relational experiences.

At first glance, the literature on the longitudinal predictiveness of early attachment status and the literature on the low concordance of attachment classifications with different figures would seem to lead to different conclusions. However, the strength of the observed longitudinal relations should not be overstated; although certainly important, the links are usually moderate in size, with attachment relationship history typically accounting for 5% to 15% of the variance. Thus the existing findings suggest that there is modest, yet noteworthy, consistency across different types of relationships.

We believe that the consistency of views may be greater within each particular type of relationship, such as romantic relationships. That is, people may have general views of a type of relationship and specific views for each relationship. Both guide behavior. In the sections that follow, we will refer to "romantic views," "views of friendships," and so forth when referring to these general views.

Another distinguishing point is that we believe that views are not views of attachment per se, but instead are views of all behavioral systems. That is, there are not separate views for each of the different systems; rather, views reflect a composite picture of the functioning of different systems in each relationship. For example, dismissing views are not only reflected in rarely turning to the partner as a secure base, but also in not wanting to provide care to the other, seeing sex as primarily an opportunity for experimentation and self-gratification, and valuing the activity rather than the companionship of the other. Similarly, preoccupied views may be manifested in terms of going along with the other's wishes (vs. expressing one's own), providing too much or poorly timed care, and using sex as a means to enhance one's own esteem as well as in terms of being quite concerned and worried about the other's availability at times of distress. Certainly, attachment experiences in relationships will be critical in the development of views, but we do not believe that they are the exclusive determinant of views. All of the systems play an important role and are integrated in views. Although each of the systems is reflected in views, it is important to recognize that a particular relationship may be more salient for one system's functioning than another. For example, close friends are likely to be more salient in the functioning of the affiliative system than the attachment system.

Finally, views are conceptualized as incorporating two distinct components: (a) conscious styles or perceptions of relationships and (b) unconscious or internal working models, which reflect more automated processing in social relationships. Styles can be assessed by self-report measures, whereas working models can be tapped by techniques, such as adult attachment interviews (Main et al., 1985). By their use of self-report measures, adult romantic attachment theorists seem to want to equate conscious styles and unconscious working models of relationships, but the existing data suggest that the two are only moderately related at most (Bartholomew, 1991; Crowell, Treboux, & Waters, 1993). We are not simply saying that conscious styles do not correspond on a surface level to unconscious models. Attachment theorists, as well as ourselves, recognize that individuals who have experienced rejecting experiences from a parent do not necessarily consciously acknowledge such experiences, and instead may protect themselves from these emotionally distressing experiences by developing defensive strategies, such as denigrating the importance of the relationship. Our conceptualization of styles goes further, however, in that we believe that conscious styles not only reflect defensive strategies that emerge from unconscious working models, but also are influenced by other variables, such as sex roles and cultural factors. For that matter, unconscious models may be influenced by other factors as well. Of course, conscious styles and unconscious working models are expected to be related to each other because they influence one another.

It is important to emphasize that our intention is not to denigrate the significance of conscious styles. To understand the phenomenology of romantic love, both components of views—conscious styles and unconscious internal working models—need to be examined because each seems to be associated with distinct facets of the romantic experience and perhaps adjustment (Kobak & Hazan, under review).

Cross-Relationship Links

We have proposed that there is a relatively high degree of consistency in views of specific relationships of one type (e.g., different romantic relationships) and a moderate degree of consistency in views of different types of relationships. As adolescents establish romantic relationships, they are likely to be influenced by their views of and experiences in other types of relationships. That is, when the different behavioral systems are activated, adolescents are likely to be predisposed to respond to romantic partners as they have in other relationships. For example, if an adolescent has tended not to turn to others as a secure base, she or he may tend not to turn to romantic partners as well.

Because the parent-child relationship is most central to the development of the attachment and caregiving systems, attachment experiences with parents are expected to have a stronger influence on the use of romantic partners as attachment figures than attachment experiences with other individuals. On the other hand, peers are the key figures for the affiliative system, and thus affiliative experiences in peer relationships, particularly friendships, are expected to be a stronger predictor of the affiliative aspects of romantic relationships than experiences in other relationships are.

At the same time, a simple recreation of past relationships is not expected for two reasons. First, the qualitative features of romantic relationships typically differ in some respects from those with friends or parents. The different features of the relationships lead to different experiences in the relationships. Second, the specific partners are obviously not the same in the different relationships. Clearly, the partners, as well as the adolescent, will shape the course of the relationships. Thus we expect views of different types of relationships to be moderately related—not highly related and not unrelated. Working models of different types of relationships may be more related to one another than the different styles are because unconscious perceptions may be less open to new information and thus may change more slowly.

Certainly, attachment theorists recognize that working models reflect present as well as past conditions (Sroufe, Egeland, & Kreutzer, 1990), but we believe that the current framework places more emphasis on the specificity of views of particular relationships. Attachment theorists emphasize continuity unless there is a major change in general life circumstances or new relational experience, such as successful therapy or having a good marital partner. In the present conceptualization, views of a particular relationship always develop because they are strongly influenced by the ongoing experiences in that relationship.

A DEVELOPMENTAL PERSPECTIVE

As developmental psychologists, we think that one of the most interesting aspects of romantic relationships is that they are not static but evolve over adolescence and adulthood. Developmental changes may occur both within the course of a particular relationship and over the course of a series of relationships. Moreover, developmental changes can be seen in a number of different respects, which include: (a) changes in the hierarchy of figures, (b) changes in the behavioral systems, (c) changes in dating life, and (d) changes in romantic views. Each is discussed subsequently.

Changes in the Hierarchy of Figures

The social context of the development of the attachment and other behavioral systems in adolescence or adulthood is fundamentally different from that in infancy. In early infancy at least, one can talk about the development of the first or primary attachment relationship. In adolescence or adulthood, however, there are preexisting attachment, affiliative, and caretaking figures that differ in their importance as sources of attachment, affiliation, and caretaking. A key idea in our conceptualization is that the romantic partner becomes part of this hierarchy of figures and then moves up in importance in the hierarchy of figures. Thus as a relationship with a romantic partner begins to develop, an adolescent starts to turn to this person as an attachment and affiliation figure and starts to serve as a caretaker to him or her. Moreover, if the relationship develops further, the adolescent is expected to become increasingly likely to turn to this person rather than to other individuals. One would expect the partner to reach the top of the hierarchy by at least the time of a marriage or a potentially permanent arrangement. This pattern is also hypothesized to occur over the course of different relationships. In early adolescence romantic partners probably do not move up very far in the hierarchy, but as the adolescent gains more experience in romantic relationships, romantic partners are likely to move up the hierarchy more quickly and occupy a higher place in the hierarchy. This hypothesized general normative trend may not, however, hold true for particular adolescents if their past experiences have been relatively negative—a point elaborated on in the subsequent section on views. Some support for the hypothesized common pattern, however, is provided by our finding that the romantic partner's place in the hierarchy of perceived support figures goes from fourth in the 7th grade to third in the 10th grade, and then to first in college (Furman & Buhrmester, 1992).

Changes in the Behavioral Systems

One of the reasons that developmental changes are expected to occur in the hierarchy of figures is that changes are hypothesized to occur in the skill and frequency of the acts involved in the functioning of a behavioral system. For example, once part of the hierarchy, a romantic partner may sometimes serve as a secure base to turn to in times of distress. As an adolescent learns how to use a partner as a secure base, he or she is likely to do so more frequently and more skillfully. Not only may these changes occur over the course of a long-term relationship, but they are also likely to be apparent over the course of a series of relationships. That is, some of the learning about what does and does not work may carry over to subsequent relationships. Certainly, most of us feel more comfortable and skillful in our interactions with current romantic partners than we did as early adolescents!

During the course of a particular relationship, a romantic partner is expected to emerge as a sexual figure and an affiliative figure before becoming an attachment figure or recipient of caretaking. This order is expected to be relatively consistent across particular relationships, but the attachment and caregiving systems are expected to become more salient in relationships in late adolescence or adulthood as ties with parents are transformed and the push to find a new primary attachment figure increases. Typically, it is not until mid- to late adolescence that a romantic partner becomes a relevant figure for all four behavioral systems.

Changes in Dating Life

In studying romantic relationships in modern Western cultures, one must also take into account dating life and its development. Feinstein and Ardon's (1973) and Dunphy's (1963) observations suggest a four-step sequence in heterosexual dating. With the onset of adolescence there is a new interest in opposite-sex peers brought on by puberty and the emergence of the sexual/reproductive system. Unfortunately, adolescents have not yet had an opportunity to develop basic skills for interacting with opposite-sex peers and must first develop a sense of comfort interacting with them, which often occurs within the context of the crowd (Dunphy, 1963). As an adolescent develops comfort and skill in these Simple Interchanges, she or he may move to Casual Dating. Here, affiliative behavior and sexual experimentation may occur in a number of short-term relationships. Romantic partners are not expected to emerge as attachment figures or recipients of caretaking until an adolescent begins to develop Stable Relationships—exclusive, longer term relationships. In fact, their full emergence is not likely to occur until the appearance of a Committed Relationship, a long-term relationship, which, if everything goes well, is likely to become a marriage or potentially permanent arrangement—a step that typically does not occur until late adolescence or adulthood. As the romantic partner becomes a more salient attachment figure and the self becomes a more salient attachment figure for the partner, the length of relationships is predicted to increase. Relationship commitments, both short and long term, are ventures into being consistently available and responsive to a romantic partner much as one has been with chums and as one's parents have been to oneself.

Distinctions among the four steps are important not only in terms of understanding the developmental course of romantic relationships but also to ensure that appropriate comparisons are made. For example, differences in how secure two adolescents' romantic views are could occur because of differences in past relationship histories, but they could also occur because one adolescent is casually dating and the other has a stable relationship. We believe that this clouding of comparisons may have led to potential underestimations of links among relationships in past research.

The Development of Views

Romantic views are not static traits of the individual. As noted previously, we expect that one's views of romantic relationships are influenced by experiences in other types of relationships. Importantly, romantic views develop further as a function of their romantic experiences. With the accumulation of experience, they become more elaborated and ultimately less prone to change.

A thornier question is whether romantic views typically become more secure, remain consistent, or perhaps even become less secure with development. All three paths are likely to occur in specific instances. For example, as an adolescent becomes more skillful in providing care or seeking attachment, affiliation, or sexual gratification, she or he is likely to be more successful and thus to develop more secure views concerning such a relationship. On the other hand, some individuals may re-create the insecure relationships they expect consciously or unconsciously. For example, dismissing individuals may tend to select partners or establish relationships that reinforce a dismissing view. Such a person may become more skillful, but more skillful in developing relationships characterized by dismissing patterns. Finally, less secure views may develop as a result of a series of negative events or relationships. Certainly, date rapes or other forms of sexual assault seem likely to lead to insecure views.

Is one path more likely than the others? Interestingly, in the study we describe subsequently the proportion of high school students endorsing Hazan and Shaver's description of a secure style (46%) was lower than typically found in college samples (55% to 60%), which in turn is lower than that found in a married sample (72%) (Kobak & Hazan, 1991). Perhaps the increase in skill and the selection of appropriate partners lead to a moderate increase in secure styles. Whether such changes will occur in underlying models remains to be seen, although the ideas of increased skillfulness, partner selection, and the potential impact of styles on working models would suggest it could. Whatever proves to be the case, the key idea is that views are affected by romantic experiences and in turn affect romantic experiences.

Timing

Although we have discussed a series of developmental changes that are at least somewhat normative in nature, it is important to recognize that the timing or onset of romantic life is likely to vary widely from individual to individual. Similarly, some may date more frequently than others. Consistent with the work on sexual behavior (Miller & Moore, 1990; Smith, 1989), it is expected that the timing of the steps to Simple Interactions and to Casual Dating are strongly influenced by family norms, peer norms, peer prestige variables, and psychobiological maturity (McCabe, 1984; Smith, 1989), and not strongly related to relational experiences with parents or friends. Similar predictions are made for the frequency of dating.

The steps to Stable Relationships and particularly Committed Relationships are, however, more likely to be related to relational experiences, particularly romantic ones and particularly as one gets older. For example, late adolescents or young adults who are dismissing of romantic relationships may be less likely to establish Committed Relationships. Moreover, the length of these relationships and the nature of their termination is expected to be related to romantic views. In particular, adolescents or adults with secure views of romantic relationships are expected to have had more lasting relationships than those with insecure views (Davis & Kirkpatrick, in press). Dismissing adolescents are expected to be more likely to terminate their relationships, whereas those with preoccupied views are more likely to have their partners terminate them.

Although we have proposed some links between views and dating history, the preceding comments should also make it clear that the concept of views or other indices of relational quality should not be equated with the quantitative indices of onset and frequency of dating life that have been the primary focus of research to date. With few exceptions, less-than-optimal developmental experiences, such as insecure attachments to caretakers, do not arrest development, but rather direct it along a less desirable path. Thus for the majority of children, regardless of past relationship history, the entrance into adolescence will lead to the search for romantic partners. The timing of that search will be influenced by family norms, peer norms, peer prestige variables, and psychobiological maturity and not by the quality of the past relationships. Past relational experiences with romantic partners and other individuals are likely to have their impact on the quality of the romantic relationships that emerge, when they do emerge.

A TEST OF THE CONCEPT OF VIEWS

Recently we tested some of our key ideas concerning views in a study of 165 middle adolescent females in the 10th to 12th grades. A self-report measure, the Behavioral Systems Questionnaire, was developed to assess adolescents' conscious styles or perceptions concerning attachment, caregiving, and affiliative behaviors in their relationships with their mothers, fathers, closest friends, and romantic partners. Separate scales assessing Secure, Dismissing, and Preoccupied styles were derived for each behavioral system in each type of relationship.

First, we tested the idea that perceptions of attachment, caregiving, and affiliation are significantly related to one another within each type of relationship. Consistent with our expectations, we found that the corresponding attachment, caregiving, and affiliative scales for each of the three styles were significantly correlated with one another in each of the four relationships (mean $r = .51$). This pattern suggests that the functioning of the three systems within a particular type of relationship is coordinated, and that one can fruitfully refer to general relationship styles. The correlations among the corresponding scales assessing the different types of behaviors were not, however, as high as the internal consistencies of the scales. Thus there is also some variance associated with the functioning of particular behavioral systems that is not accounted for by a general relationship style.

Next we tested the idea that styles are specific to the type of relationship. General style scores for each type of relationship were derived by averaging the scores across the attachment, caretaking, and affiliative ratings for each relationship. Consistent with our expectations, the correlations were moderate in size (see Table 7.1). Moreover, the magnitude of correlations was more varied across relationship pairs than one would expect if the styles generalized across types of relationships. Thus the results suggest that romantic styles or other styles are influenced by the experiences within particular types of relationships. At the same time, there are moderate links among the styles for different relationships. Particularly noteworthy were the correlations between friendships and romantic relationships. Clearly, an account of romantic relationships will need to include the role of friendships as well as parent-child relationships.

In the initial study, we only examined the pattern of relations among perceptions of types of relationships. In a small follow-up study, however, we examined the relations among specific relationships of one type. In particular, 20 college students completed four versions of the Behavioral Systems Questionnaire—one that referred to close friends in general and three others, each of which

Table 7.1   Across-Relationship Correlations for General Relationship
                Styles

Relationships	Secure	Dismissing	Preoccupied
Mother-Father	.29**	.35**	.39**
Mother-Friends	.14	.25**	.28**
Mother-Romantic	.02	.01	.23**
Father-Friends	.16*	.25**	.26**
Father-Romantic	.07	.18*	.08
Friends-Romantic	.25**	.35**	.40**

*p < .05; **p < .01.

referred to a particular friendship. To reduce carryover effects, the
administration of the four versions was interspersed over a 6-to
8-week period.

General stylistic perceptions were highly related to corresponding perceptions of specific relationships (mean r = .58), supporting
the idea that a general view may influence or be influenced by views
of particular relationships. Additionally, perceptions of dismissing
and preoccupied styles in one friendship were related to corresponding scores for another friendship (mean r = .42 and .47, respectively), but secure scores were not (mean r = .02). The difference in
consistency fits with the idea that insecure styles reflect rigidly held
beliefs that are less open to new information. The results also provide some very preliminary evidence that the degree of correspon-
dence for at least insecure scores may be greater within a particular
type of relationship.

FUTURE DIRECTIONS

The preceding sections underscore the complexity of the issues
involved in studying adolescent romantic relationships. Conceptualizing romantic relationships as attachment relationships was a
useful first step, but does not completely capture the richness of these
relationships. We have tried to make the next step by noting the
importance of the affiliative behavioral system and peer relationships,
introducing the idea of views being specific to particular relationships and only relatively concordant within types of relationships,

distinguishing between conscious styles and unconscious internal working models, and providing a developmental perspective. Even with these additions, we do not believe that the picture is complete. The different behavioral systems and their manifestations at different developmental periods require further attention, both theoretically and empirically. Similarly, we need to further articulate how the manifestation of these systems may change over the course of the development of a relationship.

Up to this point, we have not addressed the issue of whether chums or close adolescent friends serve as secondary attachment figures. The literature contains several discussions of which relationships should be conceptualized as attachments. For example, Weiss (1991) argued that romantic pair bonds and some relationships of patients to therapists are likely to be attachments, whereas most friendships, work relationships, and kin ties are not. Hazan and Zeifman (in press) have argued that intimate physical contact, such as that between caregiver and infant or sexual contact between lovers, may be needed for attachment formation. Although their argument has some appealing features, it does have difficulty accounting for any attachment relationships with therapists.

More importantly, we believe that the question of who is and who is not an attachment figure misses the point. The close relationships individuals have with various people have some similarities and differences with one another. We need to develop models that can account for the processes underlying such similarities and differences. For example, if one wants to argue that most friendships are not attachment relationships, one still has to account for the proximity seeking, emotional support, and other "attachment-like" features that characterize these relationships. Conversely, if one argues that they are attachment relationships, one has to account for the differences between these and other attachment relationships. Similarly, we need more detailed accounts of how developmental status of the individual, the nature of the relationship, and the context within which a behavioral system is activated may alter the manifestations of attachment, affiliative, or caregiving behaviors. Thus further conceptual and empirical work is needed to understand the role of different behavioral systems and relationships in adolescents' or adults' social world.

It is important to remember that we have primarily focused on a theory of romantic views and the four behavioral systems. Although we believe that romantic views and the four behavioral systems are central components of romantic relationships, that's not all there is to romantic relationships or love! Romantic relationships serve other functions than attachment, affiliation, or sex, particularly in adolescence. For example, the relationships may serve as a means of status grading and status achievement (Skipper & Nass, 1966). Such functions are likely to influence the nature and significance of these relationships.

Another topic that needs to be addressed is whom one selects as dating or romantic partners. In the adult romantic literature, investigators have found some concordance in the attachment styles of dating and marital partners (Senchak & Leonard, 1992; Simpson, 1990), but it is not clear if such matching would be found in adolescent romantic pairs. In any case, it is unlikely that the concordance in views would be high. Interpersonal attraction, the selection of dating partners, and one's status in the dating world involve much, much more than one's romantic views. A comprehensive theory would need to include a consideration of the other factors that are predictive of partner selection. Romantic views may be more predictive of the nature of the relationship than whom the relationship is with. For example, the adult literature has found that certain pairs, particularly secure-secure ones, are more likely to have satisfying and enduring relationships (Senchak & Leonard, 1992; Simpson, 1990). An important task for investigators is to identify the impact of romantic views on patterns of interactions.

Although an attachment or behavioral systems perspective may seem to focus primarily on the characteristics of individuals (vs. relationship characteristics), such is not actually the case. The romantic views of individuals are thought to be important because they are expected to affect the patterns of interactions. Moreover, one of the key features of the current conceptualization is the emphasis on the role of relationship history on the development of romantic views.

Finally, this formulation has focused on biologically-based features that we believe are typically characteristic of romantic relationships. There is much diversity in romantic relationships that also needs to be acknowledged. As noted earlier, we need to remember that romantic relationships, like all relationships, occur within a particular historical and cultural context. The role of cultural factors and their interface with biological ones requires further attention. Similarly, the literature on romantic relationships is replete with gender differences (Buss & Schmitt, 1993; Peplau & Gordon, 1985). Such differences have in fact been found in attachment styles (Brennan et al., 1991), but as yet the bases for such differences is not clear.

We believe, however, that the preceding points do not detract from the appeal of a behavioral systems perspective. They simply point out the complexity of the task we still face. It is hoped, however, that our effort to integrate the insights of the attachment and Sullivanian theories can move us toward a theory of the mysterious phenomenon of adolescent love.

REFERENCES

Ainsworth, M. D. S. (1989). Attachments beyond infancy. *American Psychologist, 44,* 709-716.

Bartholomew, K. (1990). Avoidance of intimacy: An attachment perspective. *Journal of Social and Personal Relationships, 7,* 147-178.

Bartholomew, K. (1991). Attachment styles among young adults: A test of a four-category model. *Journal of Personality and Social Psychology, 61,* 226-244.

Berndt, T. (1982). The features and effects of friendship in early adolescence. *Child Development, 53,* 1447-1460.

Blyth, D. A., Hill, J. P., & Thiel, K. S. (1982). Early adolescents' significant others: Grade and gender differences in perceived relationships with familial and nonfamilial adults and young people. *Journal of Youth and Adolescence, 11,* 425-449.

Bowlby, J. (1969). *Attachment and Loss: Vol. 1. Attachment.* New York: Basic Books.

Bowlby, J. (1979). *The making and breaking of affectional bonds.* London: Tavistock.

Brennan, K. A., Shaver, P. R., & Tobey, A. E. (1991). Attachment styles, gender, and parental problem drinking. *Journal of Social and Personal Relationships, 8,* 451-466.

Bretherton, I. (1985). Attachment theory: Retrospect and prospect. In I. Bretherton & E. Waters (Eds.), Growing points of attachment theory and research, *Monographs of the Society for Research in Child Development, 50,* No. 209, pp. 3-35.

Bretherton, I., & Ainsworth, M. D. S. (1974). Responses of one-year-olds to a stranger in a strange situation. In M. Lewis & L. A. Rosenblum (Eds.), *The origins of fear.* New York: John Wiley.

Buhrmester, D., & Furman, W. (1986). The changing functions of friends in childhood: A neo-Sullivanian perspective. In V. J. Derlega & B. A. Winstead (Eds.), *Friendship and social interaction* (pp. 41-62). New York: Springer-Verlag.

Buss, D. M. (1988). Love acts: The evolutionary biology of love. In R. J. Sternberg & M. L. Barnes (Eds.), *The psychology of love* (pp. 100-118). New Haven: Yale University Press.

Buss, D. M., & Schmitt, D. P. (1993). Sexual strategies theory: An evolutionary perspective on human mating. *Psychological Review, 100,* 204-232.

Cassidy, J., & Kobak, R. (1988). Avoidance and its relation to other defensive processes. In J. Belsky & T. Neworski (Eds.), *Clinical implications of attachment* (pp. 300-323). Hillsdale, NJ: Lawrence Erlbaum.

Collins, N. L., & Read, S. J. (1990). Adult attachment, working models, and relationship quality in dating couples. *Journal of Personality and Social Psychology, 58,* 644-663.

Crowell, J., Treboux, D., & Waters, E. (1993, March). *Alternatives to the Adult Attachment Interview: Self-reports of attachment style and relationships with mothers and partners.* Poster presented at the meetings of the Society for Research in Child Development, New Orleans.

Davis, K. E., & Kirkpatrick, L. A. (in press). Attachment style, gender, and relationship stability: A longitudinal analysis. *Journal of Personality and Social Psychology.*

Dunphy, D. C. (1963). The social structure of urban adolescent peer groups. *Sociometry, 26,* 230-246.

Elicker, J., Englund, M., & Sroufe, L. A. (1992). Predicting peer competence and peer relationships in childhood from early parent-child relationships. In R. D. Parke & G. W. Ladd (Eds.), *Family-peer relationships: Modes of linkage* (pp. 77-108). Hillsdale, NJ: Lawrence Erlbaum.

Erikson, E. H. (1968). *Identity: Youth and crisis.* NY: Norton.

Feeney, J. A., & Noller, P. (1990). Attachment style as a predictor of adult romantic relationships. *Journal of Personality and Social Psychology, 58,* 281-291.

Feinstein, S. C., & Ardon, M. S. (1973). Trends in dating patterns and adolescent development. *Journal of Youth and Adolescence, 2,* 157-166.

Fox, N. A., Kimmerly, N. L., & Schafer, W. D. (1991). Attachment to mother/attachment to father: A meta-analysis. *Child Development, 62,* 210-225.

Furman, W. (1987, March). *Social support, stress, and adjustment in adolescence.* Paper presented at the Society for Research in Child Development, Baltimore.

Furman, W., & Buhrmester, D. (1992). Age and sex differences in perceptions of networks of personal relationships. *Child Development, 63,* 103-115.

Goosens, F. A., & van IJzendoorn, M. H. (1990). Quality of infants' attachments to professional caregivers: Relation to infant-parent attachment and day-care characteristics. *Child Development, 61,* 832-837.

Hansen, S. L. (1977). Dating choices of high school students. *The Family Coordinator, 26,* 133-138.

Hardy, S. B. (1981). *The woman that never evolved.* Cambridge, MA: Harvard University Press.

Hazan, C., & Shaver, P. (1987). Conceptualizing romantic love as an attachment process. *Journal of Personality and Social Psychology, 52,* 511-524.

Hazan, C., & Zeifman, D. (in press). Sex and the psychological tether. In D. Perlman & K. Bartholomew (Eds.), *Advances in personal relationships* (Vol. 5).

Howes, C., & Hamilton, C. E. (1992). Children's relationship with child care teachers: Stability and concordance with parental attachments. *Child Development, 63,* 867-878.

Jankowiak, W. R., & Fischer, E. F. (1992). A cross-cultural perspective on romantic love. *Ethos, 31,* 149-156.

Kobak, R. R., & Hazan, C. (1991). Attachment in marriage: Effects of security and accuracy of working models. *Journal of Personality and Social Psychology, 60,* 861-869.

Kobak, R. R., & Hazan, C. (under review). *Parents and spouses: Attachment strategies and marital functioning.*

MacDonald, K. B. (1988). *Social and personality development: An evolutionary synthesis.* New York: Plenum.

MacDonald, K. (1989). The plasticity of human social organization and behavior: Contextual variables and proximal mechanisms. *Ethology and Sociobiology, 12,* 449-480.

MacDonald, K. (1992). Warmth as a developmental construct: An evolutionary analysis. *Child Development, 63,* 753-773.

Main, M., DeMoss, A., & Hesse, E. (1989). *A system for assessing lack of resolution of mourning from interview transcripts.* Unpublished manuscript, University of California, Berkeley, Department of Psychology.

Main, M., & Hesse, E. (1990). Parents' unresolved traumatic experiences are related to infant disorganized attachment status: Is frightened and/or frightening parental behavior the linking mechanism? In M. T. Greenberg, D. Cicchetti, & E. M. Cummings (Eds.), *Attachment in the preschool years: Theory, research, and intervention* (pp. 161-182). Chicago: University of Chicago Press.

Main, M., Kaplan, N., & Cassidy, J. (1985). Security in infancy, childhood and adulthood: A move to the level of representation. In I. Bretherton & E. Waters (Eds.), Growing points of attachment theory and research, *Monographs for the Society for Research in Child Development, 50,* No. 209, pp. 66-104.

McCabe, M. P. (1984). Toward a theory of adolescent dating. *Adolescence, 19,* 159-170.

Miller, B. C., & Moore, K. A. (1990). Adolescent sexual behavior, pregnancy, and parenting: Research through the 1980s. *Journal of Marriage and the Family, 52,* 1025-1044.

Orlofsky, J. L., Marcia, J. E., & Lesser, I. M. (1973). Ego identity status and the intimacy versus isolation crisis of young adulthood. *Journal of Personality and Social Psychology, 27,* 211-219.

Paul, E. L., & White, K. M. (1990). The development of intimate relationships in late adolescence. *Adolescence, 25,* 375-400.

Peplau, L. A., & Gordon, S. L. (1985). Women and men in love: Sex differences in close heterosexual relationships. In V. E. O'Leary, R. K. Unger, & B. S. Wallston (Eds.), *Women, gender, and social psychology.* Hillsdale, NJ: Lawrence Erlbaum.

Pomeroy, S. B. (1975). *Goddesses, whores, wives, and slaves: Women in classical antiquity.* New York: Schocken.

Sagi, A., Lamb, M. E., Lewkowicz, K. S., Shoham, R., Dvir, R., & Estes, D. (1985). Security of infant-mother, father, metapelet attachments among kibbutz-reared Israeli children. In I. Bretherton & E. Waters (Eds.), Growing points of attachment theory and research, *Monographs of the Society for Research in Child Development, 50,* No. 209, pp. 257-275.

Senchak, M., & Leonard, K. E. (1992). Attachment styles and marriage. *Journal of Social and Personal Relationships, 9,* 51-64.

Sharabany, R., Gershoni, R., & Hoffman, J. E. (1981). Girlfriend, boyfriend: Age and sex differences in intimate friendship. *Developmental Psychology, 17,* 691-703.

Shaver, P., & Hazan, C. (1988). A biased overview of the study of love. *Journal of Social and Personal Relationships, 5,* 473-501.

Shaver, P., Hazan, C., & Bradshaw, D. (1988). Love as attachment: The integration of three behavioral systems. In R. J. Sternberg & M. L. Barnes (Eds.), *The psychology of love* (pp. 193-219). New Haven: Yale University Press.

Simpson, J. A. (1990). Influence of attachment styles on romantic relationships. *Journal of Personality and Social Psychology, 16,* 265-273.

Skipper, J. K., & Nass, G. (1966). Dating behavior: A framework for analysis and an illustration. *Journal of Marriage and the Family, 28,* 412-420.

Smith, E. A. (1989). A biosocial model of adolescent sexual behavior. In G. R. Adams, R. Montemayor, & T. P. Gullotta (Eds.), *Advances in adolescent development: Vol. 1. Biology of adolescent behavior and development* (pp. 143-167). Newbury Park, CA: Sage.

Snyder, M., Tanke, E. D., & Berscheid, E. (1977). Social perception and interpersonal behavior: On the self-fulfilling nature of social stereotypes. *Journal of Personality and Social Psychology, 33,* 656-666.

Sroufe, L. A. (1988). The role of infant-caregiver attachment in development. In J. Belsky & T. Nezworski (Eds.), *Clinical implications of attachment* (pp. 18-38). Hillsdale, NJ: Lawrence Erlbaum.

Sroufe, L. A., Egeland, B., & Kreutzer, T. (1990). The fate of early experience following developmental change: Longitudinal approaches to individual adaptation in childhood. *Child Development, 61,* 1363-1373.

Sullivan, H. S. (1953). *The interpersonal theory of psychiatry.* New York: Norton.

Waters, E., Kondo-Ikemura, K., Posada, G., & Richters, J. E. (1991). Learning to love. In M. R. Gunnar & L. A. Sroufe (Eds.), *Self processes and development: The Minnesota symposium in child development* (pp. 217-255). Hillsdale, NJ: Lawrence Erlbaum.

Weiss, R. S. (1991). The attachment bond in childhood and adulthood. In C. M. Parkes, J. Stevenson-Hinde, & P. Marris (Eds.), *Attachment across the life cycle* (pp. 66-76). London: Routledge.

Wright, L. S. (1982). Parental permission to date and its relationship to drug use and suicidal thought among adolescents. *Adolescence, 17,* 409-418.

8. Dating Those You Can't Love and Loving Those You Can't Date

Ritch C. Savin-Williams
Cornell University

When the narrator of Felice Picano's novel, *Ambidextrous,* was 11 years old, he had his first sexual encounter:

> It progressed fairly quickly from us drinking weak highballs to us French kissing to Susan's bra coming off to my pants coming down and her rubbing my wee-wee until—miracle of miracles!—it too became a boner, just like Edward's. Or rather almost like Edward's. While hard enough to qualify, mine just wasn't sensitive enough: or perhaps it was too sensitive. Susan tugged at it, she rubbed it, she stroked it, she did everything she could to it to elicit the preordained result. I lay back on the pillow and watched. Nothing happened. True it felt strange—as though something new and uncomfortable was suddenly attached to me. It was like a new leg or hand or something that refused to take mental direction. I did feel both lightheaded and congested in my lower torso, but nothing at all to provide her with moans and grunts.
>
> Beth was called downstairs and she tried too. Again nothing. But I had survived their dare—so I made both Flaherty sisters take off their own underpants and show me *theirs.* They did, with some trepidation, and although I wasn't allowed to touch, I inspected these barely existent organs for a long time—enough to be able to memorize them for discussion later with my friends. When I finally packed my boner into my shorts and trousers and went home, it was with a feeling of triumph. (Picano, 1985, pp. 23-24)

It was not love but it was sex, within the context of a friendship. Both love and sex would come into his life 3 years later, with Ricky.

> I joined him and we began kissing sitting up, then wrapped our arms around each other and slowly floated down to the bedspread in a kiss that seemed to last forever and to merge us completely into each other

so that we were pilot and copilot zooming lightning swift through
the lower atmosphere, high as a meteorite. . . .
   We kissed without sniffing the glue and for an even longer time,
our hands all over each other's necks and backs and ears, our
tongues deep inside each other's mouths—those soft pink caves,
where we explored every crevasse, perambulated every ridge, tried
out every tastebud of spongy tongue. . . . (p. 88)

They wished they were "brothers and could live together." Their
last night together they "made love most of that night, not getting
to sleep until after dawn" (p. 98). He and Ricky were soon to be
torn apart by their parents and circumstances, plunging "into an
instant and near total grief that all Ricky's soothing words and
kisses couldn't completely assuage" (p. 98).

   Ambidextrous is one of the most insightful works reflecting on the
dilemmas of growing up "other than heterosexual" in our culture.
I begin this chapter with Picano's work not only because of its
beauty but also because there is little else to guide our understanding of the plight of sexual minority youth struggling with
issues of identity and intimacy. They encounter a world that denies
their very existence and disbelieves their capability to develop
same-sex romantic relationships. We, as social scientists, have also
been silent for far too long.

   When asked by the senior editor to contribute a chapter for this
volume, I was surprised when the request was for a manuscript
focusing on dating relationships among lesbian and gay male youth.
How could I refuse, but what would I write about? This could be a
very short chapter, I mused, especially if I relied solely on the
publications of social and behavioral researchers on the dating
behavior of bisexual, lesbian, and gay male youth. I decided to
expand my topic.

   First, I discuss difficulties in defining and finding bisexual, lesbian, and gay male youth. They are frequently invisible not only to
us but also to themselves. Romantic relationships serve important
developmental functions in the life of not only heterosexual youth
but also sexual minority youth. Yet there are important impedi-
ments, such as our cultural zeitgeist, that prevent sexual minority
youth from dating those they love and instead encourage them to
date those they cannot love. There is limited research on heterosexual and same-sex dating among lesbian, gay male, and bisexual

youth; what I was able to find is reviewed. Final reflections on specific dilemmas faced by those who, against their desires, are sexual outcasts in our culture close the chapter.

EXISTENCE OF SEXUAL MINORITY YOUTH

There is an increasing willingness among social and behavioral scientists to recognize the existence of bisexual, gay male, and lesbian *adults*. What these individuals were before adulthood seems to perplex us. Perhaps they were also gay earlier, as children and adolescents. Although we have great difficulty finding and then naming these youths, they must exist. That is, they exist independent of our ability to document them.

Remafedi, Resnick, Blum, and Harris (1992) published a demography of sexual orientation among 34,706 Minnesota public school youths in Grades 7 through 12. This representative sample came from diverse ethnic, geographic, and socioeconomic strata and was evenly split between males and females and urban and rural. They discovered that a low percentage of junior and senior high school students *defined* themselves as bisexual (0.9%) or gay/lesbian (0.4%). Almost 11%, however, were "unsure" of their sexual orientation. This declined from 26% among 12-year-olds to 9% among 18-year-olds; the percentage of adolescents who labeled themselves lesbian or gay remained fairly constant across the ages of 12 to 18 years. When questioned regarding homosexual *attractions*, the percentages escalated, a threefold increase with age—from 2% at age 12 years to 6% at age 18 years. Thus adolescents are far more likely to report homoerotic attractions than to label themselves the socially "disgraced" term *homosexual*. In fact, only 5% of those with homosexual attractions labeled themselves as gay or lesbian.

The number of Minnesota teens who reported homosexual *sexual activity* increased from less than 1% at age 12 years to almost 3% at age 18 years. Again, a minority of such youths (27%) identified themselves as gay male, lesbian, or bisexual; these youths were just as likely as "heterosexual" adolescents to report having had heterosexual sexual encounters. Nearly 3% of all youths reported bisexual or homosexual *sexual fantasies*. Three in ten of these youths also identified themselves as gay male or lesbian and had homosexual sexual experiences.

Remafedi et al. (1992, p. 720) concluded that "uncertainty about sexual orientation and perceptions of bisexuality gradually give way to heterosexual or homosexual identification with the passage of time and/or with increasing sexual experience." Relatively few of the youths who reported homoerotically oriented fantasies, attractions, or behaviors labeled themselves as lesbian, gay male, or bisexual; most maintained that they were heterosexual.

Although one is more likely to experience cross-orientation sexual behavior while an adolescent than as an adult, there is a paucity of self-defined gay male, lesbian, and bisexual youths (Remafedi et al., 1992; Savin-Williams, 1990). In Coles and Stokes' 1985 survey of youths, only one of more than 1,000 youths checked the "homosexual identity" box. Many more, 5%, had engaged in same-sex behavior. Of more than five hundred 16- to 18-year-olds attending Cornell University's summer high school program in 1985 and 1986, only eight said they were lesbian, bisexual, or gay male. Four times as many had adolescent homosexual sexual encounters (Savin-Williams, 1990). Thus sexual minority youth are difficult to find not only because of our own ignorance and silence, but because their future sexual status and identity are frequently invisible to themselves. They may have same-sex fantasies, attractions, and sexual activity, but they do not want to view themselves or to be viewed by others as lesbian or gay.

This disinclination of youth to say "I'm lesbian/gay" is in large part the result of the pervasive homophobia and heterosexism that characterizes their world. My position is that there is nothing inherently confusing or uncertain about a homosexual sexual orientation—at least no more so than for heterosexual youth. Most of the latter know that they are attracted to other-sex individuals, even if they have same-sex experiences. At a core level most youths know if they are attracted to same-sex partners. Their hesitancy is simply in saying it out loud to themselves and to others because of the repercussions that such statements have in their culture. This is the homophobia that affects youths' ability to integrate their sexuality with other aspects of their identity. Same-sex oriented youth sometimes report that they are or were "confused," but when probed, most will say they knew what they were attracted to from first memories. Their confusion represents the fears, anxieties, isolation, and harassments that they want to avoid when internal pressures to be authentic and honest with themselves and others threaten to become manifest and demand recognition and action. Thus Picano's narrator knew what he was attracted to but also that he was not supposed to love Ricky but to love girls. It is very challenging for a youth to say, "Yes, I'm one of those you love to hate. Please persecute me and call me 'faggot' or 'dyke.'" Homosexuality is frequently condemned and heterosexuality glorified in their families and peer cultures. In fact, heterosexuality is more than glorified; it is assumed to be the youth's present and future.

Despite the obstacles, lesbian, bisexual, and gay male youths are making their presence felt. Many are now coming out to themselves and to others while in junior and senior high school. Many remember feeling "different" from others in their earliest memories. The growing realization that this differentness means that one is other than heterosexual usually emerges during early adolescence and increases exponentially through young adulthood (see Savin-Williams, 1990, for a review of this literature). For example, Rodriguez (1988) found among self-identified Utah gay men that first awareness of same-sex attractions occurred on the average during early adolescence (11 years old); same-sex erotic fantasies, 3 years later; labeling feelings as homosexual at 16 years of age; first consensual orgasm achieved with another male at 17 years; and identifying self as gay, at age 23 years. In a Chicago study of gay youth (Boxer, 1988; Boxer, Cook, & Herdt, 1989), these achievements were reported to occur at essentially the same ages (in years):

	Males	Females
First memory of same-sex attractions	9.6	10.1
First homosexual fantasy	11.2	11.9
First homosexual activity	13.1	15.2
Age at first disclosure	16.0	16.0

Two significant findings emerge from these studies: the relatively nonexistent gender difference on all dimensions except for the boys' earlier onset of homosexual sexual activity and the young ages on all aspects. Both of these are discrepant from previous research (Savin-Williams, 1990). In regard to gender differences, many studies conducted in the 1960s, 1970s, and early 1980s reported the emergence of same-sex attractions, fantasies, activities, labels, and identities 1 to 4 years later for lesbians than for gay males. Explanations included the reduced importance of the erotic aspects of sexuality for females, whether for biological or cultural reasons, and the ease by which females can deny their homoerotic life because it is easier for them to be "masculine" and to express same-sex attractions and feelings outside of a sexual context (Ponse, 1980). Bisexuality also appears to be more of an option for females, thus prolonging the recognition and expression of lesbian attractions and activities ("I'm attracted to men so I can't have lesbian feelings").

Compared to earlier studies (see review in McDonald, 1982), sexual minority youth appear to be reaching various coming out milestones at younger ages. In large part this is probably due to the increased visibility of lesbians, gay males, and bisexuals and homosexuality in our culture. It is now considerably easier for children and youth of any sexual orientation to view models of homosexuality that drastically expand the stereotypic images that were the only ones available to previous generations of youth. Gay characters are routinely appearing on television shows ("Roseanne," "The Simpsons," "thirtysomething," and "Kids in the Hall"), radio (National Public Radio's "Gay and Lesbian Teens" on March 11, 1990), and movies ("My Own Private Idaho," "Poison," "The Wedding Banquet," "Paris Is Burning"). If a youth does not want to be a female athlete or a male hairdresser, she or he can still identify with a lesbian or gay male character in the media or public arena (e.g., doctors, lawyers, politicians). The net effect may very well be a lowering of barriers that prevent youths from experiencing and naming their own realities.

In past generations there was a wide separation in time between a youth's recognition of two different phenomena: "I am attracted to other males/females" and "I am gay/lesbian." In large part this was the result of the silence in our culture regarding what it meant to be gay or lesbian. Without the concept of homosexuality—or a very narrow definition of it as flaming queens and man-haters—it was relatively easy for a youth to avoid labeling himself or herself as gay or lesbian.

My belief is that this temporal gap is vastly narrowing as the direct result of the visibility of sexual minorities and cultures in our present day society. Thus for many teenagers, with the recognition of homoeroticism comes the inevitable "That must mean I'm gay/lesbian." The homophobia still present in our society may make that label difficult to accept and unwarranted, but it does little to deny the reality for youths of their sexual orientation.

The increased visibility of homosexuality in our society has not been paralleled by a decrease in cultural homphobia. Even as more sexual minority youth are able to see themselves for what they are, their worst fear is still present: rejection from parents and peers. Some youths survive and become healthy, well-functioning adolescents and adults. They have faced the acid test and they have survived. But far too many do not and they become the victims of parental abuse, peer harassment, substance abuse, and suicide. The visibility of homosexuality in our society helps youth to define themselves as bisexual, lesbian, or gay, but the cultural homophobia makes those lives far more difficult than they should be to live.

Although more social science and clinical attention has focused on the problems of sexual minority youth than the promises, it is visibility nevertheless. Our greatest, but still insufficient, attention has focused on suicide among sexual minority youth (in regard to mental health issues in general, see Cohen, in press, and Savin-Williams, in press). This is needed attention, but so is the ability of many sexual minority youths to persevere and cope with their hostile world to lead happy, productive lives with a healthy sense of self. For this to occur they must have a "successful" adolescence, which includes resolving issues of same-sex identity and intimacy.

An earlier publication in this series (Savin-Williams & Rodriguez, 1993) addresses the issue of identity. In this chapter, I turn to the limited research that focuses on the difficulties of developing age-appropriate intimate, same-sex romantic relationships.

THE IMPORTANCE OF DATING

Love, Intimacy, and Dating

One essential aspect of developing a healthy sense of self is having "opportunities for extensive social involvements and interpersonal attachments with peers" (Malyon, 1981, p. 326). Isay, a psychiatrist, argued that same-sex oriented youth need romantic relationships with each other: "The self-affirming value of a mutual relationship over time cannot be overemphasized" (1989, p. 50). Love and intimacy can thus emerge. Scarf (1987) has written extensively on these two topics. An intimate relationship "helps us contact archaic, dimly perceived and yet powerfully meaningful aspects of our inner selves" (p. 79). The need for closeness in the context of a "trusting, mutually self-revelatory relationship" is a replay of the intense emotional bond of the first attachment figure in infancy. Scarf maintains, based on the attachment literature, that we are prewired for loving—strongly felt emotional attachments that are experienced "as the need to be near to the loved one" (p. 75). When established, we feel comfortable, safe, secure, and nurtured. These early attachments set an "internal blueprint" that affects the development of intimate peer friendships in early adolescence (L. A. Sroufe, personal communication) and romance in adulthood (Hazan & Shaver, 1987).

Romantic relationships are practiced and pursued during adolescence through the process of dating. Skipper and Nass (1966) summarized the major functions of dating:

1. entertainment and recreation
2. socialization so that the sexes can "get to know each other, learn to adjust to each other, and to develop appropriate techniques of interactions" (pp. 412-413)
3. peer group status achievement
4. selection of mate

Dating stages have been proposed, including sexual awakening, practice, acceptance, and permanent object choice (Feinstein & Ardon, 1973). Dating adjustment, which involves confidence about dating abilities, having dates, and satisfaction with dating, was best predicted in a college sample by an early onset of dating, a high frequency of dating, and involvement in a "committed" dating relationship (Herold, 1979).

Most lesbian and gay male adolescents are deprived of such opportunities because they are unable to date those they feel most erotically attracted to.

That is, because of the antipathy associated with homosexuality, many critical social experiences are not available to homosexual adolescents. For example, their most charged sexual desires are usually seen as perverted, and their deepest feelings of psychological attachment are regarded as unacceptable. This social disapproval interferes with the preintimacy involvement that fosters the evolution of maturity and self-respect in the domain of object relations. (Malyon, 1981, p. 326)

Our culture is far more tolerant of homosexual sex than it is of romantic relationships among same-sex adolescent partners. Homosexual sex seems "temporary," an experiment, a phase, a source of fun, and somehow not real. But to fall in love with someone of the same gender and to maintain a sustained involvement implies irreversible "deviancy." Youth clearly learn this message from the culture that surrounds them.

One example of how culture influences our views is a book that might well represent the child-rearing messages that today's adolescents' parents received and perhaps incorporated in their youth. In her book, *The Normal Sex Interests of Children*, Frances Bruce Strain (1948) wrote that "attachments within the same sex are bound to arise to a greater or less degree" (p. 178) because of same-sex associations during this age. But these should be "transitional," normative schoolgirl crushes and boy hero-worship, that are "steppingstones to intersex love affairs. . . . If the natural, legitimate love objects are at hand, they will find each other, but if they are not, love will find a way, some way" (pp. 179-180). Youths are to be kept from same-sex boarding schools, negative statements about the other sex, and "confirmed homosexuals" who recruit impressionable youths during this "critical period" of development.

This attitude can be seen among youths who fear developing even close friendships with same-sex peers for fear that these will be viewed as homosexual relationships or as sexually intimate (Eder & Sanford, 1986). In a paper addressed to school personnel concerning high school students' attitudes toward homosexuality, Price (1982, p. 472) concluded, "Adolescents can be very cruel to others who are different, who do not conform to the expectations of the peer group." This assessment echoed an earlier view (Norton, 1976, p. 376) that the lesbian or gay male adolescent is "the loneliest person . . . in the typical high school of today."

Peer Harassment as a Barrier to Dating

Very little has apparently changed in the last decade. The Harvey Milk School, an alternative public school for sexual minority youths in New York City, was established in large part because of the harassment that youths received in the public schools because of their "differentness." The youths failed to live up to cultural ideals of sex-appropriate behaviors and roles (Martin & Hetrick, 1988).

Gonsiorek (1988) noted that sex roles and the consequences are particularly polarized and problematic during adolescence:

> Males experience intense peer pressure to be "tough" and "macho," and females to be passive and compliant. Although social sex roles are not intrinsically related to sexual orientation, the distinction is poorly understood by most adolescents, as well as by most adults. Adolescents are frequently intolerant of differentness in others and may castigate or ostracize peers, particularly if the perceived differentness is in the arena of sexuality or sex roles. (p. 116)

The rejection may not be expressed directly but is nevertheless felt by youths in many subtle ways. The rules of socially appropriate behavior and the consequences of nonconformity are known implicitly. Many of the students who attend the Harvey Milk School report that they frequently feel separated and emotionally isolated from their peers because of their differentness (Martin & Hetrick, 1988).

The school problems experienced by sexual minority students are often the result of verbal and physical abuse that they receive from peers. In one study more than two thirds of gay and bisexual male youths said they had experienced school related problems, many of which derived from peer harassment; 40% had lost a friend because of their homosexuality (Remafedi, 1987a). More than one half of Latino and African-American gay and bisexual male adolescents said that they had been ridiculed because of their sexuality (Rotheram-Borus, Rosario, & Koopman, 1991). Forty percent of the youths who sought assistance from the Hetrick-Martin Institute, which established the Harvey Milk School, had suffered abuse as the result of their sexual orientation (Martin & Hetrick, 1988). A survey of the Los Angeles County school system found a high prevalence of antigay abuse inflicted by classmates on sexual minority youths. Most were apparently premeditated, rather than a chance occurrence, and the incidence appears to be escalating dramatically (Peterson, 1989). These data correspond to the antigay violence occurring on college campuses and elsewhere (Herek, 1989). The consequences for sexual minority youth may be quite severe, including running away, engaging in prostitution, attempting suicide, and acting out sexually.

Adolescents may thus monitor their interpersonal interactions: "Am I standing too close? . . . Do I appear too happy to see him(her)?" (Anderson, 1987, p. 174). Hetrick and Martin (1987, p. 31) reflected, "They may feel afraid to show friendship for a friend of the same sex for fear of being misunderstood or giving away their secretly held sexual orientation." If erotic feelings become too aroused, same-sex oriented youth may decide to terminate friendships in order to protect their secret and maintain their peer status. Friendships with the other sex are easier because they avoid the issue of physical and sexual intimacy and will be viewed by peers as heterosexual "interest." The result may be heterosexual dating and, later, marriage, which are not uncommon among sexual minority youth. Dating is used not only for recreation and status enhancement but also as a cover for an emerging same-sex sexual identity. It may serve as self-deception as well as a means of diverting the attention of others. Little research has focused on heterosexual dating among sexual minority youth. More common is documentation of the fact that lesbian, bisexual, and gay youth have heterosexual sex. This may or may not be within the context of a romantic relationship.

Heterosexual Sex and Dating

Early retrospective research (Saghir & Robins, 1973; Schafer, 1976; Troiden & Goode, 1979) reported that gay men and lesbians engaged in heterosexual dating during their adolescence and young adulthood. These might be brief "romances" or ones of a long duration. Motivations were proposed, including denial of homosexual feelings and desires, curiosity, societal insistence on heterosexual norms and behaviors, reduction of personal strains of coming out, and internalization of heterosexist norms. For most, emotional intensity appeared to exceed erotic intensity. A lower level of sexual gratification was worth accepting in order to conform with peer pressures. It was not until later in life that they had opportunities to compare these heterosexual relationships with same-sex ones.

Many lesbian and gay male youths can perform adequately, and with physical enjoyment, as sexual partners of the other sex. Their heterosexual activity has been well documented. Early research with lesbian and gay male adults (Bell & Weinberg, 1978; Gundlach & Riess, 1968; Saghir & Robins, 1973; Weinberg & Williams, 1974) reported the widespread frequency of heterosexual activity: From one half to two thirds of gay men and 70% to 85% of lesbians had at least one heterosexual experience.

In three samples, 50% to 54% of the gay and bisexual male youths had past heterosexual experiences (Boxer et al., 1989; Remafedi, 1987b;

Savin-Williams, 1990). Few, however, had extensive sexual contact with females. Less than 1% of 214 gay and bisexual male youths had more than 50 female partners; the median was 1 (Savin-Williams, 1990). A larger percentage of lesbian and bisexual female youths have had heterosexual sexual experiences—2 of every 3 in one study (Boxer et al., 1989) and 8 of 10 in another (Savin-Williams, 1990). In the latter study of 103 female youths, only one had more than 50 male partners; the median was 2 or 3.

There is little gender difference in age of first heterosexual activity (Boxer et al., 1989). Males in the Chicago study, however, responded more positively than did females to their first heterosexual activity. Boxer et al. (1989) concluded:

> The males in our sample may fit the pattern of using heterosexual behavior to deny their homosexual attractions, while the females appear to have less need to engage in this denial (perhaps because of their more positive reaction to lesbian sex initially). (p. 12)

For most, "It was 'sex without feelings' which they 'kept trying' to enjoy without success" (p. 19). It felt unnatural without the expected and wanted emotional intensity. Many of the gay male youths actively sought heterosexual experiences, in contrast to the lesbian youths, who felt that it was something that happened to them as the result of cultural pressure and coercion from males. Heterosexual sex for many bisexual and lesbian teens was less of a choice and more of an obligation. Thus, for both physical (less erotic attraction) and social (coercion) reasons, heterosexual sex may be less pleasurable than same-sex encounters for sexual minority youth.

Consequences

Because they have learned that emotional intimacy can only be achieved with members of the other sex, same-sex oriented youth may never realize that sexual and emotional intimacy can be merged within a same-sex relationship. If they have same-sex activity it may, by necessity, be within an anonymous, guilt-ridden context. Youth may thus have same-sex oral and anal sex but never kiss their partner because the former is considered sexual and the latter intimate. Preliminary data analysis of 300 gay and bisexual male youths under the age of 21 indicates that this is indeed often true (Remafedi, personal communication).

Other youths may turn to prostitution to meet their intimacy needs (Coleman, 1989). Besides money, sex, adventure, and socializing, underlying motivations for prostituting oneself may include the need for affection and finding someone to take care of them (Maloney, as reported in Coleman, 1989).

Most common, however, is that sexual minority youth feel social and emotional isolation. The two men who began the Harvey Milk School for sexual minority youth, Emery Hetrick and Damien Martin (1988) wrote of this consequence:

> Feelings of being alone, of being the only one who feels this way, of having no one to share feelings with, are reported by over 95% of our clients. . . . When the young person has the example of adult as well as peer role models, when the adolescent has someone to talk to openly and has access to accurate information, emotional isolation tends to resolve. (pp. 171-172)

Many of the youths believed that they would never have the opportunity to develop committed, loving relationships with members of their gender. The isolation impairs their self-esteem and self-worth and reinforces feelings that they are unworthy of receiving love and affection. In adulthood, Hetrick and Martin propose that the result may be fusion in lesbian relationships, which handicaps the development of friendships and other relationships, and promiscuity in gay male relationships, with attending physical and mental health concerns.

RELATIONSHIP RESEARCH WITH LESBIAN, BISEXUAL, AND GAY MALE SAMPLES

Studies of Adult Gay Men and Lesbians

Research with adults documents the connection between being in a romantic relationship and having high levels of self-esteem and self-acceptance—but the causal pathway is unclear (Savin-Williams, 1990). That is, being in a same-sex romance may increase and build positive self-views, or perhaps individuals with high self-esteem are more likely to form and stay in intimate relationships. Establishing a relationship with another man or woman may help to resolve one's sexual identity and make one feel more complete and chosen (Silverstein, 1981).

In one study (Wilkins, 1981), single men who were "cruisers" were more likely to be insecure, emotionally labile, and sociopathic than were those in ongoing romantic relationships. Among men but not women, those who are coupled tend to be more publicly out concerning their sexual orientation (P. Peterson, personal communication). Harry and DeVall's (1978) study of gay men reported that those who were out to themselves and to others at an early age developed crushes on other males when they were adolescents; by contrast, those who experienced heterosexual dating, crushes, and interests while adolescents took much longer to define themselves as gay.

The extent to which being coupled and positive self-esteem are related, however, is debatable. For example, Harry and DeVall (1978) found self-esteem was unrelated among gay men to being (a) always single, (b) "divorced" from a gay man, or (c) coupled with a gay man for over a year. Bell and Weinberg (1978) found evidence for both positions: the two highest self-acceptance groups of gay men were the "happily marrieds" and the "swinging singles"; the latter reported little intention of establishing a romantic relationship. The lowest self-esteem groups with poor psychological adjustment were gay men and lesbians (Legier, 1986) who were not romantically involved with others—the "dysfunctionals," "asexuals," and "unmarrieds-unsettleds."

Whatever the causal pathway and the empirical research findings, it is clear that sexual minority youth, whether in Detroit (Harry & DeVall, 1978), Minneapolis (Remafedi, 1987b), New York State (Savin-Williams, 1990), or the Netherlands (Sanders, 1980), desire to have a long-lasting, committed romantic relationship in their future. Living with a partner of the same gender for life is perceived as an ideal lifestyle for most lesbian, bisexual, and gay male youths. Yet we know relatively little about such relationships.

Same-Sex Relationships Among Youths

There is little published data with teenagers that focus primarily on their same-sex romantic relationships. There is suggestive data from the Chicago, Minnesota, and New York studies. In the former, 202 youths between the ages of 14 and 21 years were interviewed. Of the total number of first homosexual sexual experiences, 17% occurred in the context of dating or a romance. This was more true for the lesbians (22%) than it was for the gay males (15%) (Pratch, Boxer, & Herdt, in preparation). The boys (24%) were more likely than girls (5%) to have their first encounters in a sexual context. More typical, however, was that same-sex friendships evolved into sexual relationships, especially for the girls (45% of the total number of first homosexual activity and 23% for boys). Although it is not clear from the data, many of these same-sex friendships with sex may have evolved into romances for the youths.

Of Remafedi's (1987b) 29 gay and bisexual male youths, 10 had a steady male partner at the time of the interview. Four relationships had lasted less than a month and one exceeded 1 year's duration. The only data published on these relationships indicate that the partners tended to be older than the youths (25 years vs. the youths' average age of 18 years). Of the 19 not currently in a relationship, 11 had been in one in the past. All but two of the 29 hoped for a steady male partner in the future.

In my initial research on gay male, bisexual, and lesbian youth (Savin-Williams, 1990) between the ages of 14 and 23 years, the youths listed their romantic relationships in terms of ages when the relationship began, sex of the partner, and how long the relationship lasted. Two thirds of the males and 86% of the females reported having romantic relationships. Six of 10 romantic relationships for the youths were with a same-sex rather than an other-sex peer. Compared to the gay and bisexual male youths, lesbians and bisexual females reported having (a) more romances (2.4 vs. 1.4); (b) relationships that began at an earlier age (16.6 years vs. 17.2 years); (c) relationships that lasted a longer time (15 months, with range of days to nearly 10 years vs. 12 months, with range of days to 7 years); and (d) a relationship at data collection time (67% of the females vs. 41% of the males). Males were slightly more likely to begin their romantic careers with a member of the same sex.

Lesbian and bisexual female youths with a high proportion of lesbian romances were likely to be in a current relationship, to have had their first romance with a girl, to have had brief relationships, and to be out to others; their self-esteem was essentially the same as the self-esteem of those who had a higher percentage of heterosex-

ual romances. Lesbian and bisexual female youths who began romances early in their lives were also likely to be in a current relationship and to have had multiple and long-lasting romances. Being
publicly out was highly related to having one's first romance be
with another girl.

Gay and bisexual male youths who had a large percentage of gay
rather than heterosexual romances also had a large number of
relationships, were in a current relationship, had had their first
romance with another boy, and had high self-esteem. They were not
more likely to be publicly out. Beginning romances at an early age
was significantly correlated with having long-term and multiple
relationships, having many relationships, having high self-esteem,
and being publicly out.

REFLECTIONS

As in the case of the narrator in Picano's *Ambidextrous,* heterosexual dating among same-sex-oriented youth is clearly defined and
recognizable. His relationship with Ricky was perceived by family
and friends as an adolescent chumship and not as a sexual romance.
Yet the intensity of the sex and the romantic feelings clearly placed
this relationship as a marker in his life: It defined for him his sexual
identity.

As a profession our silence on sexual minority youth is deaden-
ing—in both abstract and concrete senses. We ignore them in our
conferences, our journals, our textbooks, our teaching, and our
awareness. As clinicians and developmental psychologists, we must
be concerned about this silence and its subsequent consequences,
such as encouraging youth to develop intimate relationships with
those to whom they are not particularly erotically attracted.

Garnets, Hancock, Cochran, Goodchilds, and Peplau (1991) recently recommended that therapists recognize the existence, nature,
and concerns of lesbian and gay male relationships. Therapists
should educate themselves, especially in regard to the diversity of
relationships that are possible, and support and validate the importance of these relationships. I believe this to be applicable to researchers and teachers as well.

Sexual minority youth are attempting, like other adolescents, to
find a sense of authenticity and connection with those similar to

themselves. How long can a gay male, bisexual, or lesbian adolescent pretend before she or he begins to have difficulty separating the pretensions from the realities? Many bisexual, lesbian, and gay male youths "use" heterosexual dating to avoid stigma and discrimination. When dating, the "faggot" and "dyke" name calling lessens and peer status increases. Some also date heterosexually as an attempt to disconfirm to themselves the growing encroachment of their homoerotic attractions. The incidence of heterosexual sex and relationships in the lives of gay male and lesbian youths attest to these conflicts.

The difficulties of dating same-sex partners during adolescence are monumental. First is the very simple difficulty of finding each other. The vast majority of those who will eventually identify as bisexual, gay male, or lesbian are not out to themselves, let alone to others. A second prohibition is the consequences of same-sex dating, such as family and peer verbal and physical harassment. A third impediment is the lack of public recognition or "celebration" of those who are romantically involved with a member of the same gender. Unlike heterosexual dating, there is little social advantage, such as peer popularity or acceptance, to be gained by holding hands and kissing another girl or boy in the school hallways. The benefit is purely psychological—a sense of authenticity, intimacy, love, support, and nurturance.

A vivid account of these difficulties is in the seminal autobiography of Aaron Fricke, *Reflections of a Rock Lobster* (1981). He fell in love with a classmate, Paul.

> With Paul's help, I started to challenge all the prejudice I had encountered during 16½ years of life. Sure, it was scary to think that half my classmates might hate me if they knew my secret, but from Paul's example I knew it was possible to one day be strong and face them without apprehension. (p. 44)

Through Paul, Aaron was becoming more resilient, self-confident, warm, and loving of life.

> His strengths were my strengths. . . . I realized that my feelings for him were unlike anything I had felt before. The sense of camaraderie was familiar from other friendships; the deep spiritual love I felt for Paul was new. So was the openness, the sense of communication with another. (p. 45)

Life was significant. Poems were written and a future was planned. Kindness and strength were freed. Aaron was in love, with another boy.
But there were no guidelines or models.

Heterosexuals learn early in life what behavior is expected of them. They get practice in their early teens having crushes, talking to their friends about their feelings, going on first dates and to chaperoned parties, and figuring out their feelings. Paul and I hadn't gotten all that practice; our relationship was formed without much of a model to base it on. It was the first time either of us had been in love like this and we spent much of our time just figuring out what that meant for us. (p. 46)

Eventually, after a court case, Paul and Aaron attended the Senior Prom. Although the book is filled with horrid examples of the reception lesbian, gay male, and bisexual youth receive from peers, teachers, and parents, the couple encountered more support than destruction from their fellow seniors.

As social scientists we need to listen to Aaron and to Picano's narrator, to hear their concerns, insights, and solutions. Most of all, we need to end the invisibility of romantic relationships among gay male, lesbian, and bisexual youth and to validate and support their existence. The well-being of millions of youths would be enhanced.

REFERENCES

Anderson, D. (1987). Family and peer relations of gay adolescents. In S. C. Geinstein (Ed.), *Adolescent psychiatry: Developmental and clinical studies* (Vol. 14, pp. 162-178). Chicago: University of Chicago Press.

Bell, A. P., & Weinberg, M. S. (1978). *Homosexualities: A study of diversity among men and women.* New York: Simon & Schuster.

Boxer, A. M. (1988, March). *Betwixt and between: Developmental discontinuities of gay and lesbian youth.* Paper presented at the Society for Research on Adolescence, Alexandria, VA.

Boxer, A. M., Cook, J. A., & Herdt, G. (1989, August). *First homosexual and heterosexual experiences reported by gay and lesbian youth in a urban community.* Paper presented at the Annual Meeting of the American Sociological Association, San Francisco.

Cohen, K. M. (in press). Living a life of secrets and lies: Psychosocial stressors among sexual minority youth. In R. Savin-Williams & K. M. Cohen (Eds.), *Understanding diversity among lesbians, gay males, and bisexuals: Clinical, developmental, and social issues.* Forth Worth, TX: Harcourt Brace.

Coleman, E. (1989). The development of male prostitution activity among gay and bisexual adolescence. *Journal of Homosexuality, 17,* 131-149.

Coles, R., & Stokes, G. (1985). *Sex and the American teenager.* New York: Harper & Row.

Eder, D., & Sanford, S. (1986). The development and maintenance of interactional norms among early adolescents. In P. Adler (Ed.), *Sociological studies of child development* (Vol. 1, pp. 283-300). Greenwich, CT: JAI Press.

Feinstein, S. C., & Ardon, M. S. (1973). Trends in dating patterns and adolescent development. *Journal of Youth and Adolescence, 2,* 157-166.

Fricke, A. (1981). *Reflections of a rock lobster: A story about growing up gay.* Boston: Alyson.

Garnets, L., Hancock, K. A., Cochran, S. D., Goodchilds, J., & Peplau, L. A. (1991). Issues in psychotherapy with lesbians and gay men: A survey of psychologists. *American Psychologist, 46,* 964-972.

Gonsiorek, J. C. (1988). Mental health issues of gay and lesbian adolescents. *Journal of Adolescent Health Care, 9,* 114-122.

Gundlach, R. H., & Riess, B. F. (1968). Self and sexual identity in the female: A study of female homosexuals. In B. F. Riess (Ed.), *New directions in mental health* (pp. 205-231). New York: Grune & Stratton.

Harry, J., & DeVall, W. B. (1978). *The social organization of gay males.* New York: Praeger.

Hazan, C., & Shaver, P. (1987). Romantic love conceptualized as an attachment process. *Journal of Personality and Social Psychology, 52,* 511-524.

Herek, G. M. (1989). Hate crimes against lesbians and gay men: Issues for research and policy. *American Psychologist, 44,* 948-955.

Herold, E. S. (1979). Variables influencing the dating adjustment of university students. *Journal of Youth and Adolescence, 8,* 73-79.

Hetrick, E. S., & Martin, A. D. (1987). Developmental issues and their resolution for gay and lesbian adolescents. *Journal of Homosexuality, 14,* 25-44.

Isay, R. A. (1989). *Being homosexual: Gay men and their development.* New York: Avon.

Legier, D. (1986). Patterns of diversity among homosexual and heterosexual women. *Dissertation Abstracts International, 46,* 4018B.

Malyon, A. K. (1981). The homosexual adolescent: Developmental issues and social bias. *Child Welfare, 60,* 321-330.

Martin, A. D., & Hetrick, E. S. (1988). The stigmatization of the gay and lesbian adolescent. *Journal of Homosexuality, 15,* 163-183.

McDonald, G. J. (1982). Individual differences in the coming out process for gay men: Implications for theoretical models. *Journal of Homosexuality, 8,* 47-60.

Norton, J. L. (1976). The homosexual and counseling. *Personnel and Guidance Journal, 54,* 374-377.

Peterson, J. W. (1989, April 11). Gay runaways are in more danger than ever, and gay adults won't help. *The Advocate,* pp. 8-10.

Picano, F. (1985). *Ambidextrous.* New York: Penguin.

Ponse, B. (1980). Lesbians and their worlds. In J. Marmor (Ed.), *Homosexual behavior: A modern reappraisal* (pp. 157-175). New York: Basic Books.

Pratch, L., Boxer, A. M., & Herdt, G. (in preparation). *First sexual experiences among gay and lesbian youth: Person, age, and context.*

Price, J. H. (1982). High school students' attitudes toward homosexuality. *Journal of School Health, 52,* 469-474.

Remafedi, G. (1987a). Male homosexuality: The adolescent's perspective. *Pediatrics, 79,* 326-330.

Remafedi, G. (1987b). Adolescent homosexuality: Psychosocial and medical implications. *Pediatrics, 79,* 331-337.

Remafedi, G., Resnick, M., Blum, R., & Harris, L. (1992). Demography of sexual orientation in adolescents. *Pediatrics, 89, 714-721.*

Rodriguez, R. (1988, June). *Significant events in gay identity development: Gay men in Utah.* Paper presented at the annual meetings of the American Psychological Association, Atlanta, GA.

Rotheram-Borus, M. J., Rosario, M., & Koopman, C. (1991). Minority youths at high risk: Gay males and runaways. In M. E. Colten & S. Gore (Eds.), *Adolescent stress: Causes and consequences* (pp. 181-200). New York: Aldine.

Saghir, M. T., & Robins, E. (1973). *Male and female homosexuality.* Baltimore: Williams & Wilkins.

Sanders, G. (1980). Homosexualities in the Netherlands. *Alternative Lifestyles, 3,* 278-311.

Savin-Williams, R. C. (1990). *Gay and lesbian youth: Expressions of identity.* Washington, DC: Hemisphere.

Savin-Williams, R. C. (1994). Verbal and physical abuse as stressors in the lives of sexual minority youth: Associations with school problems, running away, substance abuse, prostitution, and suicide. *Journal of Counseling and Clinical Psychology, 62.*

Savin-Williams, R. C., & Rodriguez, R. G. (1993). A developmental, clinical perspective on lesbian, gay male, and bisexual youths. In T. P. Gullotta, G. R. Adams, & R. Montemayor (Eds.), *Adolescent sexuality: Advances in adolescent development* (Vol. 5, pp. 77-101). Newbury Park, CA: Sage.

Scarf, M. (1987). *Intimate partners: Patterns in love and marriage.* New York: Random House.

Schafer, S. (1976). Sexual and social problems of lesbians. *Journal of Sex Research, 12,* 50-69.

Silverstein, C. (1981). *Man to man: Gay couples in America.* New York: William Morrow.

Skipper, J. K. Jr., & Nass, G. (1966). Dating behavior: A framework for analysis and an illustration. *Journal of Marriage and the Family, 27,* 412-420.

Strain, F. B. (1948). *The normal sex interests of children: From infancy to adolescence.* New York: Appleton-Century-Crofts.

Troiden, R. R., & Goode, E. (1979). Variables related to the acquisition of a gay identity. *Journal of Homosexuality, 5,* 383-392.

Weinberg, M., & Williams, C. J. (1974). *Male homosexuals: Their problems and adaptations.* New York: Penguin.

Wilkens, J. L. (1981). A comparative study of male homosexuality personality factors: Brief cruising encounters vs. ongoing relationships. *Dissertation Abstracts International, 42,* 2555B.

9. Adolescents' Relations With Adults Outside the Family

Nancy Darling
Dickinson College

Stephen F. Hamilton
Cornell University

Starr Niego
Cornell University

Whom we develop relations with, what those relations are like, and how those relations affect us depends upon our own characteristics, the characteristics of other persons, and the social roles that define our relationship to one another. Most research and theorizing about adolescents' social relations have been directed toward people in two classes of social roles: parents and peers. In this chapter, we discuss adolescents' relations with another class of associates—unrelated adults. How frequent are such relationships? What are they like? How do differences in social context change their character and influence?

Adolescence is a transitional period between embeddedness within the family and the relative independence of adulthood. Among its defining qualities are an expanding awareness of social relations, greater ability to actively shape the social environment, and the development of a self-concept that includes an awareness of both the current self and potential adult selves. Adolescents' relations with parents shape subsequent adult relations, and they undergo a transformation during adolescence; relations with peers take on new qualities of reciprocity and intimacy during the same period. Therefore these relations have been explored in greatest depth. As increasing attention has been placed on community influences on adolescent development and on the potentially ameliorative properties of adolescents' relations with adults outside the family, however, a greater understanding of the role of unrelated adults is needed.

This chapter discusses the role of unrelated adults in adolescent development. Although evidence suggests that casual contact between youths and adults who support community standards seems to reduce delinquency and gang activity (Sampson, 1992) and support the development of school-related skills and positive attitudes toward school (Coleman & Hoffer, 1987; Darling, Gringlas, & Steinberg, 1993; Fletcher, Steinberg, & Darling, 1993), it is not this type of relationship that is our focus. This chapter will review literature pertaining to adolescents' relationships with adults whom the adolescent regards as "important" or "significant."

Significant others influence adolescents both through the interaction they engage in with the adolescent and their ability to serve as role models (Bell, 1970). Thus a favorite biology teacher might facilitate a girl's entering a science career because the challenging discussions between teacher and student helped her develop sophisticated cognitive and problem-solving capabilities and a solid understanding of course material, because success in this area contributed to the girl developing an image of herself as a capable and intelligent student, but also because the positive relationship between student and teacher allowed the girl to project herself into the role of scientist.

Like interactions with persons in other social roles, the components of adolescents' relations with unrelated adults may be divided into those that are primarily affective and those that are primarily instrumental. Each component has different developmental implications, and they may combine in ways that either undermine or support each other. Focusing on the processes through which significant others influence development allows researchers to detect those influences. In this chapter, we argue that one reason for the neglect of unrelated adults as a developmental influence on youths is that traditionally American researchers have focused on the affective qualities of relationships rather than on their instrumental and activity-centered components. It is the latter, we contend, that distinguish the influence of unrelated adults from that of significant others in other social roles.

SYMBOLIC INTERACTIONISM AND SELF-EVALUATION

One process through which significant others are thought to influence development is through the direct and indirect feedback they provide about the self (Cooley, 1902/1964; Dewey, 1940; James, 1890/1950; Mead, 1934; for a review see Stryker, 1981). Symbolic interactionist theorists provided impressive empirical support for the contention that what we believe about ourselves reflects this feedback and that our beliefs about ourselves are important determinants of our emotional states and how we interact with our environments.

Two types of distinctions have been used to explain social role variability in the association between perception of one's relations with significant others and self-concept: variability in one's perception of the information source and variability in the aspect of the self that one perceives the source to reflect upon. People occupying different social roles differ in their influence on our self-concept because of the *value* we place upon their opinion and because of their *credibility* (Rosenberg, 1973). Value refers to the extent to which we desire the other to think well of us. For example, the opinion of her mother is probably more important to an adolescent girl than the opinion of her math teacher. Credibility refers to the extent to which we place faith in the truth or validity of the person's evaluation. The same adolescent girl might place more faith in her math teacher's evaluation of her academic ability than she does in her mother's evaluation. Thus an adolescent's self-image could be influenced by a significant other either because the other is emotionally important (i.e., is highly valued) or because the adolescent believes that the other is a credible source of information on the behavior in question.

The feedback the girl receives from her mother and her math teacher may affect different components of her self-concept. Social roles vary in the extent to which people filling those roles will tend to be "orientational significant others" or "role-specific significant others" (Denzin, 1966). Orientational significant others are those whose opinions influence global self-evaluation, such as one's sense of the self as a good person or a hard worker. Parents are the prototypic orientational significant other. The influence of role-specific significant others is limited to their evaluation of specific qualities or characteristics that are delimited to a particular role or role set. For example, the evaluation of a basketball coach might affect one's opinion of oneself as a basketball player or an athlete, but not affect one's general self-esteem.

REFERENCE GROUPS AND ROLE MODELS

A second set of processes through which unrelated adults and other significant others may influence development is through their shaping of adolescents' normative beliefs and expectations. Specifically, significant others perform several functions of reference groups.[1] The first of these is that of a role model (Daloz, 1987; Erkut & Mokros, 1984). As defined by Kemper (1968), a role model is one

> who demonstrates for the individual how something is done in the technical sense. . . . [The role model] is concerned with the "how" question. The essential quality of the role model is that he possesses skills and displays techniques which the actor lacks (or thinks he lacks) and from whom, by observation and comparison with his own performance, the actor can learn. (p. 33)

A role model provides students with observational learning opportunities that include imitation of new behaviors, inhibition of unsuccessful behaviors through observation of negative consequences, and the disinhibition of formerly constrained behaviors and increasing use of successful behaviors through observation of positive consequences (Bandura, 1977).

Adolescents can also assimilate the values of a significant other through the other's influence on their experience of the normative group and through the other's acting as an audience[2] (Kemper, 1968). Conformity to group norms offers the minimal acceptable criteria for performance. To the extent that significant others raise the standards to which adolescents compare themselves, adolescents will raise their minimal standards of performance. Kemper's concept of the audience, in contrast, encompasses "those for whom one performs in an attempt to assure recognition" (Kemper, 1968, p. 33). The actor attributes values to the audience and attempts to behave in accordance to those values, actively seeking their attention. Significant others may both serve as an audience and help define the audience to whom a student plays.

SCAFFOLDING

Both symbolic interactionism and reference group theory are based upon processes that change developing persons' perceptions of themselves and their worlds. In contrast, the interest that researchers working from both the Piagetian and Vygotskian perspectives place on interactions with others centers upon the potential influence that others have on basic skills and cognitive abilities. For example, Piaget has argued that social interaction in which contrasting views are presented and discussed facilitates the process of disequilibration and thus cognitive growth (Piaget, 1983). Vygotsky argues that cognitive development proceeds through the internalization of increasingly complex interactions taking place in a social context (Wertsch, 1981). For example, engaging in a joint activity with another person is thought to enable an adolescent to engage in more complex interactions with the physical environment than he or she could alone and thus to facilitate cognitive growth. This type of joint interaction is called scaffolding. From this perspective, the primary mechanism through which adults or other significant others would influence adolescent development would be through social interactions that would hinder or facilitate basic cognitive changes in adolescents' ability to manipulate their environment rather than through their perceptions.

ORGANIZATION

How do unrelated adults function in adolescents' lives, and through what processes are they likely to influence adolescents' development? What makes the influence of unrelated adults different from that of significant others in other social roles? In examining the research on the role that significant unrelated adults play in adolescents' lives and the potential developmental impact of these adults, we will draw upon four types of studies: descriptive studies of adolescents' perceptions of their relations with significant others; retrospective studies of the role of significant adults in the lives of "resilient" youth; intervention research on the efficacy of introducing potentially significant others into adolescents' lives; and correlational studies of the association between interaction patterns in adolescents' naturally occurring relations with adults and adolescent outcomes.

These studies address the following questions: How often do adolescents establish close relations with unrelated adults? How do adolescents describe their relations with unrelated adults, and how do they compare with their relations with significant others in other social roles? What is the developmental impact of adolescents' relations with nonkin adults? We will present information relevant to each question in turn. This information will be used to reflect upon the processes through which significant others are thought to influence development and to discuss a possible model for examining the special role played by unrelated adults.

REVIEW OF THE LITERATURE

How Often Do Adolescents Establish Close Relations With Unrelated Adults?

When asked to list the adults who are important in their lives, adolescents name parents, adult siblings, grandparents and other relatives, neighbors, family friends, teachers, coaches, and religious figures. Variations across gender, race, and the setting in which the research is conducted confound efforts to draw a definitive picture of the nature of youths' social ties. However, a few findings are common across studies. (See Galbo, 1984, 1986, for extensive reviews.)

Nearly all youth cite at least one significant adult, most often of their own gender. Not surprisingly, parents and other relatives are mentioned more often than adults outside the family. Although unrelated adults comprise only a small proportion of the social network members of 7th to 10th graders (approximately 10% in one study by Blyth, Hill, & Thiel [1982]), most adolescents will name at least one unrelated adult who is important to them. For example, in one retrospective study, 82% of college juniors named an unrelated adult as one of the 10 most important people in their lives prior to entering college (Hamilton & Darling, 1989). When allowed to name adult associates separately from peer associates, 69% of seventh to eighth graders named an unrelated adult as currently important to them (Darling, 1990), and Blyth et. al (1982) reported that adolescent boys named an average of 1.89 and girls an average of 2.31 significant nonkin adults. When confronted with a stressful life event, 56% of seventh and eighth graders said that they asked an unrelated adult for help with their problem (Munsch & Blyth, 1993). Thus although unrelated adults are less commonly nominated as significant network members than parents, adult kin, or unrelated peers, they are perceived as important by large numbers of adolescents.

Girls tend to name more unrelated adults as significant others than boys do, and context may also help determine both the likelihood that adolescents will encounter and develop meaningful relationships with unrelated adults and the type of adult with whom they come to associate. Garbarino and his colleagues found that urban children included more unrelated adults in their networks than their suburban or rural peers. However, when asked to name the individuals to whom they could turn for help with a problem, the urban sample named fewer adults than their nonurban peers (Garbarino, Burston, Raber, Russell, & Crouter, 1978). Such variability has been found both across neighborhoods within the same city (Furstenberg, 1990) and across schools in the same community (Coleman & Hoffer, 1987) and appears to be one way in which communities contribute to variation in the development of adolescent problem behavior. Children from families in which parents are divorced are also more likely to name unrelated adults as part of their social network than are their peers from intact families (Stinson, 1991). Many of the adults named were friends of the children's mothers whom they had met while accompanying their mothers on social visits.

Cross-national comparisons call attention to differences in social arrangements that are taken for granted in any one country. Customary practices and the structure of social institutions, especially educational systems and social services, create varying opportunities for young people to interact with adults (Hamilton, 1991; Matsuda, 1989). A good illustration is the institution of apprenticeship found in Germany, Switzerland, Austria, and Denmark and in some Eastern European countries. Apprentices, who include half or more of the older adolescent population, spend a majority of their waking hours at work, in the company of adults (Hamilton, 1990). This places them in direct and sustained contact with adults far more regularly than their agemates who attend school full time. In Germany, other social arrangements also reduce the segregation of adolescents that is characteristic of U.S. communities. For example, most of the activities that are sponsored by schools in the United States as "extracurricular" activities, including sports teams and music groups, are sponsored by community clubs in Germany, in which members are drawn from the entire age spectrum. Instead of the high school band, a parade features the community band, in which one trumpeter may be 16 and another 61.

Although availability changes the number and social roles of adults with whom the adolescent may form relationships, even within the range of available adults, it is unclear exactly what qualities will cause a particular adult to come to be regarded as "significant." In the research reviewed by Galbo (1984, 1986), adults were valued for their honesty, understanding, openness, encouragement, and support. Yet because many of the researchers presented youth with lists of adults assumed by the researchers to be significant, we cannot be certain how accurate or meaningful the findings are. Moreover, lists of important attributes tell us little about the kinds of relationships that develop between adolescents and adults and what consequences they might have for development.

How Do Adolescents Describe Their Relations
With Unrelated Adults, and
How Do These Compare With
Their Relations With Significant
Others in Other Social Roles?

The normative qualities that adolescents attribute to their relations with nonkin adults are different from those they ascribe to either parents or peers. This is true both when adolescents are asked to describe their relations with adults, such as teachers, who are chosen by investigators because they are presumed to be important (for example, Rosenberg, 1973, or Lempers & Clark-Lempers, 1992) or when the described relations are with adults who were chosen by adolescents as among the most important in their lives (for example, see Blyth et. al, 1982; Darling, 1990; Darling, Hamilton, & Matsuda, 1990; Hamilton & Darling, 1989).

Two key findings emerge from this literature. First, adolescents describe their relations with nonkin adults as less emotionally supportive or companionable than their relations with other classes of associates. For example, in a study of adolescents' descriptions of their relations with mothers, fathers, siblings, best friends, and most important teachers, Lempers and Clark-Lempers (1992) conclude, "Relations with teachers were, in general, ranked lowest . . . by all adolescent groups for affection, reliable alliance, companionship, intimacy, and nurturance" (p. 91). Teachers were also ranked among the lowest in admiration, conflict, and satisfaction. The only exception to this pattern was that teachers were ranked moderately high in their provision of instrumental aid. These results are consistent with the literature reviewed by Galbo (1984) with regard to teachers and are used to support the contention that "most adolescents do not perceive teachers as important to them, especially if they have parents or other relatives who are supportive" (p. 92). The word "important," however, is relative, and what is important differs in different theoretical contexts. The results of another study of seventh and eighth graders' relations with fathers, mothers, unrelated adults, siblings, and peers also suggest that adolescent-adult relations are less affect laden than those with other associates (Darling, 1990). Associates in each category were selected by the adolescent from among all those elicited during a social network interview and were chosen because they were the associate in that category with whom the adolescent described the most intense relationship. Unrelated adults were less likely to be described as antagonists or controllers than were other associates, and were seen as less supportive than parents (Darling, 1990). Importantly, however, when a broader range of relationship qualities that included instrumental functions was included, unrelated adults took on a more prominent role. Unrelated adults were perceived more as teachers, role models, challengers, and guides than were peers or siblings, although not as much as parents.

A series of studies comparing U.S. and Japanese adolescents' perceptions of the "functional roles" of parents, peers, and unrelated adults came to similar conclusions (Darling et al., 1990). College students in the United States ($N = 126$) and Japan ($N = 239$) named the 10 people whom they believed had been most influential in their lives during high school and described 27 different aspects of their relationship with these significant others. Despite important cultural differences, college students in both Japan and the United States reported that the instrumental functions associated with "mentoring" (i.e., teaching, challenging, and serving as a role model) were the salient features of relations with adults outside the family. Although nonkin adults were described as companions about as much as parents (though much less than peers), they were described as less supportive and much less antagonistic than either parents or peers.

Taken together, these findings paint a portrait of adolescents' relations with unrelated adults that is quite different from their relations with either parents or peers. Whereas adolescents' relations with parents are characterized by both strong affective and instrumental components, and their relations with peers as being predominated by affect, the salient characteristics of relations with unrelated adults are instrumental.

What Is the Developmental Impact of Adolescents' Relations With Nonkin Adults?

Much attention to the study of adolescents' relations with adults outside the family stems from increasing evidence that such individuals may play a significant role in facilitating healthy development. Studies of "resilient" children and youth, those who thrive in circumstances that are devastating to most, suggest that youth who overcome serious obstacles to successfully negotiate the transition to adulthood are often guided by strong, supportive adults (Garmezy, 1987; Rutter, 1987; Werner & Smith, 1982). When parents are unavailable or unable to provide necessary care (e.g., because of illness, severe deprivation, death, or divorce), these adults step in to serve *in loco parentis*. Michael Rutter, who has devoted considerable effort to identifying how youth cope with adverse conditions in their lives, asserts that relations with supportive adults may be particularly important at turning points, when decisions are made that will shape the life course. His research, concerned primarily with features of individuals and their environments that help protect against psychopathology, is reinforced by applied studies of school performance and avoidance of problem behavior among youth in threatening circumstances (Lefkowitz, 1987; Wilson, 1987).

Reflecting on this body of research, Rutter (1987) argues strongly that we need to investigate the mechanisms and processes that protect children and youth from risk, not simply broadly defined variables or individual attributes associated with resilience. Comparing the functions performed by individuals occupying different social roles offers one way of understanding the processes at work in adolescents' interpersonal relations. For example, we might ask whether and how ties to parents and friends vary. Darling (1991) examined the association between challenge and support 8th and 11th graders experienced in their relationships with significant others and their performance on quantitative and verbal achievement tests. Challenge was conceived as the extent to which associates questioned adolescents' ideas, pushed them to think in new ways, and offered alternative points of view. Support was conceived as the extent to which a significant other validated, protected, and encouraged the adolescent.

Dramatically different patterns of association were found for the two age groups. Eleventh graders who named at least one unrelated adult challenger performed better on quantitative tests than those who did not. However, neither support nor challenge from unrelated adults predicted achievement scores of the eighth-grade students. In contrast, parental challenge and support were associated with achievement during early adolescence, but the influence waned by the eleventh grade. Also noteworthy was the finding that support provided by unrelated adults did not predict achievement for the older group of students. Yet the support (but not the challenge) characteristic of peer relations did predict performance on quantitative tests.

Similarly, a study of 92 16-year-old boys in Norway found that school performance was influenced by the father's socioeconomic status and by the number of nonkin adults in the boys' social networks (Cochran & Bo, 1989). These adults included family friends; coaches, teachers, and youth workers; adult members of peers' families; and neighbors. Subjects in this study described their relations with nonkin adults as centered on casual social interaction, activities, and information exchange, not on emotional bonds.

A Cautionary Note

Together these studies suggest that beneficial effects of youth-adult relationships are shaped in part by activities and the contexts in which they occur. The same holds true for deleterious effects. In their study of youth in the workplace, Greenberger and Steinberg (1986) found some evidence of antisocial behavior and negative work values for youth engaged in part-time employment. Closer investigation of relations between the young people and their supervisors revealed that the two groups had little regular contact. Because the jobs required few skills, there were few opportunities for the kinds of joint activities or teaching opportunities examined in Darling's research. Moreover, "adult" supervisors were often just a few years older than the youth themselves.

In a study conducted by Foster-Clark (1989), the presence of challenging unrelated adults in boys' social networks was associated with higher rates of self-reported delinquency, but only when neither or only one parent also performed this role. The researchers hypothesized that these unrelated adults may have "challenged" the boys to engage in negative or antisocial behaviors. Yet additional evidence supported a compensatory role for extended-family adults on the same measures of delinquency.

Mentoring

Intervention programs focusing on unrelated adults in informal roles often use the rubric of "mentoring." Mentoring programs match adolescents with nonkin adults whom they would be un- likely to know without the program. These programs are designed to help adolescents become more competent and responsible as they face the multiple challenges of coming of age, particularly the challenges of racial discrimination and poverty (Flaxman, Ascher, & Harrington, 1988; Freedman, 1991). As efforts to provide selected adolescents with unrelated adult significant others, these programs can be considered experiments whose results might shed light on the questions of interest here.

The most spectacular and best publicized program is Eugene Lang's "I Have a Dream" program, which grew out of a spontane- ous promise to sixth-grade students in his former elementary school in New York City. Lang agreed to pay the college tuition of all students who graduated from high school and continued with their education. In addition to offering financial support, Lang took a continuing personal interest in the young people and hired a full- time social worker to guide them through the next 6 years, helping them get the most out of their schooling, formulate plans for the future, and cope with personal crises. It is the mentoring aspect of the program to which Lang attributes the high rate of success among students. The rate of high school graduation, college entrance, and college completion of the "Dreamers" far exceeds what would have been expected from an ordinary sixth-grade class in Harlem.

Public/Private Ventures, a research and development organiza- tion, has undertaken the first extensive evaluation of I Have a Dream and other mentoring programs (Higgins, Toso, Furano, & Branch, 1991; Styles & Morrow, 1992).[3] Some of the difficulties in evaluating programs like these were noted in Hamilton's (1981) study of the Learning Web, a program matching youth with adult volunteers who can teach them a skill. Although parents were convinced that their children benefited, Hamilton found the program to be a different experience for each participant. Such variability hindered any attempts to draw firm conclusions about its impact.[4]

Hamilton and Hamilton (1992a) warned that mentoring programs are not as simple and inexpensive as their most enthusiastic proponents claim. Indeed, the same barriers that keep adolescents apart from adults under normal circumstances interfere with the creation of mentoring relationships. Simply keeping in touch and finding time to be together were overwhelming tasks for many pairs.

In the program they studied, the researchers found that mentoring relationships failed to develop when mentors viewed the relationship as predominantly emotional. Adults who worried about whether their proteges liked them were stymied by such adolescent behavior as not returning telephone calls. Mentor-youth pairs would engage in a recreational activity together, enjoy it, but not be willing or able to get together regularly. If, on the other hand, the mentor set an instrumental goal, which could often be described in terms of building character and competence in the protege, the pair met more frequently and expressed greater satisfaction with their relationship. The successful mentors, in other words, wanted to teach something, not just get to know a young person. Ironically, relationships were built when building a relationship was *not* the main purpose for getting together.

Another conclusion from that study was that mentoring needs a context. Hamilton and Hamilton suggested that career interests seemed to be a constructive focus for mentoring and thus workplaces would be fruitful locations. The efforts of mentors who took protegés to a movie or engaged in other "entertaining" activities were successful only when the activity was directed toward an instrumental purpose: for example, discussing the personal implications of a film about a successful woman, or planning and preparing a meal together.

Summary: Instrumental Versus Affective Relations

A common theme emerges from each of these four strands of research. In comparison with adolescents' peer and parental relations, significant relations with nonkin adults are characterized more by instrumental components than by affect. When asked to name adults outside the family who are or were important to them, adolescents tend to identify adults filling roles with explicit social-izing functions, such as teacher, coach, or youth group leader. One distinguishing feature of these relations is the extent to which the adults set out to nurture the talents and abilities of the adolescent. From what we have seen in the available research, engaging youth in challenging, goal-directed joint activities appears particularly beneficial to their development. This is not to say that such relations are without emotion. In fact, a strong tone of mutual caring is frequently present. Challenging, teaching, and pushing adolescents to do their best is an expression of caring as much as is the emotional warmth we often associate with emotional bonds. What distinguishes relations with unrelated adults, however, is that the emotional relationship with a particular teacher or coach appears to grow out of that adult's validation of the adolescent's effort and ability. For example, a boy who receives special attention from his basketball coach that centers on the teach-ing of skills may interpret the positive affect in the relationship in that context. Thus he may believe that one reason the coach likes him is that he is a good basketball player and a hard worker—that is, because of what he *does*. He may work to enhance that part of his identity by working harder at those skills. This is clearly different from relations with friends or parents, social roles that prescribe that affection is to be based on who he *is*.

The distinction made between role-specific and orientational sig-nificant others is quite similar. When the social roles unrelated adults occupy begin as delimited to a particular sphere (as in the case of the coach or most other adults adolescents name), the feed-back they provide to adolescents may be delimited as well. How-ever, as they become more important (i.e., increase in value), their influence may spread to broader domains of the self-concept, such as the self as hard working or intelligent.

The often delimited and instrumental basis of adolescents rela-tions with nonkin adults may change the way adolescents evaluate the credibility of their feedback. When a particular teacher or coach becomes important to an adolescent, it is either because the adoles-cent sees in that person qualities the adolescent admires and wants to emulate or because the person holds a vision of the adolescent that the adolescent wants to share. These qualities may be either personal or solely skill related. This admired person's validation of the adolescent's abilities may be especially valuable if the adolescent believes that the admired person's evaluation is unbiased by prior emotional bonds. Thus when adolescents and unrelated adults do form strong bonds of mutual affection, the adolescent may interpret them as resulting, first, from his or her abilities, and, second, from his or her qualities as a human being. Thus, unlike the praise of a mother or a best friend, which is in some senses obligatory, praise from an unrelated adult is less easy to dismiss and more likely to be taken to heart. This is particularly true when it refers to observable performance, as in athletics or music, where standards are more visible and praise for the sake of encouragement is easier to detect.

Another result of the social roles that usually define the relations between adolescents and unrelated adults is that equal reciprocity is less likely to characterize relations between adolescents and non-kin adults than relations between adolescents and unrelated friends. The typical roles in which adolescents encounter unrelated adults are those like teacher or coach, which obligate the adult to be responsive to the adolescents for whom they are responsible. Thus the quality of relations between adolescents and nonkin adults is much less dependent upon the adolescent's skill in maintaining the relationship than are adolescents' relations with peers, for example.

FUTURE RESEARCH DIRECTIONS

Reflecting back to the processes through which significant others are thought to influence adolescent development, it seems possible that research on the role of unrelated adults in adolescent development has failed to produce compelling results partly because researchers have been looking in the wrong place. Most research on the role of significant others has been an extension of research on the influence of parents and peers, both social roles in which affective components exert a strong influence. Uncovering the role of nonkin adults may necessitate a different approach.

First, researchers must expand the characterization of relationships beyond purely affective qualities (such as warmth, companionship, antagonism, and support) that are clearly important to also include other qualities such as challenging, teaching, and introducing to new ideas. Second, researchers should pay closer attention to the content of interactions, including specific standards and joint activities. One way in which significant others may influence adolescents during critical periods is by introducing them to new settings and activities. These settings and activities may have developmental consequences long beyond the emotional relationship between adolescent and the other. Third, researchers need to focus on both role-specific and global self-concept and to look at the developmental consequences of specific components of relations with significant others on each. Finally, the affective and instrumental components of social relations must be looked at interactively as well as additively.

Another set of implications for research is also clear. The topic of adolescents' relations with nonkin adults is worthy of further exploration, and that exploration should be sensitive to individual and contextual variation in the frequency and form of such relations. In particular, future research should distinguish among adolescent subjects, especially in terms of their gender, age, social class, and family form. It should attempt to identify who the unrelated adults are with whom adolescents interact and the nature of that interaction. The most useful research will not take snapshots but videotapes, tracing the process of interaction and relationship development over time. International comparisons offer useful contrasts and should be pursued as a complement to conventional single-country studies. Evaluations of mentoring programs should be exploited for their potential to add a significant unrelated adult to an adolescent's social network.

This is the route now being taken by the second author and his colleagues at Cornell; that is, social experimentation designed to introduce potentially significant adults into adolescents' lives. Finding that the goals of program mentors were too easily displaced toward emotional ties and too often without a context, we turned instead to the institution of apprenticeship, which is traditionally based on a close and enduring relationship between an adolescent and an adult outside the family.

Current work investigates how elements of German apprenticeship can be adapted to the United States and what impact apprenticeship might have on adolescents' relations with adults. The program development side of this effort has been reported elsewhere (Hamilton & Hamilton, 1992b; Hamilton & Hamilton, 1993; Hamilton, Hamilton, & Wood, 1991). Here we will briefly describe plans for studying youth apprentices' relations with adult "coaches" and "mentors."[5]

In the Youth Apprenticeship Demonstration Project, young people, beginning in their junior year of high school, spend part of the school day (10 to 15 hours per week) in a workplace where they are not simply part-time employees but also learners. Adult workers have a formal responsibility for teaching and supervising them. These adults must also initiate the apprentices into the social system of the workplace. One question for research is what and how the apprentices learn and adults teach. Another is how and to what extent close relations develop between adolescent apprentices and their adult coaches and mentors. Observations of interactions in the workplace and interviews with all parties provide data that serve to trace the development of relationships over time. Because the apprenticeships are located in four different firms, the influence of context can also be analyzed. For example, interviews with the first-year cohort (n = 22) indicate systematic differences among workplaces in the extent to which apprentices identify adults there as important to them. Those differences can be related to different program structures and to differing corporate cultures in the sense of prevailing norms, values, and behaviors.

Finally, because the program is intended to last for 4 years (spanning 2 years of high school and 2 more of community college), changes in relations with the same adult and with a range of adults, both in the firm and elsewhere, can be tracked over an extended period.

Intimately connected as it is with a complex social experiment, this research will not soon yield generalizable results. The initial numbers are too limited and the conditions too unusual, at least in the United States. However, because so little is known about the subject, we are hopeful of providing new insights by exploring apprenticeship as an exemplar of relations between adolescents and nonkin adults.

NOTES

1. A reference group helps to orient an actor in a certain course, whether of action or attitude (Kemper, 1968, p. 32).
2. Freud (1933) ascribed these same functions to role models.
3. In the first P/PV study of mentoring programs, Freedman (1988) visited five programs linking youth with senior citizens and interviewed 47 pairs of youth and adults. Concluding that both parties benefited, and strongly recommending further research and development, he also offered useful insights into the processes at work in the program. One was a proposed typology of relationships between mentors and their protegés. He characterized 10 of the relationships as "nonsignificant," meaning

that the people involved failed to interact regularly and well. The remaining 37 pairs were named "significant" and further distinguished as either "primary" or "secondary" relationships. Youth and adults involved in the 21 secondary relationships showed evidence of closeness and considered their ties important, but bounded. The 16 pairs engaged in primary relationships, on the other hand, viewed their connection as central to the lives of both parties and unlimited by the program's definitions of their roles. Participants in these relationships treated each other like family members.

4. An intriguing finding of this study, though the sample was too small to support generalization, was that about half of the Learning Web participants named their mentor or a Learning Web staff person as one of the five most important adults in their lives, and these additions accounted for the larger number of important adults named by participants than were named by comparable students who were not enrolled in the program.

5. The two teams reflect a different level of emphasis on instrumental teaching (i.e., coaching) and support, advice, and more diffuse assistance (i.e., mentoring). Normally both functions are performed by the same individuals but not to the same extent.

REFERENCES

Bandura, A. (1977). *Social learning theory.* Englewood Cliffs, NJ: Prentice Hall.

Bell, A. P. (1970). Role modelship and interaction in adolescence and young adulthood. *Developmental Psychology, 2,* 123-128.

Blyth, D., Hill, J. P., & Thiel, K. P. (1982). Early adolescents' significant others. *Journal of Youth and Adolescence, 11,* 425-450.

Cochran, M., & Bo, I. (1989). The social networks, family involvement, and pro- and antisocial behavior of adolescent males in Norway. *Journal of Youth and Adolescence, 18,* 377-398.

Coleman, J., & Hoffer, T. (1987). *Public and private high schools: The impact of communities.* New York: Basic Books.

Cooley, C. H. (1902/1964). *Human nature and the social order.* New York: Scribner's.

Daloz, L. A. (1986). *Effective teaching and mentoring: Realizing the transformational power of adult learning experiences.* San Francisco: Jossey-Bass.

Darling, N. (1990, March). Control beliefs during early adolescence: A comparison of the niche formation and socialization models of development. *Dissertation Abstracts International, 51*(9), 4615-B.

Darling, N. (1991). The influence of challenging and supportive relationships on the academic achievement of adolescents. In S. F. Hamilton (Ed.), *Unrelated adults in adolescents' lives* (pp. 12-30) (Occasional Paper #29). Ithaca, NY: Western Societies Program.

Darling, N., Hamilton, S. F., & Matsuda, S. (1990, March). *Functional roles and social roles: Adolescents' significant others in the United States and Japan.* Paper presented at the meeting of the Society for Research in Adolescence, Atlanta, Georgia (ERIC Document Reproduction Service No. ED 322 453).

Darling, N., Steinberg, L., & Gringlas, M. (March, 1993). Community integration and value consensus as forces for socialization: A test of the functional community hypothesis. In L. Steinberg (Chair), *Community and neighborhood influences on adolescent behavior.* Symposium conducted at the meetings of the Society for Research on Child Development, New Orleans.

Denzin, N. K. (1966, Summer). The significant others of a college population. *Sociological Quarterly, 7*(3), pp. 298-310.

Dewey, J. (1940). *Human nature and conduct.* New York: Modern Library.

Erkut, S., & Mokros, J. R. (1984). Professors as models and mentors for college students. *American Educational Research Journal, 21,* 399-417.

Flaxman, E., Ascher, C., & Harrington, C. (1988). *Youth mentoring: Programs and practices.* Urban Diversity Series No. 97, ERIC Clearinghouse on Urban Education, Institute for Urban and Minority Education. New York: Teachers College, Columbia University.

Fletcher, A., Steinberg, L., & Darling, N. (1993, March). Influence of parental authoritativeness in adolescent peer networks on adolescent misconduct. In L. Steinberg (Chair), *Interactive influences of parents and peers on adolescent misbehavior.* Symposium conducted at the meetings of the Society for Research on Child Development, New Orleans.

Foster-Clark, F. S. (1989, March). Influences on adolescent problem behavior: Individual and social network factors conditioning the impact of deviant peers. *Dissertation Abstracts International, 50*(9), 4244-B.

Freedman, M. (1988). *Partners in growth: Elder mentors and at-risk youth.* Philadelphia: Public/Private Ventures.

Freedman, M. (1991). *The kindness of strangers: Reflections on the mentoring movement.* Philadelphia: Public/Private Ventures.

Freud, S. (1933). *New introductory lectures in psyschoanalysis.* New York: Norton.

Furstenburg, F. (1990, August). *How families manage risk and opportunity in dangerous neighborhoods.* Paper presented at the 84th annual meeting of the American Sociological Association, Washington DC.

Galbo, J. J. (1984). Adolescents' perceptions of significant adults: A review of the literature. *Adolescence, 19* (76), 951-970.

Galbo, J. J. (1986). Adolescents' perceptions of significant adults: Implications for the family, the school, and youth serving agencies. *Children and Youth Services Review, 8,* 37-51.

Garbarino, J., Burston, N., Raber, S., Russell, R., & Crouter, A. (1978). The social maps of children approaching adolescence: Studying the ecology of youth development. *Journal of Youth and Adolescence, 7,* 417-428.

Garmezy, N. (1987). Stress, competence, and development: Continuities in the study of schizophrenic adults, children vulnerable to psychopathology, and the search for stress-resistant children. *American Journal of Orthopsychiatry, 57*(2), 159-174.

Greenberger, E., & Steinberg, L. (1986). *When teenagers work: The psychological and social costs of adolescent employment.* New York: Basic Books.

Hamilton, S. F. (1981). Adolescents in community settings: What is to be learned? *Theory and Research in Social Education, 9,* 23-38.

Hamilton, S. F. (1990). *Apprenticeship for adulthood: Preparing youth for the future.* New York: Free Press.

Hamilton, S. F. (Ed.). (1991). *Unrelated adults in adolescents' lives* (Occasional Paper #29). Ithaca, NY: Western Societies Program.

Hamilton, S. F., & Darling, N. (1989). Mentors in adolescents' lives. In K. Hurrelmann & U. Engel (Eds.), *The social world of adolescents: International perspectives* (pp. 199-209). Berlin: Walter deGruyter.

Hamilton, S. F., & Hamilton, M. A. (1992a). Mentoring programs: Promise and paradox. *Phi Delta Kappan 73*(7), 546-550.

Hamilton, S. F., & Hamilton, M. A. (1992b). Bridging the school-to-work gap. *School Administrator, 49*(3), 8-15.

Hamilton, M. A., & Hamilton, S. F. (1993). Toward a youth apprenticeship system: A progress report from the Youth Apprenticeship Demonstration Project in Broome County, New York. Ithaca, NY: Cornell University.

Hamilton, S. F., Hamilton, M. A., & Wood, B. J. (1991). *Creating apprenticeship opportunities for youth.* Ithaca, NY: Cornell Youth and Work Program.

Higgins, C., Toso, C., Furano, K., & Branch, A. Y. (1991). *I Have a Dream in Washington, DC: Interim report.* Philadelphia, PA: Public/Private Ventures.

Kemper, T. (1968). Reference groups, socialization and achievement. *American Sociological Review, 33*, 31-45.

Lempers, J. D., & Clark-Lempers, D. S. (1992). Young, middle, and late adolescents' comparisons of the functional importance of five significant relationships. *Journal of Youth and Adolescence, 21*, 53-96.

Lefkowitz, B. (1987). *Tough change: Growing up on your own in America.* New York: Free Press.

Matsuda, S. (1989). Significant partners in childhood and adolescence. In K. Hurrelman & U. Engel (Eds.), *The social world of adolescents: International perspectives* (pp. 100-209). New York: Walter de Gruyter.

Mead, G. H. (1934). *Mind, self, and society.* Chicago: University of Chicago Press.

Munsch, J., & Blyth, D. A. (1993). *An analysis of the functional nature of adolescents' supportive relationships.* Manuscript submitted for publication.

Piaget, J. (1983). Piaget's theory. In P. H. Mussen (Ed.), *Handbook of child psychology* (4th ed.) (Vol. 1, pp. 103-128). New York: John Wiley.

Rosenberg, M. (1973). Which significant others? *American Behavioral Scientist, 16,* 829-860.

Rutter, M. (1987). Psychosocial resilience and protective mechanisms. *American Journal of Orthopsychiatry, 57*(3), 316-331.

Sampson, R. J. (1992). Family management and child development: Insights from social disorganization theory. In J. McCord (Ed.), *Advances in Criminological Theory* (Vol. 3, pp. 63-93). New Brunswick, NJ: Transaction Publishers.

Stinson, K. M. (1991). *Adolescents, family, and friends: Social support after parents' divorce or remarriage.* New York: Praeger.

Stryker, S. (1981). Symbolic interactionism: Themes and variations. In M. Rosenberg & R. H. Turner (Eds.), *Social psychology: Sociological perspectives* (pp. 3-29). New York: Basic Books.

Styles, M., & Morrow, K. V. (1992). *Linking lifetimes: Understanding how youth and elders form relationships.* Philadelphia: Public/Private Ventures.

Vygotsky, L. S. (1978). *Mind in society.* Cambridge, MA: Harvard University Press.

Werner, E. E., & Smith, R. S. (1982). *Vulnerable but invincible: A longitudinal study of resilient children and youth.* New York: McGraw-Hill.

Wertsch, J. V. (1981). The concept of activity in soviet psychology. In J. V. Wertsch (Ed.), *The concept of activity in soviet psychology* (pp. 3-36). Armonk, NY: M. E. Sharpe, Inc.

Wilson, W. J. (1987). *The truly disadvantaged: The inner city, the underclass, and public policy.* Chicago: University of Chicago Press.

10. Current Theory and Research on Personal Relationships During Adolescence

Raymond Montemayor
Ohio State University

Virginia R. Gregg
Ohio State University

In the history of the study of relationships during adolescence three trends are evident: First, theorists and researchers have mainly focused on two relationships, parents and peers; second, they have investigated a small number of specific questions about these relationships; and third, the primary framework for examining relationships has been to search for the impact parents and peers have on adolescents. Much has been learned from these research traditions, which remain viable and continue to stimulate empirical research, as many of the chapters in this volume demonstrate. What also emerges from this book, however, is a hint of a new relational perspective from which new questions and methodologies may emerge. In this last chapter we highlight and bring to the forefront some of the key points made in previous chapters, attempt to identify themes running through the chapters, and offer suggestions for future theorizing and research on adolescent relationships.

Scholars interested in the period of adolescence traditionally have emphasized the importance of parents and peers in defining the adolescent experience and in influencing its outcome. Such an emphasis has been and remains justified, given the depth and breadth of influence parents and peers have on adolescents. One of the new and exciting developments in the study of adolescent relationships, however, has been to open up the interpersonal world to include the study of relationships other than those with parents and peers. As the contributions to this volume demonstrate, contemporary research on adolescent relationships is a vital area of investigation that includes the study of same- and opposite-sex romantic relationships and relationships with unrelated adults. It is only because of a lack of space that chapters in this volume did not include other important adolescent relationships, such as relationships with siblings (Buhrmester & Furman, 1990), grandparents (Baranowski, 1982), and step-parents (Hetherington & Anderson, 1987).

Until very recently research on parents and peers was driven by a small number of specific questions. Researchers interested in the parent-adolescent relationship mainly focused on the development of adolescent autonomy, parent-adolescent conflict, and the influence of parent disciplinary styles on adolescents (Steinberg, 1990). Scholars interested in peers have been primarily concerned with describing the adolescent peer culture and with understanding peer pressure and peer conformity (Brown, 1990). An overlapping issue has been to examine the relative impact of parents and peers on adolescent functioning. All these issues continue to generate research and new knowledge. Although much about these issues is not well understood, recent research on parents and peers, as the contributions in this volume illustrate, moves beyond classic questions.

The "new look" in relationship research springs from an evolving relational framework in which individuals are distinguished from the relationship, making it possible to study the relationship itself (e.g., Hartup, 1989; Kelley et al., 1983). An example of this framework is based on the work of Kenny and his colleagues, who have developed a "social relations model" based on the idea that relationship factors are not entirely predictable from characteristics of individuals in a relationship (Kenny & LaVoie, 1984). The model and its analytical technique have been fruitfully applied to the study of adolescents and their parents (Cook, Kenny, & Goldstein, 1991) and to family relations in general (Kashy & Kenny, 1990).

Although research on adolescent relationships is not yet driven by relational models, one sees in some of the chapters in this volume the initial stages of movement in that direction. Traditional research has focused on relationships as independent or dependent variables, primarily investigating the impact of parents and peers on adolescents or examining relationships as a function of adolescent, parent, or peer characteristics. In contrast, contemporary approaches to the study of relationships focus on relational issues, such as relationship development, continuity, and change.

A relationship perspective is clearly evident in Chapter 2 by Collins and Repinski. They argue that autonomy and closeness have been the key constructs used by theorists and researchers to examine and describe relations between parents and adolescents. Further, they show that several constructs within each of these two categories are similar, although different theoretical underpinnings have resulted in different measures, empirical predictions, results, and interpretations of findings. As a result, confusion exists about how to integrate the available literature. (See Lamborn & Steinberg, 1993, for a recent example of this type of controversy.)

The new perspective Collins and Repinski offer as one solution to some of this confusion is based on a paradigmatic shift away from a focus on individuals to one based on the relationship itself. In particular they propose an "interdependency perspective" as one useful way to describe relations between parents and peers and to characterize relationship change during adolescence. Interdependency emphasizes joint patterns of behavior and the mutual impact relationship partners have on each other. An important interdependency concept that Collins and Repinski describe is "closeness," which they define as the "frequency, diversity, strength, and duration of mutual impact."

An interdependency perspective and the relationship dimension of closeness can be applied to any relationship, although the definition and measurement of closeness will differ from relationship to relationship. For example, Brown, Mory, and Kinney in this volume apply an explicit relational perspective to the study of adolescent groups, in which the focus of study is not relationships between individuals but relationships between groups. From their perspective the dyadic issue of closeness becomes translated into the group issue of loyalty. Further work applying a relational perspective to parents and peers and to adolescent relationships in general should yield insights into relationship formation and transformation.

Several relationship issues emerge from Chapter 3, in which Noller describes and integrates her own research and the research of others on the impact of parent-adolescent relations on adolescents. The important contribution she makes in this chapter is to lay out a framework of a process model to specify relationship factors implicated in adolescent outcomes. The primary factors she identifies as important are parent-adolescent communication patterns, frequency of conflict, conflict resolution styles, parental punishment and control, family decision making, and adolescent autonomy and closeness. Important adolescent outcomes that are influenced by parent-adolescent relationship style include adolescent adjustment, psychopathology, and problem behaviors such as smoking, alcohol and drug use, and early sexual intercourse. Noller highlights the need to develop process models to understand the impact of adolescent relationships on adolescent behavior. She focuses on the parent-adolescent relationship. Gerald Patterson and his colleagues also have focused on this relationship and have developed and tested elaborate and complex models of the impact of parents on male adolescent antisocial behavior (Patterson, Reid, & Dishion, 1992). This work might be used as a stepping stone to model other parent-adolescent processes and other adolescent outcomes. Process models of relationship continuity and change are also needed. Much research has examined relationship change, especially between parents and children as children enter adolescence (Montemayor, Adams, & Gullotta, 1990), but less is known about why these changes occur, which is a process question.

One issue of concern to researchers interested in adolescent relationships is how to take into account the possibly differing perspectives individuals in a relationship have about their relationship. Noller focuses on parents and adolescents and shows that, in general, adolescents have more negative views about their parents and other family members than do parents. Understanding these differences, how they develop and what impact they have on relationships, could be a fruitful line of research on several parent-adolescent relationship issues, such as conflict negotiation and the development of closeness. In general, the issue of differing relationship perspectives is a fundamental one to the conceptualization, data collection, and analysis of relationships (Paikoff, 1991). As well as the differing perspectives of the two individuals in a relationship, there also must be added the perspective of an outside observer. How to integrate behavioral observations with participants' perceptions remains a thorny, unsolved issue.

Another way a relational perspective adds to the study of parent-adolescent relations is that it focuses attention not only on the impact of parents on adolescents but also on the influence of adolescents on the parent-adolescent relationship. Traditional research on the parent-adolescent relationship is driven by a unidirectional conception of causality that emphasizes the impact of parents on adolescents. This is a one-sided view, however, because adolescents bring their own history into relations with parents, who also have a history, and it is out of this interaction that a relationship emerges that influences both parent and adolescent. Understanding the emergence of this relationship and its impact on both parents and adolescents are questions that follow from a relational approach. Most research on the "adolescent experience" has examined white middle-class adolescents, but has been applied to adolescents in general. Only recently have researchers become sensitive to the diversity of adolescent experiences. In particular, ethnic background exerts a powerful impact on adolescents. In a growing body of work, writers and researchers have begun to examine the impact of ethnicity on adolescents (e.g., Spencer & Dornbusch, 1990), and further work on these issues continues. With the exception of Cooper's Chapter 4, however, authors in this volume do not examine cultural variation in adolescent relationships. There may be many good reasons for this neglect: For example, the data base is small, and authors are focused on what they see as core relationship issues and not on variation. Yet the absence of explicit attention to ethnic variation limits generalization not only in the traditional quantitative sense, but also, as Cooper illustrates, in a qualitative sense. For example, according to Cooper, ethnic variation exists not only on *how* close parents and adolescents feel toward each other but, more importantly, on the *way* closeness is expressed. Attending to ethnicity enriches our understanding of adolescents and, in addition, deepens our knowledge about the constructs in which we are interested.

In her chapter on culture, Cooper goes beyond a traditional emphasis on the importance of examining development within a cultural context. The new point Cooper makes is that cultures are not monolithic and cannot be described by simple generalizations. Cultures are multidimensional and include a range of norms and values, some contradictory. Further, individuals are influenced by different cultural values and adhere to these values to different degrees. Another source of variation is the result of the enculturation of adolescents and their parents, the degree to which they subscribe to the norms of the majority culture and participate in it. As a result of these different sources of variation, individual differences within a culture are great. Put in statistical terms, Cooper's point is that although culture is a main effect, within-group differences are large. This point is a general one, not specifically about relationship issues, but it is especially important when examining relationship development to investigate both within- and between-group differences.

In Chapter 5 on adolescent peer groups, Youniss and his colleagues continue previous work on describing adolescent peer relations. From a relational perspective Youniss makes the point early in his chapter that the relations adolescents have with parents and peers are distinct in form and content. According to Youniss, peer relations are marked by the use of "symmetrical reciprocity" and focus on making and maintaining friendship. In contrast, relations with parents, and adults in general, are based on "reciprocity of complement" and are structured around issues of obedience. Youniss is not concerned with examining and contrasting these two social worlds here, having done that elsewhere (Youniss & Smollar, 1985). The point that relationships with peers may be structurally different from those with parents complements Cooper's similar point about qualitative differences in relationships across ethnic groups. A focus on the qualitatively different ways relations are organized and on their different functions leads to research questions that have not been addressed adequately in the past. For example, instead of asking to whom adolescents are closer, parents or peers, one might ask how closeness is defined and expressed with parents and peers. Such an approach recognizes the integrity of different types of relationships and leads to a deeper understanding of relationship variation.

Brown, Mory, and Kinney develop a relational perspective on adolescent crowd behavior, which they use to examine several crowd phenomena. Among their many interesting points, two seem especially noteworthy in regard to relationships. They show that crowd labeling—what they refer to as "crowd caricaturing"—is inherently a relational activity in two important senses: First, the labeling itself is co-constructed among peers who are members of relational groups; and second, the attributions about crowds are often about relational styles. The observation that relationships are a context within which ideas about the world develop, ideas which in turn influence relationships, is an intriguing framework to examine relationships and cognitions. Some work exists in this area (e.g., Hinde, Perret-Clermont, & Stevenson-Hinde, 1985), but it primarily focuses on parents and preadolescent-aged children. Little has been done on the impact of peers on adolescent intellectual and cognitive development, although a large literature exists on peer influences, primarily in the social area.

A second point Brown and his colleagues make is that crowd membership influences relational styles and so serves as a context for the development and expression of interpersonal behavior. Being identified as a member of a crowd by oneself, other crowd members, and others is based on several characteristics, such as adherence to a certain style of dress, degree of academic orientation, leisure interests, and, most importantly, on styles of interaction with peers. Brown and his coauthors go on to examine some ways crowds might influence relational styles, and they suggest that this influence exists even when adolescents are not interacting with members of their own crowd. This intriguing idea that a relational style learned in one context is expressed in other contexts with other people helps explain why it is difficult for adolescents to change their image or to gain entrance into other crowds even if they alter their appearance. This idea also has important implications for interventions with adolescents in deviant peer groups. Removing an adolescent from the influence of antisocial peers is only the first step in a long-term process of change that must also include altering an interpersonal style that identifies the adolescent as a troublemaker and interferes with his ability to interact with nondeviant peers.

Research on opposite-sex relationships during adolescence has focused primarily on sexuality and to a lesser extent on friendship. As a result we know much about adolescent sexuality as an activity, but little about it as an outcome of a romantic relationship, although much research on adolescent sexuality suggests that it is embedded within a relational context (Zelnik, 1983). For this reason alone we need to know more about adolescent romantic relationships, in addition to the fact that dating and the formation of romantic relationships are central features of adolescent life.

Furman and Wehner single out romantic relationships for study and propose an intriguing conceptualization from which they discuss several hypotheses about determinants of romantic relationship styles. Much of their focus is compatible with a relational perspective, although they are mainly concerned with examining the association between characteristics of individuals and relationship styles. The perspective that a relational approach adds to this framework is to explicitly focus on the relationship as an emergent phenomenon, as an outcome of the developmental histories of the two individuals, and that is not entirely predictable from characteristics of either individual alone. An important point clearly made by Furman and Wehner, and by no other authors in this volume, is that relationships are essentially developmental phenomena. This is true in two ways. First, a current relationship is at least partly an outcome of the previous relationships of the two people involved. This point, which seems obvious, has been surprisingly ignored in research on adolescent relationships. For example, we know little about how parents' relationships with their parents influence the current parent-adolescent relationship. Nor do we know how relations with peers in childhood influence peer relations in adolescence. Furman and Wehner bring a strong developmental perspective to the study of romantic relationship formation and propose that a current romantic relationship is highly influenced by an individual's attachment history and previous romantic relationships.

A developmental perspective also is helpful for understanding relationship change. A relationship is not static but changes and is altered in both subtle and profound ways by internal individual changes and external social and environmental alterations. Virtually nothing is known about variation in trajectories of adolescent romantic relationships, although understanding the determinants of these trajectories may increase our knowledge about why some adolescent relationships become sexual while others do not—an understanding that might lead to more effective pregnancy prevention programs.

Several themes relevant to an understanding of relationships run through Savin-Williams' description of the romantic relationships of gay, lesbian, and bisexual youth. According to Savin-Williams the fundamental dilemma gay youth face is that negative social attitudes about homosexuality make it difficult for these youth to form healthy identities as gay individuals. Gay youth, no less than heterosexual youth, desire peer acceptance and so conceal their sexual orientation for fear of ostracism and even violence. As a result of this fear of revealing themselves, gay youth find it difficult to pursue and establish romantic relationships with individuals of their own sex.

The general issue raised by Savin-Williams' Chapter 8 is: How is identity formation related to relationship expression during adolescence? One framework from which to address this question was proposed by Erikson (1968), who has a developmental model in which identity formation is a prerequisite for the expression of true interpersonal intimacy. Using this linear model, one would expect relationship variation, especially along some maturity dimension, based on variation in identity status. Out of Savin-Williams' discussion of the romantic relationships of gay youth, a relational model emerges in which relationships are both influenced by identity development and influence its outcome. According to this model, identity formation occurs within a relational context in which an adolescent projects a diffused self-image onto another and, by seeing it reflected back, gradually clarifies that image. Based on this model, relationships are not simply another developmental outcome, derived from personality development, but are the arena in which the self is constructed and expressed.

Most of the writing and research on the relationships adolescents have with adults has focused on parents, and very little is known about relationships between adolescents and unrelated adults. Darling, Hamilton, and Niego discuss the relationships adolescents have with teachers, coaches, activity leaders, and so forth, and make the point that these relationships provide adolescents with experiences that they do not, and cannot, receive from their parents. According to Darling and her colleagues, the parent-adolescent relationship is primarily about emotional closeness and support. Relationships with unrelated adults, in contrast, focus on skill learning and the expression of those skills, and provide adolescents with an arena for accomplishment, for the acquisition of knowledge about the self, and for the development of self-esteem.

Most writers about relationships, whether writing about relationships during adolescence or during other periods of the life cycle, focus on emotional and affective issues. As can be seen from the chapters in this volume, relationships are viewed as the contexts in which feelings of closeness, support, attachment, love, esteem, and acceptance develop. This is a legitimate view of relationships, but by focusing exclusively on emotional affect we have neglected the instrumental dimension of relationships. Darling and her colleagues remind us that relationships are also contexts in which adolescents learn about the world and acquire academic, social, and athletic skills. Clearly, relationship researchers need to incorporate these aspects of relationships in conceptualizations of adolescent relationship development.

REFERENCES

Baranowski, M. D. (1982). Grandparent-adolescent relations: Beyond the nuclear family. *Adolescence, 17,* 575-584.

Brown, B. B. (1990). Peer groups and peer cultures. In S. S. Feldman & G. R. Elliott (Eds.), *At the threshold* (pp. 171-196). Cambridge, MA: Harvard University Press.

Buhrmester, D., & Furman, W. (1990). Perceptions of sibling relationships during middle childhood and adolescence. *Child Development, 61,* 1387-1398.

Cook, W. L., Kenny, D. A., & Goldstein, M. J. (1991). Parental affective style risk and the family system: A social relations model analysis. *Journal of Abnormal Psychology, 100,* 492-501.

Erikson, E. R. (1968). *Identity: Youth and crisis.* New York: Norton.

Hartup, W. W. (1989). Social relationships and their developmental significance. *American Psychologist, 44,* 120-126.

Hetherington, E. M., & Anderson, E. R. (1987). The effects of divorce and remarriage on early adolescents and their families. In M. D. Levine & E. R. McAnarney (Eds.), *Early adolescent transitions* (pp. 49-67). Lexington, MA: Heath.

Hinde, R. A., Perret-Clermont, A. N., & Stevenson-Hinde, J. (Eds.) (1985). *Social relationships and cognitive development.* New York: Oxford University Press.

Kashy, D. A., & Kenny, D. A. (1990). Analysis of family research designs: A model of interdependence. *Communication Research, 17,* 462-482.

Kelley, H. H., Berscheid, E., Christensen, A., Harvey, J. H., Huston, T. L., Levinger, G., McClintock, E., Peplau, L. A., & Peterson, D. R. (1983). *Close relationships.* New York: Freeman.

Kenny, D. A., & LaVoie, L. (1984). The social relations model. In L. Berkowitz (Ed.), *Advances in experimental social psychology* (Vol. 18, pp. 141-182). New York: Academic Press.

Lamborn, S. D., & Steinberg, L. (1993). Emotional autonomy redux: Revisiting Ryan and Lynch. *Child Development, 64,* 483-499.

Montemayor, R., Adams, G. R., & Gullotta, T. P. (Eds.) (1990). *From childhood to adolescence.* Newbury Park, CA: Sage.

Paikoff, R. L. (Ed.). (1991). *New directions for child development: No. 51. Shared views of the family during adolescence.* San Francisco, CA: Jossey-Bass.

Patterson, G. R., Reid, J. B., & Dishion, T. J. (1992). *Antisocial boys.* Eugene, OR: Castalia.

Spencer, M. B., & Dornbusch, S. M. (1990). Challenges in studying minority youth. In S. S. Feldman & G. R. Elliott (Eds.), *At the threshold* (pp. 123-146). Cambridge, MA: Harvard University Press.

Steinberg, L. (1990). Autonomy, conflict, and harmony in the family relationship. In S. S. Feldman & G. R. Elliott (Eds.), *At the threshold* (pp. 255-276). Cambridge, MA: Harvard University Press.

Youniss, J., & Smollar, J. (1985). *Adolescent relations with mothers, fathers, and friends.* Chicago: University of Chicago Press.

Zelnik, M. (1983). Sexual activity among adolescents: Perspective of a decade. In E. R. McAnarney (Ed.), *Premature adolescent pregnancy and parenthood* (pp. 21-33). New York: Grune & Stratton.

Index

About the Editors

Raymond Montemayor is Associate Professor of Psychology at The Ohio State University. His research interests include behavioral approaches to the study of adolescence, especially parent-adolescent relations, and the study of conflict and stress between parents and adolescents. In addition, he is interested in the impact of peer relations on adolescent social development. He is Associate Editor for the *Journal of Early Adolescence* and is an editorial board member for the *Journal of Adolescent Research*.

Gerald R. Adams is a Professor in the Department of Family Studies at the University of Guelph. He is a Fellow of the American Psychological Association and has been awarded the James D. Moral Research Award from the American Home Economics Association. Currently he has editorial assignments with the *Journal of Adolescence, Journal of Primary Prevention, Journal of Early Adolescence*, and *Social Psychology Quarterly*.

Thomas P. Gullotta is CEO of the Child and Family Agency in Connecticut. He currently is the editor of the *Journal of Primary Prevention* and is the senior book series editor for *Issues in Children's and Families' Lives*. In addition, he serves on the editorial boards of the *Journal of Early Adolescence* and *Adolescence* and is an adjunct faculty member in the psychology department of Eastern Connecticut State University. His 59 published works include 2 textbooks, 6 edited books, and numerous articles focusing on primary prevention and youth.

About the Contributors

B. Bradford Brown is a Professor of Human Development in the Department of Educational Psychology and Research Scientist in the Wisconsin Center for Education Research at the University of Wisconsin-Madison, where he has been since receiving his Ph.D. from the University of Chicago in 1979. His research focuses on adolescent social development, especially teenage peer relationships and peer influence processes. Brown is particularly well known for his work on the formation and operation of teenage peer cultures (or "crowds"), and on the impact of peer pressure on school achievement and deviant behavior.

W. Andrew Collins is a Professor in the Institute of Child Development, University of Minnesota. He received his Ph.D. from Stanford University in 1971. A fellow of the American Psychological Association and the American Psychological Society, he is associate editor of *Child Development* and a member of the Executive Council of the Society for Research on Adolescence. From 1976 to 1980, he was editor of the *Minnesota Symposia on Child Psychology,* and he is the author or editor of several other scholarly volumes and textbooks on child and adolescent psychology. His research has focused on mass media influences on children and youth and, more recently, on changes in family relationships during middle childhood and adolescence.

Catherine R. Cooper is Professor of Psychology and Education at the University of California at Santa Cruz, and was the founding director of the graduate program in developmental psychology there. She received her Ph.D. from the Institute of Child Development at the University of Minnesota. Her current research concerns cultural perspectives on adolescents' self and relational development in the United States and in Japan, with particular focus on linkages among adolescents' experiences with their families, peers, schools, and communities.

Nancy Darling is an Assistant Professor at Dickinson College. Her current work involves an investigation of how community parenting and network structural characteristics change the effectiveness of parents' efforts to socialize children. This work relies on individual, family, neighborhood, and census tract information, in addition to social network analyses, in an effort to understand variability in adolescent psychosocial well-being, academic performance, and deviance. Future work will examine within-family variability in the experience and influence of parenting style and practices.

Wyndol Furman is a Full Professor in the Department of Psychology at the University of Denver. He received his Ph.D. from the University of Minnesota. His research is concerned with children's and adolescents' personal relationships. He has conducted studies on peer, parental, and sibling relationships as well as romantic relationships.

Virginia R. Gregg is a Ph.D. candidate in the Developmental Psychology program at Ohio State University. She obtained her B.S. and M.A. degrees from Ohio State University in 1989 and 1991, respectively. Her research interests include changes that occur in parent-child relationships during adolescence, particularly changes in closeness and separation.

Stephen F. Hamilton is Professor and Chair of Human Development and Family Studies at Cornell. His research investigates the interaction of school, community, and work during the transition from adolescence to adulthood. The author of *Apprenticeship for Adulthood: Preparing Youth for the Future* (1990), he has investigated the school-to-career transition in the United States, Germany, Sweden, Denmark, Austria, and Switzerland. Hamilton directs the Cornell Youth and Work Program, which operates a youth apprenticeship demonstration project testing the adaptation of European apprenticeship in the United States. Research on this project addresses informal teaching and learning in workplaces.

David Kinney received his Ph.D. from the Department of Sociology at Indiana University in 1990. Prior to assuming his current position at Research for Better Schools, Inc., in Philadelphia, Dr. Kinney was a Project Coordinator at the Consortium on Chicago School Research and Center for the Study of Urban Inequality at the University of Chicago. His main fields of interest are adolescent peer culture, education, deviance, and socialization. He has conducted several ethnographic investigations of peer culture, identity formation, and academic achievement of American adolescents in diverse cultural and educational settings.

Jeffrey A. McLellan is a Ph.D. candidate in the Human Development program at the Catholic University of America. His prior research looked at adolescents' rules for maintaining interpersonal relationships as well as adolescents' understandings of economic transactions.

Margaret S. Mory is a doctoral candidate in Human Development in the Department of Educational Psychology at the University of Wisconsin-Madison. Her research involves an examination of the intersection between adolescent social development, social cognitive development, and intergroup relations. She is particularly interested in the "crowd" as an emergent social category through which adolescents forge interpretations of their peer world and of their own social identities.

Starr Niego earned a master's degree in developmental psychology in 1992. At present she is a doctoral candidate in the Department of Human Development and Family Studies at Cornell University. She is particularly interested in applying participatory research methods to bridge theory and practice in human development. Her dissertation focuses upon the dynamics between individual and social change as girls move from adolescence into adulthood. Together with a group of high school girls she is conducting a collaborative investigation of adolescent identity and critical consciousness.

Patricia Noller is Reader in Psychology at the University of Queensland, having obtained her Ph.D from the same university in 1981. Her doctoral research was about nonverbal communication in married couples. She is author of *Nonverbal Communication and Marital Interaction*, coauthor with Victor Callan of *Marriage and the Family* and *The Adolescent in the Family* and with Victor Callan, Cynthia Gallois, and Yoshi Kashima of *Social Psychology*. She also coedited with Mary Anne Fitzpatrick *Perspectives on Marital Interaction*, and they have coauthored the recently published *Communication in Family Relationships*. Her research has been published in international journals such as *Journal of Personality and Social Psychology, Developmental Psychology, Journal of Marriage and the Family, Journal of Social and Personal Relationships, Multivariate Behavioral Research*, and *Journal of Adolescence* and as chapters in a number of books. She has recently been appointed foundation editor of *Personal Relationships, Journal of the International Society for the Study of Personal Relationships*, to be published by Cambridge University Press.

Daniel J. Repinski is Assistant Professor of Psychology at the State University of New York at Geneseo. He received his Ph.D. in 1993 from the Institute of Child Development at the University of Minnesota. He obtained his B.A. from St. John's University in 1984 and his M.S. from Iowa State University in 1989. His major research interests include adolescent social and personality development, change during adolescence in close relationships with parents and friends, and the significance of close relationships for adolescents' psychosocial development.

Ritch C. Savin-Williams is a Clinical and Developmental Psychologist in the Department of Human Development at Cornell University. His early research, summarized in *Adolescence: An Ethological Perspective* (1987), focused on peer relationships and friendships. Most recently, his teaching, research, and clinical interests have centered on gay youth (see *Gay and Lesbian Youth: Expressions of Identity* [1990]), especially their self-esteem, coming out to self and others, and sexuality. Two books are in progress: *Sex and Sexual Identity Among Gay and Bisexual Males* and *Developmental and Clinical Issues Facing Lesbians, Gay Males, and Bisexuals* (with K. M. Cohen).

Darcy Strouse is a Ph.D. candidate in the Human Development program at the Catholic University of America. She is studying adolescent females' attitudes and interests in science and engineering careers. She is looking at the contributions of parents, friends, and peer groups in sustaining these career interests.

Elizabeth A. Wehner is a postdoctoral fellow at the University of Colorado Health Sciences Center. She received her Ph.D. from the University of Denver. Her primary research interests involve the study of children's social networks, with a particular interest in parent-child attachment relationships.

James Youniss, Professor of Psychology and Director of the Life Cycle Institute at the Catholic University of America, has been studying the role of interpersonal relationships in social development for the past 15 years. His work has focused on parental and friend relations. The present chapter represents his first look at adolescent peer groups.

20002

220002